TEMPLES OF SOUTH INDIA

India—The Land and the People

TEMPLES OF
SOUTH INDIA

K.R. SRINIVASAN

NATIONAL BOOK TRUST, INDIA

ISBN 81-237-2251-6

Editions 1972, 1979, 1985, 1998
Reprinted in 1991, 2001, 2003 (*Saka* 1925)

© K.R. Srinivasan, 1972

Rs 55.00

Published by the Director, National Book Trust, India
A-5 Green Park, New Delhi - 110 016

Contents

Preface to the Fourth Edition

This book attempts to present a comprehensive picture of the chronologically uninterrupted chain of extant South Indian temples, covering a vast period of time and wide area, exhibiting regional idioms and variations and perceptible evolutionary trends. In such a general narration, following a chronological sequence and regional order, representative or outstanding examples have come in for a fuller description.

The first edition of the book appeared in 1972. Though intended primarily for the lay reader, it has also been found useful as an elementary reference manual. The second revised edition was published in 1979.

In this fourth edition, further revised material has been added in various places.

1

INTRODUCTION

As a religious institution and place of worship, the temple in India has had a hoary past. As a structure that enshrines a god or some other object of veneration, circumambulation (*pradakshina*), adoration and worship (*puja*), it has had a varied growth in different parts of the subcontinent. This was according to the local needs and credal requirements and subject, of course, to the interplay or exchange of thoughts and ideas. Though fundamentally the basic elements of the temples and the worship in them derived mostly from *Vedic* and *Puranic* sources, in course of centuries they assumed different styles and patterns during their diffusion over wide areas from the cradle centres of the great Indian religions in north India. The rise of the protestant cults of Jainism and Buddhism during the pre-Christian epoch and the development of their own versions of the legends, creeds, forms of deities, rituals and the like, resulted in their adaptation of one kind or another of the temple form and its adjuncts as suited the object of their particular worship and its glorification, for essentially the temple in its form and layout depended on the object of veneration installed and the method adopted for its worship. The three creeds being indigenous, and not exotic, had not to derive the basic forms of their temples from anywhere except from their own land of origin. All the three, while retaining the common Indian plans and elevations, and the native principles and techniques of construction, had, however, to show their credal distinctions by suitable adaptations of their forms and through emphasis on the features of the cognitions of the respective creeds in the general make-up and content of the structure.

The builders or the craftsmen—*sthapatis* and the *silpins*—who belonged to the same guilds of artisans, had common principles and set methods of design and construction and they worked in collaboration with the priesthood which knew the rituals, the nature of the object of veneration, and the modes of their worship. They together determined the forms of the temples with such modifications as suited the respective cases, as also the fixation of the features of the principal deities and the decorations of the structure with iconic and other sculptural embellishments. As a result, the *Vastu*, *Silpa* and *Agama* texts and canons as described in the *sastras* were evolved. All that was known and necessary in the creation of the temple and the conduct of worship therein was codified. Thus to the Indian mind the indigenous architecture remains basically and essentially Indian. It cannot be sub-divided into what is usually attempted to be made out as Hindu, Jain, or Buddhist architecture.

The organized religions, Hinduism, Jainism and Buddhism, did, in their early stages of growth, spread into the southern peninsula across the Vindhyan barrier of mountains and forests, because of their own vitality, in successive waves, merging into the religions of the south which had viable cultures, social patterns, traditions and religious beliefs of their own, not to speak of a language that could flower into its own literature, independently of every other factor. A greater impetus to these contacts was given by the Mauryan conquests that reached the northern borders of the Mysore plateau, beyond which Asoka, the great patron of Buddhism, recognized viable, stable and organized kingdoms of the far south, with their own indigenous culture. He treated them as friendly neighbours across the border among whom he could spread his message through his southern administrators.

The tradition of rock-cut architecture and excavation into living rocks of *chaityas* and *viharas* of the Buddhists initiated by Asoka near Gaya was soon taken up in the trap-rock regions of the Deccan and western India, reproducing aspects of contemporary brick-and-timber originals which, because of the perishable nature of the fabric of their construction, did not survive the march of time. This expression of forms of architecture and sculpture through the permanent medium of stone, adopted earlier by the Buddhists, then by the Hindus and the Jains, has enabled the monuments to last for centuries and give us a fairly good idea of what the contemporary religious architecture and sculpture in general was. The brick-built *stupas* and *chaityas*, which are in essence temples, in the eastern Andhra and northern Karnataka regions, too, have survived because of the adoption of stone for their protective casing and sculptured veneer, not to mention the stone railings which totally imitated timberwork in their joinery and fixtures. In these cases stone cannot be said to have gone into actual construction which was still of brick. These *stupas* and *chaityas* show their own distinct regional characters as against their compeers in north and north-western India.

From the sixth and seventh centuries AD, the Hindus and Jains of the south too adopted the stone medium, and started excavating rock-cut cave-temples, or carving out rock-cut monolithic temple forms, and ultimately building them of stone. We have a long series of such stone temples created in close succession and extending uninterruptedly through the past thirteen centuries, surviving in their thousands all over the peninsula, more to the far south where most of them are still in use. The comparative freedom from foreign invasions and disruption in this part of India and the relative strength of the kingdoms and society were some of the contributing factors. Even the early Hindu and Jain temples came into being under the royal patronage of the rulers of the three great empires of the south—the Chalukyas, the Pallavas and the Pandyas—along with the lesser kingdoms wedged in between. The spirit was soon caught up by the nobility, the mercantile corporations and the agricultural trade, and artisan guilds that flourished during those times. The result was that a chain of temples, great and small, studded every village and town of the south, which thus came to be known as the land of temples. The temples were documented by their own expressive and detailed inscriptions, again in their thousands. Temples from the Chola times (ninth-tenth centuries) became the very hub of the rural and urban life in all its aspects—religious, cultural, social, economic and educational—and thus became the repository of all that was best in fabric, architecture, sculpture and other arts.

Buddhism almost went into complete eclipse soon; the Hindu temples to a greater extent and the Jain ones to a lesser extent predominating. There had been, of course, a natural interchange of ideas and usages among the three during their periods of development and growth in the region on a matrix that was essentially indigenous. The Buddha, for instance, was adopted as the ninth of the ten incarnations of Vishnu in the Hindu pantheon in place of Krishna, who came to be considered as the whole aspect of Vishnu. This is testified by a Pallava inscription of the seventh centrury AD in one of the early cave-temples at Mahabalipuram. Then again, Buddhist *tantric* rituals percolated into the Hindu modes of worship. The Jains had by then established their *sangas* at Madurai, and even earlier their creed of the Digambara persuasion had centred principally in Sravana Belagola in Mysore with its affiliates and branches—the *guchchhas*— radiating into Andhra, Karnataka, Tamil Nadu and Kerala. Hinduism witnessed a great revival under the Saiva saints (Nayanmars) and the Vaishnava saints (Alvars) who were soon defined and became part and parcel of the pantheon and in the ritual and calendar of festivals. Sankara, the great philosopher and teacher, also reformed the popular Hindu creeds—the Shanmata and the model of the related worship. With such a background the growth of temples and organized temple worship became truly phenomenal.

The southern temples with their characteristic tiered *vimana* shrines, major and minor, their axial and peripheral *mandapa* adjuncts, which are flat-roofed halls, and the towering *gopura* entrances form a distinct class by themselves as against the northern *prasada* temples with their curvilinear superstructures, the crowning *amalaka* and *mandapas* with rising tiered roofs. That the *vimana* form in its various plans and elevations built of brick and timber had been already developed in the south before the seventh century will be only too evident from the maturity shown by the first monolithic replicas as reproduced in the so-called *rathas* of Mahabalipuram and the earliest of the stone structural *vimanas*. The *mandapa* forms are likewise evident from the cave-temple types, while the *gopura* in its simplest form is also to be found in the early temple units. They could not have arisen in stone spontaneously.

The prevailing maritime contacts with the regions of the east in the Indian Ocean, which were actuated more by trade and emigration than by motives of political aggrandisement and were, therefore, peaceful and the resultant emigrations of colonists, lent much to the contemporary make-up of the religion, culture, art and architecture of these lands. South Indian temple architecture, sculpture and iconography may be said to have had a great share in this. In fact, it may be said that many of the greatest achievements in the fields of religion, art and architecture are said to be found in regions beyond the cradle centres of the great religions in south India—as at Thanjavur and Madurai, and in other lands, as in Java and Cambodia.

Thus in an integrated scheme of a study of the temples of India, the southern temples have perforce to be studied independently in order to understand not only their origin and mode of development through time and space into the varied regional styles, but also the similarities and differences and the mutual influences of the two great traditions, northern and southern. An attempt has been made in the following pages to portray in outline the temples of the south. Since even the simplest architectural and art terms of the European classical origin, often employed in the description of Indian temples, are inadequate and not always apt, the barest use of Indian technical terms of common Sanskrit origin for the most important parts, as used in the *Vastu* and *Silpa* manuals, has been made. The terms most of which are familiar to temple-goers of the south are not only explained in the course of the running description but also collected in a glossary at the end, so that they can eventually be put to a more purposeful use.

2

THE BEGINNINGS—EARLY TEMPLES

The cult of worship of objects or phenomena considered super-human in a specified manner and in specified places has been one of the traits of mankind from very remote times. The early form of such practices can only be deduced from literary evidences, traditions and material relics that have come down to us in the course of the centuries. A fairly vivid picture of life and organized worship in the the ancient Tamilakam, the country of the Tamils, in the southernmost part of the peninsula that included what is now Kerala also, is supplied by the earliest available literature in Tamil, dating from the commencement of the Christian era, if not before it. The extant portion of this vast literature embodies in itself earlier and contemporary traditions, many of which still persist. The material evidence would be the numerous megalithic monuments of diverse variety and shape that have survived. These monuments which are funerary or sepulchral in character are, by far, the largest group of extant early monuments in the south and are very widely distributed all over the area south of the Vindhyas. These monuments, characterized by the association of large stones, reveal by their character and content a highly evolved material culture, as can also be deduced from the numerous references found in the early Tamil literatures of the *Sangam* epoch and later. Here is mention of the erection and veneration with accompanying ritual of the monuments raised in honour of the dead, for example, the *nadukal* or 'stone-erection'. This culture which had its beginnings somewhere in the middle of the first millennium BC, if not earlier, prevailed in the south till the middle of the first millennium AD and continued in some modified or restricted form for centuries thereafter.

In the same body of literature we also get glimpses of other gods and spirits worshipped by the common people, as also their religious practices prevalent, perhaps, much before the advent of the great proselytizing religions of Brahmanism (more conveniently denoted as Hinduism), Jainism and Buddhism, not to mention another important religion, that of the Ajivikas. The worship of local gods and the animistic worship of spirits inhabiting trees, rivers and hills, or of the guardians of villages, cities, cross-roads, sea-shores, and river ports or *ghats*, lakes and tanks were similar in essence to what obtained in north India (*yakshas*, *bhutas* and *devatas*), where we have the classic instance of the infant Buddha being taken soon after birth to the shrine of *yaksha*, Sakya Vardhana.

THE HYPAETHRAL TEMPLES[1]

The worship of trees as the abode of spirits and gods was once very popular. These spirits were associated with many trees, such as the *AI* (banyan), *Arasu* (pipal), *Iratti* (zizyphus or the jujube), *Ilanji, Kadamba, Pala* (jack), *Vakai* (Albizzia), *Vanni* (prosopis), *Velli* (wood-apple), *Vembu* (neem), *Vengai* (pterocarpus), etc. The *Kadamba* tree is said to be the abode of Murugan (Kartikeya), and the *AI* (banyan) that of Siva. The *Ahananuru*, one of the earliest Tamil works, describes a banyan tree in worship as surrounded by a brick enclosure and to which offerings were made. This would appear to be an instance of a tree-temple or *vriksha-chaitya* that was not particularly Buddhistic. The Tamil epic *Silappadikaram*, a work somewhat later in point of time, however, mentions a *Podi-manram*, or temple of the *Bodhi*-tree, a *vriksha-chaitya* of Buddhist affiliations designated as *Bodhi-ghara* (*Bodhi-griha*) in Buddhist literature. All these would constitute a class of hypaethral temples, that is, temples open to the air and devoid of a roof over the object of worship.

From archaeological evidence, it would be clear that this conception of tree-worship is very ancient, dating back to the Harappan times. As in the south, so also in north India there are references in early Buddhist texts to their existence even prior to the Buddha. In Buddhist literature such tree-shrines, with or without a temple structure and not specifically Buddhistic, are referred to as *rukka-chaitya* (*vriksha-chaityas* or *chaitya-vrikshas*) or

---

[1] Open temples, with no roof.

tree-temples, while those around the *Bodhi*-tree that had become sacred to the Buddhists are called *Bodhi-gharas*. The *Bodhi*-tree at Uruvela was considered sacred, even before Buddhist times, as the abode of a *devata* or divine being *(yaksha)* to whom offerings were made and from whom marriage and fertility boons were prayed for. The honour or worship offered to other sacred trees was similar, as, for example, in regard to the offering of flowers and garlands, bathing or purification with scented water, spreading of clean sand around their trunks to enable perambulation and the performance of the other functions and rituals as mentioned above. Sometimes even railings or enclosure walls were constructed and decked with flags, buntings and parasols.

Since construction around the sacred tree was meant not only to be honorific but also to meet the needs of the rituals of worship, it took definite architectural shapes in different plans. This is evident from the sculptural representations in relief of *Bodhi-gharas* in north and south Indian Buddhist sites, dating back as early as the second century BC. The *Bodhi-ghara* is always represented as a high gallery, open or roofed, immediately surrounding the *Bodhi*-tree and the *vajrasana* at its foot, with definitely posed entrances, into the enclosed sacred area, the *Bodhi-manda*. In *Asokavadana*, the emperor, Asoka, in fulfilment of his vow, is stated to have poured scented water from a thousand vessels by mounting on an enclosure *(varam)* which he had erected on all the four sides of the celebrated *Bodhi*-tree at Bodh Gaya. Of the two Amaravati versions of the *Bodhi-ghara* in south India, one is intact, though poorly preserved, and the other is fragmentary. The former, essentially square in plan, with the ends of the sides extended slightly beyond at each intersecting corner, has an unusually high second floor or gallery over the ground level. This was perhaps made accessible, as should be the case also in the other examples, by suitably placed flight of steps not seen in the relief representations. On plan it would have four sets of eight pillars, each at the four corners, four of each set occupying each of the real corners, while four more are placed in advance of each set in two pairs in front of the corners. The other Amaravati relief is triple storeyed and circular on plan. This too has tall pillars on the ground floor, supporting the two storeys above. The celebrated *Bahuputra-chaitya* of Vaisali, which was one of the Buddha's favourite resorts during his many visits to Vaisali, is depicted on one face of an Amaravati stele,[1] to indicate Vaisali in the narrative depiction of the Buddha's last visit to that place, though he did not stay at this *chaitya* that time. This part of the scene has three trees, with the bases of two of them enclosed by a railing. The most prominent one on the right, with the railing around it, is shown as being worshipped by two devotees, one with folded hands and the other holding out a baby towards the tree. This has also an inscription below it, calling it '*Bahuputra-chaitya* of Vaisali'. This would be a rendering of a *vriksha-chaitya* with a simple railing denoting its antiquity, for the stele and the inscriptions are of post-Asokan times. According to *Buddha-ghosha*, this was a many-branched tree where people prayed for sons. The depiction accordingly of one praying for the boon, and the other, having obtained it, presenting it in gratitude and for it to be blessed further is appropriate.[2]

In short, the *Bodhi-ghara* structures around the principal object of worship would thus anticipate the cloister galleries (or *dalans*) round the roofed temple structures, or *vimanas*, often more than one storeyed, enshrining the object of worship. These cloister galleries are designated in the Tamil inscriptions and texts as *malikai (malika)* as also in the *Silpa* and *Agama* literature on temple architecture. The only difference is that while the early examples surround hypaethral shrines which are not covered by a roof, the later *malikais* surround roofed shrines or *vimanas* containing the object of worship or the deity.

The very ancient and deep-rooted cult of tree worship contin-ued in south India, particularly the Tamil country, even after organized temple worship of the Hindu cults had grown. This would be seen in the association of religious places, or *sthalas*, with particular trees, the *sthala-vrikshas*, along with a particular water course, river, lake or tank, the *tirtha*. A place of important pilgrimage is even now called a *sthala*, or a *tirtha*, and a sacred

---

[1] *Ancient India*, Nos. 20 & 21, pp. 168-177.

[2] The *Arasu* (pipal) tree, often combined with the *Vembu* (neem) on river banks, or tank bunds, or other sacred spots, is even today an object of worship and peram-bulation by those desirous of progeny, and this *Asvattanarayana-pradakshina*, as it is called, is considered to be beneficial on Mondays which are also new-moon days.The *Arasu* is also considered sacred to Vishnu Naryana or Janardhana and the *pitris*, or departed ones, whose blessings are to be invoked for good progeny.

place must necessarily have a combination of *sthala-vriksha* and *tirtha*, along with the *murti*, or god-head. For example, the *sthala-vriksha* in Chidambaram is the *Tillai* (Aquillaria) in Jambukesvaram (near Tiruchirapalli), the *Jambu* in the Ekamranatha, at Kanchi the *Amra*, and in Madurai the *Kadamba*. There are numerous such instances, and they are mostly Saiva in association. Further, the early Tamil works associate particular trees, such as the *Kaval maram* (totem trees) with kings and ruling chiefs. The *Panai*, the *Atti* and the *Vembu* were, for example, the emblems, respectively, of the Chera, Chola and Pandya kings.

The other type of hypaethral temple brought into vogue by the Buddhists was the *stupa*, often called *maha-chaitya*. Before its advent in the south, the *stupa* which had begun as a low hemispherical solid dome or *anda* had developed into one where the *anda* was raised over a distinct cylindrical drum, the *medhi*. The *medhi*, being of a larger diameter than the *anda* above, provided a narrow circumambulatory passage, *pradakshina*, often with a low balustrade on its edge at a higher level in addition to the one on the ground level at its base. The balustrade was formed of vertical panels or slabs morticed between upright pillars planted at intervals. The *medhi* was often projected as offsets on the four cardinal sides in the shape of small platforms, the *ayaka* platforms, for the placement of offerings in simpler cases of the *stupa*. In other cases, flights of steps were provided for access. In some other cases, the *ayaka* platforms had each a set of five tall pillars planted on their outer edges. These were called *ayaka* pillars. On the top of the *anda* is the *harmika* square on plan and enclosing an umbrella (*chhatra*) or a series of them (*chhatravali*). The whole structure is often surrounded by a railing with plain openings on the four sides, and not the elaborate *torana* entrances as at Sanchi. The brick-built *stupa* had its *anda* and *medhi* and the *ayaka* platforms. In the earlier and simpler examples, these are merely plastered over, with a large looped garland girdling the *anda* picked out in stucco as an adornment. In others of the Krishna valley and adjacent areas, they were encased by a series of curved slabs of the local limestone—the marble-like soft Palnad limestone—that can be quarried into thin and large slabs and easily carved. The railing was also of the same material and carved likewise. The carvings consist of scenes from the various legends about the Buddha and also his life-story, besides other ornamental and decorative sculptures and motifs.

While the earlier larger and smaller *stupas* were solid and sometimes massive, the rest were semi-hollow and had adaptations of internal structural designs of brickwork with plans like the spoked wheel, the *swastika*, square within circles, etc., with the interspaces packed with rubble. All these were expedients designed to conserve brick and at the same time enhance the strength and stability of the structure, which was to bear the weight of the immense hemisphere and also of the casing of limestone slabs. These independent *stupas* or *maha-chaityas* contained relic caskets preserving fragmentary portions of the relics of the Buddha, or some other great master, suitably hidden and sealed inside.

The ruined *maha-chaitya* at Amaravati had its foundations laid in Asokan times. It was subsequently enlarged and encased with carved and sculptured limestone slabs with a stone railing. In the earlier phase here, as in the *stupas* at Bhattiprolu, Jaggayyapeta and Garikapadu, the *ayaka* platform alone came to be more elaborately sculptured in its stone casing as compared to the rest of the drum. This was consistent with the fact that the *ayaka* extensions served as altars for placing flowers, lamps and offerings by the devotees. The drum had more or less plain slabs with little carving, except perhaps for the low relief pilasters at the edges. These pilasters carried animal figures over their bell-shaped capitals. In addition, there were figures of devotees flanking the Buddha's symbols. Even during subsequent renovations the sculptors devoted greater attention to the *ayaka* platform, as in the case of other *stupas* elsewhere. The parapet slabs of the circumambulatory passage over the *medhi* had their inner faces finely carved as in the *maha-chaityas* of Nagarjunakonda, Jaggayyapeta, Ghantasala and Pedda-Ganjam. These slabs were morticed between uprights placed at intervals over the outer circumference with a running moulded coping on top. The stone railing dating earlier than 200 BC was also enlarged in the course of reconstruction and emerged in its final architectural and embellished form between AD 150 to 200. After this came the last phase of embellishment of the *stupa* when many of the earlier sculptured casing slabs of the basal parts were reversed and their erstwhile unsculptured inner faces trimmed and covered with some of the finest sculptures. This was done during the period AD 200 to 250.

The large *maha-chaitya* of Nagarjunakonda, built early in Ikshvaku times, belongs to the class of uncased *stupas*. Its brickwork has been mostly plastered over, and the *anda* decorated by an immense garland ornament in stuccco. But unlike the Amaravati *stupa* which was built solid, this *stupa* had a central column with eight radial walls meeting a peripheral circular wall, thus producing the appearance, on plan, of a cart-wheel with its hub, spokes and felly. There was a second concentric outer wall with further projections of the radial walls between it and the inner circular wall, the two circular walls forming, respectively, the bases of the *anda* and the *medhi*, while the inner cross-walls with fillings between them afforded the necessary structural support. It probably also had an outer circular railing. Many of the other *stupas* in this area had stone casings with sculptures and they also invariably had a stone railing. The *ayaka* platforms, though generally seen in the *stupas* of this area, are not noticed in the *stupas* at Ramatirtham and Salihundam, while they are seen only on one side of the rock-cut *stupa* at Sankaram. Likewise in the case of the Buddhist *stupas* on the east coast, lying between Nagarjunakonda and Amaravati on one side and Salihundam on the other, *stupas* like those at Sankaram have the *ayaka* platforms on one of their sides.

It is to be noted in this context, that while the Amaravati *stupa* revealed below its levels urn-burials, the site of Nagarjunakonda has shown the prevalence of the *stupas* with almost contemporaneous megalithic monuments. Such associations of megalithic sites and *stupa* sites are numerous in the Deccan, Andhra and north Mysore areas, roughly coinciding with the southern tracts of the Mauryan empire and the regions where Buddhism, among other northern religions, had a greater influence. This perhaps gave rise to the cult of the worship and reverence of the *stupa*, which is essentially funerary in content as well as by association. This was easily assimilable in this area which had an earlier megalithic tradition. For the same reason, therefore, one can assume that stone which was primarily associated with the dead and the cult of the dead for many centuries, could be adopted in the make-up of these essentially brick-built *stupas*, either as a protective veneer or as a surrounding enclosure or rail, and in columns that were free standing or structural supports. However, in contrast to the highly developed technique of brick construction, the structural patterns in stone were elementary and did not extend beyond simple casing or joining, as in the rails and balustrades, of crosspieces or slabs with tenons to morticed uprights. This was pure imitation of timberwork, a simulation of carpentry in stone. Actual stone construction involving structural principles of design, support, coursing and breaking of joints, counteraction of thrusts and loads, had not yet been developed.

In the extreme south, beyond the southernmost reaches of the Mauryan empire, where, according to the Asokan inscriptions, the Tamil kingdoms of the Cheras, Pandyas, Cholas and Satyaputas flourished, there is almost a paucity of Buddhist *stupas*. But contemporary literature speaks of Buddhism, along with the three other religions from the north which appear to have had a stronger hold in this area, particularly Hinduism and Jainism. The Ajivikas are heard of even towards the close of the first milennium AD and perhaps they merged into Jainism, which was predominantly Digambara, and had strong footholds in the southern Mysore or Kannada region also.

The megalithic cult was popular and worship and veneration of funerary monuments are frequently described, particularly the *nadukal* or stone erection (menheir or megalith) with offerings in-cluding toddy and animal sacrifice, keeping lamps lighted, and oblations of large quantities of boiled rice in heaps (*perumchoru* or *pavadai*). The dead, according to the literary evidence, were believed to have become stone itself which had acquired divine properties. A stone could be a hero, a warrior, a king, or even an ordinary person. Women, who immolated themselves on the death of their husbands, at a time when the cult of chastity and faithfulness was spreading fast, were given memorials in the nature of *sati* stones, later called in inscriptions *toru* or *masatikkal* (*maha-sati-kal*). Such memorial or *sati* stones, belonging to the second-third centuries AD, are found with inscriptions and sculp-tural reliefs in the Andhra sites, particularly at Nagarjunakonda, and are called *chhaya-khabas or chhaya-khambas*. These are also common in the Kannada country and across the borders in the peripheral regions of the Tamil country from the fourth century onwards. The early Tamil works speak of such a stone erection or *nadukal* in many contexts on which were written, evidently with ochre paint and brush, or later inscribed the name and exploits of the dead person it represented. This object of worship was surrounded by an enclosure, and a spear and shield were planted in front, and offerings of food and toddy were made. This instance of hypaethral temple is represented by a similar ancient construction on the Rangasami peak in the Coimbatore district, with a menheir or upright stone, having a trident or *trisula* planted in front and surrounded by a rubble wall.

The sculptured hero-stone slab or *virakal*, so erected in memory of, or over the grave of, the dead hero, was often flanked on either side, in front of the sculptured slab stele, by two more lateral slabs and the whole topped by a horizontally laid roof-slab, thus enclosing a roofed space. The formation can be called a dolmenshrine because it comprises three orthostatic slabs and a roof slab, like a dolmen, but contains the sculptured figure, that is venerated, on the inner face of its back wall. Such shrines called Ammankovils abound in the western districts of Tamil Nadu, in the Kongu area, and the adjoining districts of the Mysore plateau on the west in the Karnataka area. Besides the relief sculpture they carry inscriptions of the seventh-eighth centuries and later.

Temples as places of worship—the *podiyil* or *manram*, or *murram*—had objects of worship that were very often mere mounds or platforms—*medai*—under a particular tree in the village. Sometimes they were trilithons of a stone slab placed over two uprights—the *terri* which survive even today in some remote parts. Some of the platforms had a post, or *kandu*, representing the deity planted over them. These shrines are described as *kandudai-p-podiyil*, meaning the common place of worship where the *kandu* is installed. From some of the brief descriptions in the earliest Tamil works, we learn that the *kandu*, as the abode of a deity, stood in a pillared hall, or *podiyil*, on a platform that was cleansed and smeared with water and cowdung by young women who, after a dip in the bathing *ghat*, lighted an ever-burning lamp near the *kandu*. We are also told that many came here to worship with offerings or *bali*.

The *Buddha-pitikai* or *Dharma-pitikai* as the object of worship by the Buddhists is referred to in the Tamil epic, *Manimekalai*. From its brief description it would appear to have been a circular *padma-pitha*, or seat of expanding lotus petals, mounted over a square plinth, also with a lotus petal base, the whole evidently of brickwork. A solitary example of a *Buddha-pada*, the *tiruvadi* (or *punya-pada)* of the master, as an object of worship, has come up from the recent excavations of the anicient Chola port city of Kaveri-p-pattinam at the mouth of the river Kaveri. It is a carved slab of Palnad limestone of about the fourth century AD and perhaps formed the top piece of a brick platform. It was probably originally installed in a shrine for worship. These two instances would show that, in the absence of *stupas* as objects of worship in the Tamil country, it was the Buddha-*pitikai* and the Buddha-*pada* that were worshipped till the much later advent of the iconic forms of the Buddha in stone or other materials.

Recent excavations in the Gudimallam temple in Chittoor on the Tamil Nadu-Andhra border have revealed the fact that the *linga* with its *pitha,* both of sandstone, were originally hypaethral in the second century BC. A brick shrine enclosing it came up in the first-second centuries AD to be replaced by a stone apsidal one, much later. The brick shrine was apsidal too (Dr I.K. Sharma).

THE ROOFED TEMPLES

Where roofed structures were built enshrining such platforms, cult objects, symbols or iconic representations, they imitated secular buildings in the plan and style of construction. The only difference was that the temples were made of more permanent material, like brick and wrought timber, more lavishly decorated with plaster, stucco, carving and painting, and often larger in dimensions in contrast to the humbler mud-and-wattle-walled, thatch-roofed houses of the common folk.

None of these temples has survived in the Tamil land though we have enough word pictures of these simple or storeyed constructions in the Tamil *Sangam* classics. One, for example, describes a temple with high brick walls and wooden beams, containing inside, on its back wall, the painted picture of the deity or Kadavul that was worshipped, indicating that it was either a mural painting or a stucco figure, or sometimes a carved wooden plaque that constituted the principal object of worship in the more sophisticated temples of the time. Such temples or shrines, mostly of brick and timber, are variously designated in the *Sangam* works as *Kottam*, *Nagaram*, *Koyil* and *Palli*. Evidently these names indicate different plans and styles of construction. The epic *Manimekalai* speaks of temples built of brick and having imposing entrances or *gopuras*. Some of these temples were storeyed *madams*, and these included memorial shrines also.The custom of building such memorial shrines, called *Palli-p-padai* in Tamil, continued even in the ninth and tenth centuries AD as testified by the Tamil and Kannada inscriptions.

In the ancient Tamil country of the far south, as its early literature also reveals, various gods are represented as presiding over different tracts of the country, namely, the hilly, the sylvan or pastoral, the riverine or agricultural, the desert or arid zones, and the littoral or seaside. Such gods were Seyon, Mayon, Vendan, Valiyon, Korravai or Kadukal. There were, in addition, other minor gods. It was in the centuries preceding and following the Christian era that the dynamic religions of the *Vedic* Hindus, the Jains, the Ajivikas, and the Bauddhas of the north made definite and vital impacts on the cultural, linguistic and religious substratum of the south. This also coincided with the extent of the political map of the Mauryas, with the extreme south beyond its limits maintaining a strong indigenous core with a viable culture, language and a fast-growing literature under organized kingdoms. The incoming people found it expedient to cultivate the local languages in order to expound better their ideas of religion and ritual and actively contributed by taking a large share themselves in the growth of the literature and grammar of the Tamil language. There are many among the *Sangam* poets, who were Brahmins or Jains. The same happened to the Kannada language a little later. Thus, the impact resulted in the importation and infusion in various degrees of new thoughts and ideas by the incoming religious cultures, as also a simultaneous absorption of much that was local. The phenomenon that occurred as a result of such impact of the culture and religions of India in the countries of the Far East such as Ceylon, Burma, Thailand, Cambodia and Indonesia, producing a synthesis of godheads and local modified versions of the legends, iconography and ritual, occurred here also more or less. For example, Hinduism, particularly in the Tamil country, which included much of Kerala also, became eclectic by absorbing the local deities and concepts in the pantheon and ritual, or by identifying them with many of its own. The local Mayon was identified with Krishna or Vishnu, Valiyon with Balabhadra, Korravai with Durga, Seyon or Murugan with Kartikeya, and Vendan with Indra.The *Sangam* and post-*Sangam* poetry extending up to about the seventh century speaks of temples—*kottams, nagarams* and *koyils*— dedicated to these gods, besides temples for Siva, Indra's mount—Airavata, and his thunderbolt *Vajra,* the celestial boon tree *Kalpataru,* the sun and the moon. The beginnings of the slow evolution of *Agamic* worship are also to be found here. Similar, but to a much lesser degree, was the effect in the case of local Jainism, which was mainly and for long Digambara, and Buddhism. Iconic forms of Siva, Vishnu, Surya, Kartikeya, Sri, Durga and other gods were also evolved. This synthesis, in effect, resulted, after due growth during the five succeeding centuries (between the eighth and the thirteenth), in the contribution of the south to the common heritage of India of unique forms and concepts, for example, the form and concept of Siva as Nataraja and Dakshinamurti, Devi as Lalita, the *bhakti* cult of the Nayanmars and Alvars—the Saiva and Vaishnava hagiologists—and the great philosophies of *Advaita, Visishtadvaita* and *Dvaita* of Sankara, Ramanuja and Madhva. The same can be said of the contributions of the south to Jainism and Buddhism of later times.

No remains of these gods, mostly painted or carved in wood, or of their temples of brick and timber, have survived in the far south. This was because of the perishable nature of the fabric of which they were made.

The northern half of the peninsula which comprises the Deccan and the Andhra and Kannada areas, that is, roughly those parts that came under the Mauryan empire, naturally imbibed more from the penetrating cultures, religions and languages (Prakrit and Sanskrit) than others. This resulted in the delayed development of its indigenous literatures which thus do not supply much material regarding the purely local traditions and beliefs of the very early times. But many contemporary material relics indicating the religious forms and places of worship are extant and have come up, as in north India, in the latest excavations. Though the Buddhist relics are more numerous, recent excavations in Nagarjunakonda have revealed the existence also of Hindu temples side by side, showing the popularity of the Saivite, Vaishnavite, and other cults. These relics also reveal the fact that the temples or shrines had a common plan, design and mode of construction, irrespective of the creeds to which they belonged. The credal difference was marked only by the gods or objects that were installed for worship and their appropriate symbols or the plastic representations that formed the decorative elements of such temples. Jainism seems to have had more congenial homes in the Kannada, Tamil and Kerala areas. In their plans their religious structures, particularly their temples, did not differ much from those of the Hindus, a feature that has persisted through the centuries to the present day. The traces of Buddhist temples that were perhaps fewer have been lost in these areas, though a number of Buddha images of later periods have been found in different parts of south India. Had their temples survived, they too would not have differed much in form from the Hindu or Jain temples of those days.

Architecturally, these simple shrines, replicas of contemporary secular dwellings, were square, oblong, circular, elliptical and apsidal, rarely hexagonal or octagonal and were built of timber or brick. Such religious and secular structures are indicated in the early bas-relief sculptures belonging to the centuries immediately before and after Christ, e.g. Barhut and Sanchi in the north and Amaravati and Nagarjunakonda and other places in the south. They have already been indicated as being plans in the representation of tree-temples or *vriksha-chaityas*, Buddhist *stupas*, and *Bodhi-mandas* (*Podi-manram* in Tamil).

The square buildings have their roofs converging to a point (*kuta*), the circular or octagonal ones likewise have domical roofs (*kuta*), the oblong ones have vault-like or wagon-top-like (*sala*) or occasionally gabled roofs (*sabha*), as in Sitamarhi and Sone Bhandar, and the elliptical ones have inverted keel-shaped roofs with a long ridge and a number of finials (also called *sala*). The front view of the apsidal structures can be noted in many of these relief sculptures.

From the extant literary descriptions, from the sculptural representations in relief, and from the few excavated relics (as, for example, the circular shrine at Bairat, others at Nagarjunakonda and Salihundam, and the standing ones in Chejerla and Ter in Andhra and western Decccan), one can infer that the roofs of these brick-and-timber structures were either supported on their pillars, the intervening space being covered by screen walls, or they were raised totally on their walls with the pillars, if any, represented only as ornamental pilasters externally. Often the brick wall had an internal system of pillars standing close to them to form additional supports for the beams and timbering of the superstructure and the roof. The entire structure was often built over a solid masonry platform or *adhishthana*.

The apsidal Guntupalle *chaitya* (second century AD) is wholly brick-built. The entrance has brickwork jambs into which a wooden door-frame was fitted. The roof was evidently a vault made up of corbelled brickwork that was plastered and perhaps also cribbed inside with wooden ribs and crosspieces—on the analogy of an earlier rock-cut *chaitya* of the same plan. The remains of another *chaitya* noticed near Vidyadharapuram, near Vijayawada, are of like nature. A somewhat better preserved *stupa*-shrine or *stupa-chaitya*, where the central object of worship was the representation of a *stupa*, has come up from the excavations at Salihundam (Srikakulam district, Andhra Pradesh). The circular *chaitya* is brick-built. The massive wall has a stepped up base provided with a narrow vestibule for approach in front, resembling the *antarala* of later temples. Several subsidiary shrines of identical shape also exist there.

In Nagarjunakonda and other Andhra Buddhist sites, the brick-built *chaitya* temples are associated with *viharas* or monasteries, where they are often found as apsidal structures on either side of the passage behind the main *vihara* entrance, or are found in pairs in front of the major *stupas* or *maha-chaityas*, which were themselves open or hypaethral temples, facing each other. Often one of them enshrines a *stupa* and is called *stupa-chaitya*. The other enshrines the feet or, later, figures of the Buddha, and is known as Buddha-*chaitya*. Independent apsidal *chaityas* or temples, the earliest of that possibly enshrined a Buddha image, has been noticed in Nagarjunakonda. In a few other cases the shrines have a square plan.

The excavations in Nagarjunakonda have also revealed large non-Buddhist temple complexes of the Ikshvaku kings (third and fourth centuries AD) dedicated to Siva, Vishnu, Kartikeya and Devasena. They have mostly four-sided or apsidal *garbha-grihas* (sanctum) built over an elevated plinth with a large pillared *mandapa* in front of them, a raised platform at the fore part of the *mandapa* indicating a *ranga-mandapa*, and often an ambulatory court round the *mandapa*. The whole is enclosed by a brick-wall with entrance on the front side (east or west) on the *gopura* pattern, with simpler additional entrances on the south and north sides. The pillars of the *mandapa* were made from Palnad limestone, rectangular in section, chamfered at the corners for some length from a point above the middle height of the shaft, and terminating again in an apex of a rectangular section. On top is cut a wide rectangular notch for fitting the wooden beams, which were mostly longitudinal. Over the beams, the local vein schist slabs, called Macherla slabs, were laid, and this ceiling was, perhaps, covered over by a brick-and-mortar terrace. The apsidal shrines, sometimes in pairs, are entirely brick-built. Only sometimes as in the Pushpabhadrasvami temple, the superstructure is supported by a parallel row of limestone pillars set inside the straight sides of the apse with similar pillars arranged in a semi-circle at the rear curved end, the pillars carrying longitudinal beams over the parallel sides and short curved beams over the rear pillars. The intervening spaces between the pillars were walled up. In front of the shrines there is often a rectangular *ardha-mandapa* interposed between the shrine and the pillared *maha-mandapa*. The *maha-mandapa* in some cases is often extended laterally by one or more bays and, in some instances, there were pillared cloisters (*malikai* or *malika*) inside the enclosure walls surrounding the court round the three sides of the *maha-mandapa*. The temple complexes have a single main shrine or sometimes more than one main shrine. The single shrines are oblong, square or apsidal in plan. In cases with multiple shrines there are some examples with two shrines, both apsidal, and others having both rectangular and apsidal shrines. The walls of the temples do not appear to have been adorned with much sculpture. While the *mandapas* had flat roofs, the shrine superstructures, particularly of the apsidal ones, were *gaja-prishtha*, i.e. with forms resembling the hind-quarters of an elephant. It cannot be said for certain whether the square and oblong shrines were *vimana* forms with the typical storeyed superstructure as found in the later *vimanas* of the south. One cannot fail to notice from the remains of this extensive site a close similarity between the Buddhist and non-Buddhist types in architectural traditions.

The Kartikeyasvami temple had a square brick-built shrine facing east with a closed rectangular *ardha-mandapa* of bricks in front. Its longer axis north-south was preceded by a closed *maha-mandapa* with six rows of five pillars each. Another temple of Kartikeya, to the north of the Pushpabhadrasvami temple, had a rectangular closed *mandapa* with a square pedestal close to its hind wall at its centre, and a pillar at each corner. It suggested a pillared *mandapa* shrine. The image in the Pushpabhadrasvami temple, referred to by that name in the inscription on the *dvajasthamba* as 'Mahadeva Pushpabhadrasvamin', was enshrined in an apsidal *garbha-griha*.

The icon of Ashtabhujasvamin, according to the inscription relating to its installation, dated AD 278 was of wood, eight-armed, and was installed on a stone pedestal that carried the inscription. The inscription on a conch (*sankha*) found at the same site also bears the same name. The temple with its two sanctuaries, one oblong and the other apsidal, each with a pillared *mandapa* in front, distinct from the independent one of larger dimensions at the rear, had a *dvajasthamba* surmounted by the *chakra* emblem of Vishnu.

The east-facing temple complex on the river bank and close to the village of Putlagudem, near the old ferry *ghat,* is interesting, in that in the court on the south and north sides of the pillared *maha-mandapa* were found the basements of *parivara* shrines, all brick-built and topped by thin stone slabs forming the floors of the subsidiary shrines of square, circular, and octagonal plans.

Similar brick temples of the post-Ikshvaku and pre-Chalukyan (sixth century) period, have been excavated in the submersible Srisailam project area in Vivapuram, Rungapur, Gumakonda, Kudavelli and Siddesvaram, all in the Kurnool and Mahboobnagar districts. The shrines are invariably square on plan with or without an attached *ardha-mandapa* in front. The *lingas* are of rolled natural sandstone pebbles with or without *linga-pithas*. The spout of the latter where present is oriented north. Otherwise the consecrated image alone appears to be of stone, while the construction was of brick and timber. The soles (*adhishthana*) are of moulded bricks and moulded parts of the superstructures too have come out in the excavations (Dr R. Subrahmanyam and Dr I.K. Sharma).

Fortunately there are two apsidal shrines of this period of original Buddhist dedication and subsequent conversion to the Hindu creed, still existing in their entirety. They are the Trivikrama temple at Ter in western Deccan, and the Kapotesvara temple at Chejerla, in coastal Andhra. Both are dated earlier than AD 600, but not earlier than AD 300. Of the two, the Kapotesvara may be the earlier one judged from the stylistic and architectural points of view. This temple built of large-sized bricks shows no external pilaster markings on its wall, except at the two front ends which are not original. Internally the ceiling of stone slabs is supported by a system of ten stone pillars, ranged five, each along the straight sides of the apsidal structure and spanned by thick stone beams, in contrast to the Nagarjunakonda structures which had wooden beams, thus making an advance in the use of stone in construction and thereby indicating a later date. The vaulted brickwork *sikhara* is supported inside by uprights of either brick-work or stone and, perhaps also by fillings in-between over the ceiling slabs. The cornice moulding (*kapota*) and the clerestory-like *griva* as well as the blunted ridge of the *sikhara* shows a backward slope.

Recent excavations have revealed that the original founda-tion of this temple was Saivite and not Buddhist, later converted into Saivite, as was hitherto believed.

The Ter temple now containing a Trivikrama image shows more advanced features. It is entirely brick-built, without internal pillars or ceiling slabs, and the *sikhara* ridge is quite horizontal. Externally the wall surface is relieved by pilasters with evolved capital components. Internally the vault is formed by a system of corbelling-in of the successive courses of brickwork from all sides, thus gradually diminishing the gap and ultimately closing it on top. This mode is called *kadalika karana* in Indian *Silpa* parlance. The front end of the *sikhara* of the Ter *chaitya* shows the barge-board and barge-plate with a median transverse supported on four pilasters, and a central light-opening, all in imitation of timber orginals, while the Chejerla *sikhara* facade shows the relief of the shrine. In these respects, these approximate to the motifs of the *sikhara* facades of the Visvakarma at Ellora and the Nakula-Sahadeva *ratha* in Mamallapuram.

3

EARLY ROCK ARCHITECTURE

ROCK-CUT CAVE-TEMPLES—*LAYANAS* (BUDDHIST)

Side by side with the predominantly brick-and-timber architecture of early times, there arose a movement at the time of Asoka which resulted in a series of temples and other religious resorts being excavated into living rock. Being made of more permanent material, these have survived to the present day. Since they are faithful imitations of the contemporary brick-and-timber structures which served as their models, they reproduced, at least in their frontal and interior aspects, all the architectural details of the period, thus enabling us to form an idea of what the fronts and interiors of contemporary temples and places of what are called *layanas* into rock and creating partial or total imitations of structural examples, cannot be called architecture, which essentially implies construction by building up of components. They can only be regarded as sculpture on a large scale, more conveniently designated as 'rock architecture', or 'architectural sculpture'. The phase of rock architecture extended approximately over a period of more than a thousand years from the time of Asoka, and is found scattered over different parts of India, the latest of them belonging to the close of the tenth century.

The earliest caves excavated by Asoka and his grandson Dasaratha into the very hard local rock (quartzose-gneiss) are in the Barabar and Nagarjuni hills near Gaya. They were dedicated to the Ajivikas. The most important examples of this group are the Sudama (Nyagrodha) and the Lomas Rishi caves. These two caves exactly reproduce the plan of the Suddhamma Deva Sabha in the Barhut relief. This series of caves indicates that the simplest form of such temples consisted of a circular cell or shrine alone, as at Guntupalle; the porch, or *mandapa* was added later to

accommodate worshippers. This mode of rock architecture shifted in the next century mainly to the softer trap formations of the
hills of western India or western Deccan where, between 200 BC
and AD 200, a number of Buddhist excavations were made. They
include *chaitya* halls, which were really temples or places of
worship; the object of worship being a *stupa* representing the
Buddha, and *viharas*, or monasteries, each with a number of cells
opening into a large central assembly-hall. Such examples are
found in the vicinity of Poona and Nasik, and Ajanta and
Aurangabad. The choice of this area was due to.the fact that the
softer trap rocks were more easy to work on than the hard
granites or gneisses, as in Gaya. Such places of worship were also
excavated into the softer rocks on the Eastern Ghats, lying in the
northern coastal districts of Andhra and the southern districts of
Orissa, as in Guntupalle and Sankaram, both cut-in and cut-out,
the examples in Orissa being the Jain caves of Khandagiri and
Udayagiri. Among these the Buddhist cave at Kondivte in Salsette,
the Tulaja cave in Junnar, near Poona, and the cave in Guntupalle
in Andhra bear comparison with the Sudama and Lomas Rishi
caves near Gaya.

Beyond the Bombay-Poona region, where the soft trap-rock
formations were exploited for excavation of *chaityas* and *viharas*,
further north and north-west, the laterite hills as in Junagad,
afforded the venue for such excavations; laterite when freshly
exposed being equally soft and tractable. Futher south, beyond
Konkan, in the Kerala area, west of the *ghats*, again abounding in
laterite, it was excavated into, though as cave-tombs of megalithic
association in corresponding times.

The rock-cut *chaitya* at Guntupalle is not far removed from
the Gaya caves in point of time. It is a stone version of a circular
hut with a cupola-like domed roof of thatch or sheet metal resting
on a wooden frame-work resembling an inverted basket, and
enshrining a monolithic *stupa* as the object of worship in the
centre, circumambulatory passage all round, and a porch in front
of its doorway. The porch framing the entrance shows similar
imitation of timberwork in stone, including the *torana* arch above
the lintel.

The Buddhist cave-temple in Kondivte is of similar design
where the circular shrine or *garbha-griha* is occupied by a solid
stupa leaving only a narrow circumambulatory passage or

pradakshina all round within the shrine and occupying the end of a rectangular hall or *mandapa*, with a flat roof as the shrine itself. The Tulaja cave in Junnar is also an excavation after the model of a circular *chaitya*. The main roofing dome rests on a ring of twelve plain octagonal pillars, instead of on a circular wall—as in the other examples—enclosing a central *stupa*, both surrounded by a circular aisle, or *pradakshina*, which is half-domed.[1] The circular *garbha-griha* of the Suddhamma Deva Sabha in Barhut is a bas-relief representation of the same model.

The other *chaityas* are mainly apsidal in plan, consisting of a long rectangular hall like a nave, terminating at the farther end into an apse with often two narrower aisles on either side, each separated from the nave by a row of pillars and extended round the apse as a circumambulatory passage round a *stupa*, also hewn out of rock and occupying the centre of the apse. The doorway in front is a huge threshold with an arched window on top. In front of the facade of the hall, a transverse verandah with frontal pillars is often cut. The structures after which such excavations were made were, therefore, essentially apsidal temples. Such an apsidal or *chapa* form resulted perhaps from the coming together of a circular shrine and rectangular assembly-hall, which were originally distinct from each other as in the examples already described.

At Ajanta, in the Deccan, out of the thirty excavations, six consisting of two *chaitya* halls (Nos. 9 and 10), and four *viharas* (Nos. 8, 12, 13, and 30), belong to the early group, and are of the same type as some Buddhist excavations at Bhaja, Karle, Kondane, Pithalkora, Nasik, Kanheri, etc. These belong to the period between the second century BC and the second century AD. The rest belong to the period after the fourth century AD. They were excavated in the time of the Vakatakas, mostly between AD 450 and 600. The last ones were excavated around AD 650. The activity in general, and particularly the embellishments, however, continued till the times of the Rashtrakutas in the eighth-ninth centuries AD.

The early *chaityas* are large, apsidal, with an elaborate facade, having horseshoe-shaped windows on the top of the entrance,

---

[1] A temple of a similar structural plan has come to light in the excavations at Bairat, near Jaipur.

and the interior divided into a central nave and lateral aisles by two rows of columns. The aisles continued round the apse as a circumambulatory passage. A rock-cut *stupa*, in the apse portion, formed the object of worship. The ceilings of the aisle were either flat or vaulted, the whole modelled after timber constructions.

The *viharas* were astylar halls, with a number of monks' cells excavated into their three side walls, the hall having one or more main entrances in front.

The rock architecture of the second phase consists of two apsidal *chaityas* (19 and 26). It is similar to the earlier type but has a Buddha figure prominently standing out in front of the *stupa* in the apse, under a *nasika* or arch projected from the drum of the *stupa*. This suggests that the form of the *stupa* itself was conceived as a circular shrine with a domical roof, and a projected vaulted entrance porch in front in the shape of a *sukanasika*, conforming to the *Vesara* type of temples of later periods.[1] The *viharas*, except those unfinished or destroyed (3, 5, 14, 23, 24, 28, and 29), combine the characteristics of monasteries and shrines in them, the latter aspect becoming more prominent. Thus these abodes of stone, or hill-abodes, called *sailagriha* in an inscription datable between AD 450 and 525 in Cave 26, would become *vihara-chaityas*, if we equate the term *chaitya* with the shrine containing an object of worship, called also *devakula, ayatana, vimana, dhama, mandira*, etc. In fact, the inscription in *Vihara* 16, datable between AD 475 and 500, calls it a *chaitya-mandira*.

These *viharas* generally consist of an outer verandah or porch, corresponding to the *mukha-mandapa* or *agra-mandapa* of the temple complexes, a pillared hall (sometimes astylar), corresponding to the *maha-mandapa* with a shrine or *garbha-griha* at its rear, often with an *ardha-mandapa*, or transversely rectangular ante-chamber intervening between the shrine and the main hall. When the hall has pillars instead of a central nave and lateral aisles pattern, the arrangement of a central square enclosed by four or more pillars—the others forming a peripheral series— would suggest a *ranga-mandapa* on the model of or anticipating the Chalukyan *navarangas*. Into the lateral walls of the *maha-mandapa* or hall and sometimes also into the hind walls cubical cells are cut for the priestly monks. These are fewer in number than those in regular monasteries—rock-cut and brick-built—

---

[1] These would bear comparison with the similar and smaller Nalanda brick *stupas*.

thus suggesting that their use was restricted to the monks of higher ranks only, or to the priestly order immediately connected with the actual ritual worship in the principal *chaitya*. Often there are additional *chaityas* or cells on either side of the principal one on the rear wall of the hall, and also in the lateral walls of the front porch, or *agra-mandapa*. Even the two-storeyed excavation (Cave 6) has essentially the same plan. The sanctum contains a large figure of the Buddha, often with other sculptures in the *ardha-mandapa*. In the case of Cave 27, the *ardha-mandapa* is advanced into the *maha-mandapa*. The arrangement of a succession of *mandapas*, one behind the other, with one or more shrine cells at the rear, is on the pattern found in the brick-temple complexes of the Ikshvaku period in Nagarjunakonda that preceded these later excavations in Ajanta.

The hindmost part of such an axial group—consisting of the rectangular ante-chamber and square behind it, sometimes partly advanced into it—is found repeated mostly as the plan in the Hindu and Jain rock-cut cave-temples of the Chalukyas, Pallavas, Pandyas and other dynasties of south India, who continued rock-cut architecture from the sixth to about the first half of the tenth century AD or even later, as in Ellora. In few cases, as in the Ajanta examples, the cave-temple has a large and almost square *mandapa*, corresponding to the hall with the sanctum behind, the transverse rectangular *ardha-mandapa* being eliminated. In a temple complex with such an axial arrangement, the sanctum does not appear to have had a superstructure of the pyramidal type. These cave-temples, including the *chaitya-mandiras*, may as well be called *mandapa*-temples as they are designated in later inscriptions. The excavation of lateral shrines on either side of the main shrine all in a line, with a common *mandapa* in front, is one line of elaboration, while the other line would be the excavation of additional shrines into the lateral walls with all the shrines opening into a common hall or verandah as is often found in the verandahs or ante-chambers of the Ajanta *viharas*. Both the modes are found developed in the later cave-temples of the Chalukyas, Pallavas, Pandyas, and other contemporary dynasties of the south.

The Buddhist rock architecture of Ellora (in all twelve excavations) concentrated at the south end of the hill, as also the excavations at Aurangabad mark the culmination of the series, and they continue the earlier tradition of western India.

The Ellora Buddhist group falls into three sub-groups, the earliest being Caves 1, 2, 3 and 5 dating from round about the fourth century AD. Caves 4 and from 6 to 10 are assignable to the sixth-seventh centuries AD. Caves 11 and 12, which are unique, belong to the seventh century AD. In contrast Cave 1 in the first series is simple and perhaps an experimental excavation. Caves 2 and 3 are essentially similar to each other. They have a verandah or *agra-mandapa*. While the *maha-mandapa* of Cave 2 has lateral galleries on either side, that of Cave 3 is without them. The shrine cells behind both contain a seated Buddha. The shrine of Cave 2 has two lateral cells with an ante-chamber or *ardha-mandapa*. There are monastic cells on the lateral walls of the *mandapa* of Cave 3. Cave 6, the largest among single-storeyed excavations, consists of a verandah and a pillared hall with twenty-two cells on its walls. Behind the pillared *maha-mandapa* is a transverse ante-chamber or *ardha-mandapa*, with a Buddha shrine in the rear.

Cave 4 is two-storeyed. The groundfloor consists of a hall, an ante-chamber and a shrine behind, with additional cells on either side of the shrine and on the lateral walls of the hall. The upper floor is ruined and a *pradakshina-patha* and two cells alone are extant. Cave 8 has again a large hall with three monk-cells on the north wall. The shrine behind, fully cut-out, has a *pradakshina-patha*, and an ante-chamber in front. It contains a seated Buddha. On the north wall of the *pradakshina-patha* there are monastic cells.

Cave 6 as usual has a verandah and a hall behind, having a lateral hall on the south with six cells. At the rear of the main hall there are an ante-chamber and the shrine. Cave 7 has behind its verandah a hall with four central pillars and twelve unfinished cells on its three side walls. The central shrine at the rear is flanked on one side by a *prajnaparamita* and its door-frame is moulded, thus denoting that it is the main shrine.

Cave 9, strictly speaking, is a long hall or *mandapa*, with a prominent sculptured facade—a poor imitation of Cave 10. The back wall is divided into three bays by four pilasters, the central bay containing a sculpture of the seated Buddha simulating a shrine, while the lateral bays contain attendants.

Cave 10 (Visvakarma) is a large *chaitya* similar to those at Ajanta with pillars and aisles and balconies in front of the arch opening. The pillars are simple and the sculptures few. The apse consists of a *stupa* with a shrine of the seated Buddha cut into it, thus indicating the *stupa* form to be a circular *vimana* (*Vesara*) with the deity inside. The drum of the *stupa* has twelve panels all round, ten of which contain miniature Buddhas. The arch on the facade is very elaborate and different in design from that found in Ajanta and elsewhere. Its trefoil arches, and the *udgamas* and the *amalakas*, recall similar motifs characteristic of contemporary and later Brahmanical temples in the northern style.

Caves 11 and 12 of the seventh century AD, called Do-tal and Tin-tal, respectively, are perhaps the largest of this class of Buddhist excavation, remarkably original in their plans and storeys, containing interesting iconographic sculptures and architectural embellishments. Though both are three-storeyed, the Do-tal cave was so called since its groundfloor remained buried. A similar rock-cut cave excavation, now called Anantasayanagudi in Undavalli on the south bank of the Krishna, also belongs to this class. It is perhaps of the Vishnukundini times and was meant originally for a Buddhist dedication.

The Aurangabad cave-temples include a *chaitya* of the earlier Hinayana phase and a number of *viharas* (eight in two groups) and other less important excavations, all belonging to the seventh centruy AD.

In all these excavations the roughness of the texture, even of finished surface, necessitated a plaster coating to render it smooth. Further embellishments came by way of rich paintings of which we have many extant as the celebrated paintings of Ajanta.

4

LATER ROCK ARCHITECTURE

ROCK-CUT CAVE-TEMPLES — *LAYANAS* (HINDU AND JAIN)

In the beginning of the second half of the millennium after Christ, the Brahmanical and Jain creeds too started adopting the rock-cut mode of temples. This caught on quickly and in the last four centuries of the millennium a vast number of such temples had been created all over the south, from the Deccan to very near the Cape. These, incidentally, are far more numerous than similar excavations in the north. The majority of these again are Brahmanical. The Jain ones are fewer. The inauguration of this mode of rock-cut temples for the Brahmanical and Jain gods commenced with the coming to power of three great empires in the peninsula—the Chalukyas of Vatapi (Badami) in the Deccan region, with their collateral branch of the Chalukyas of Vengi (or the Eastern Chalukyas) on coastal Andhra, the Pallavas of Kanchi on the eastern coast, and the Pandyas of Madurai in the far south. The best and maximum output in this direction came during the three centuries between AD 550 and 850, when these three powerful kingdoms were not only keen political rivals but were also close competitors in the patronage of art, architecture and literature. While the early Chalukyas of Badami were replaced in the middle of this period by the Rashtrakutas of Manyakheta, the Pallavas and the Pandyas continued to hold sway right through. The intervening minor and subordinate dynasties, wedged among the three imperial powers as buffer states, also took part in the activity and contributed to this movement in their respective regions.

There had been a lingering tradition of a taboo on stone for sacred and secular structures, because of its long local association with funerary erections, as has been noted before. This was apparently broken almost simultaneously by the Chalukya King Mangalesa, and his contemporary the Pallava King, Mahendra I. Mangalesa excavated Vishnu Cave-temple No. III in Badami, in commemoration of and in association with the Narayana-bali ceremony (shraddha) of his departed and beloved brother Kirtivarman in Saka 500 (AD 578), as the related inscriptions say. Mahendra I, perhaps taking the cue, excavated his first cave-temple at Mandagappattu (South Arcot district) for the Hindu trinity— Siva, Vishnu and Brahma. While Mangalesa chose the finely-grained and horizontally stratified soft sandstone cliffs of Badami (Bijapur district), as the new capital, Mahendra I chose the very hard close-grained granite rock of Mandagappattu, far away from his capital. In Mangalesa's case, though the excavation of a cave-temple for a Hindu god and the carving of Hindu sculptures on it were altogether novel credal innovations, the mode was only a perpetuation of the earlier tradition of excavating such cave-temples into deliberately chosen soft rocks like sandstone, trap or limestone that had been in continuous existence from Mauryan times in north, central and western India as also the Deccan.[1] Thus, his craftsmen had the advantage of the long acquired know-how of such cutting into sandstone and carving them, which had been developing for nearly a millennium. The first cave-temple was, as a result, bold and ambitious in design and of larger dimensions. Close on Mangalesa's first cave-temple followed other similar cave-temples of the Chalukyas in Badami, Aihole, and other places, all excavated into the same soft rocks.

In the case of Mahendra, the excavation into hard rock and carving of the cave-temple and sculpture would almost be an innovation, since there had been no precedents, except those of Asoka and Dasaratha in the Barabar, Nagarjuni and Sitamarhi hills, near Gaya, some 900 years before. Since then the practice and tradition had been totally given up or forgotten and not attempted in that long interval of time and space. In such a context, Mahendra's gloating over his first achievement in his inscription on the Mandagappattu cave-temple became quite

---

[1] In fact, the Guptas had earlier excavated cave-temples for the Hindu gods in the sandstone cliffs of Udaigiri near Vidisa.

meaningful. The inscription states that "this brickless, timberless, metalless and mortarless abode of Lakshita was caused to be made by King Vichitrachitta for Brahma, Isvara and Vishnu." The small inscription is important also in that Mahendra's work was a departure from the contemporary usage and tradition in the matter of the creation of a stone-temple without resorting to the usual materials, such as brick, timber, metal and mortar. What was even more significant was that it was a departure from the process known till then of excavating into deliberately chosen soft rocks. This was followed by more cave-temples being excavated by him into the hard rocks of the south. They are all of a simpler design and less ambitious in size because of the hardness of the new rock material of hitherto unknown potentialities that involved greater labour, invention of new tools and skills in cutting, and longer time to complete.

Thus one may say that the Chalukyas and the Pallavas inaugurated two parallel traditions in the south. The succeeding dynasties in the Chalukyan region of the Deccan, north Mysore, and coastal Andhra continued the choice and use of soft stone rocks for their cave-temples and later for their structural temples. Those that came after the Pallavas and their contemporary Pandyas, who also excavated into hard rocks of their area, continued to choose and employ likewise hard rocks for their rock-cut and structural temples further south.

The result was that these two parallel traditions continued in the south in the respective regions till the advent of the Vijayanagar empire in the second half of the fourteenth century, which soon embraced in its ambit both these regions and in fact soon extended practically over the whole of south India. The soft stone tradition of the northern region almost came to an end and the use of hard stone for temple construction became almost universal, though the regional styles and distinguishing characters that had developed up to that time in either region were generally maintained.

The three centuries covering the rock-cut phase in the Brahmanical and Jain temple architecture coincided also with the great revivalist movements of the Hindus and the continuing hold of the Jain sects on some sections of the people. With the commencement of the seventh century, and in the wake of the revivalist movements of the Hindus, great changes were wrought and the *bhakti* cult developed. In the Tamil land the Saiva and Vaishnava hymnist saints, the Nayanmars and the Alvars, became wedded to the *Vedic* traditions and traversed the whole area visiting shrines, singing hundreds of devotional hymns in Tamil and rousing the people. This also resulted in the reformation of the extremist Saiva creeds of the Kalamukhas, Pasupatas, Mahesvaras, Saktas and the like; it curbed the strong hold that Jainism had on the people and almost led to the decline of Buddhism.

Jainism had all along been having a great hold on the Telugu and Kannada regions as a result of the patronage it received from the kings and the rich mercantile groups. The Kannada area continued to be the centre of south Indian Jainism from where the various *guchchhas* branched out into the Tamil and Telugu areas. It was again in the first half of the ninth century that the great Hindu reformer-philosopher, Sankaracharya, appeared on the scene, refined the existing creeds and their practices, established the six *mathas* (the Shanmata, viz. Ganapatya Kaumara, Saura, Saiva, Vaishnava, and Sakta) on a sound basis, and propounded the great and universal philosophy of *Advaita*. It is a curious fact that these rock-cut or stone-built temples of the period, though created by great kings or with their patronage, were almost totally ignored by the contemporary Tamil hymnists. This was perhaps because they were innovations that avoided the use of traditional materials of architecture and sculpture and as such militated against the *sampradaya*. Evidently, it took them time to become acceptable.

The output in terms of rock-cut temples of the Pallavas and after them the contemporary Pandyas and minor dynasties like the Muttaraiyars of the Thanjavur region in between, and of the rulers in the Kerala area is far greater in hard rock than it is in softer rocks of the Chalukyas, the Rashtrakutas, the Eastern Chalukyas and the Telugu Cholas of the Deccan and coastal Andhra areas. The Pallava cave-temples form a more coherent series and as such can be considered first.

THE PALLAVA: MAHENDRA STYLE CAVE-TEMPLES

The simple cave-temples of Mahendra (*c.* AD 580-630) consist of a pillared verandah with shrine-cell or cells cut into either the rear or the side walls of the verandah or hall, depending on which way the main facade of the verandah or *mandapa* faced. Thus in *mandapas* facing south or north, the single shrine-cell or cells were often cut into the lateral walls so as to face east or west , while in *madapas* facing east or west the shrine-cell or cells were cut into the hind wall of the *mandapa*. These, as all rock-cut architecture, are necessarily designed to show the interior aspect of the structural monuments they imitated. They are essentially of the *mandapa*-type of temples. The cave-temples excavated by Mahendra are authenticated by his own inscriptions which are very often single dedicatory verses or strings of his titles. Such temples are ten in number. Nine of them are: the Lakshitayatana dedicated to the *trimurti* at Madagappattu, the so-called Pancha Pandava cave-temple at Pallavaram (now converted into a Muslim *dargah)*, the Rudravalisvaram or Cave-temple No. II at Mamandur dedicated to Siva, the Kal *mandapam* cave-temple at Kuranganilmuttam, very similar to the Pallava inscriptions, the Vasantesvaram or larger cave-temple at Vallam, dedicated to Siva, the Mahendra Vishnu-*griha* cave-temple at Mahendravadi, the Vishnu cave-temple or Cave-temple No. 1 at Mamandur, the Satrumallesvaralaya cave-temple at Dalavanur dedicated to Siva, and the Avanibhajana Pallavesvara-*griha* cave-temple at Siyamangalam. All of them are located roundabout the Pallava capital of Kanchi and the port town of Mahabalipuram (Mamallapuram) in the Chingleput, North Arcot, and South Arcot districts—comprising the Pallava home province of Tondaimandalam (the region situated to the north, west and south of modern Madras). The Lalitankura Pallavesvara-*griha*, or the upper rock-cut cave-temple at Tiruchirapalli, is the solitary one farthest from the capital, situated in the Cholamandalam on the bank of the Kaveri up to which boundary Mahendravarman inherited the kingdom from his father, Simha Vishnu. This cave-temple is also the only example excavated near the summit of the hill, while the rest are nearer to the base of the rocks. The unfinished rock-cut temples at Vilappakkam (North Arcot district) and Aragandanallur (South Arcot district) would also, on stylistic grounds, belong to the Mahendra style.

Where there is only a single cell behind the *mandapa*, there are four pillars and pilasters on the facade of the rectangular *mandapa*, two pilasters *in antis* at the two extreme ends against the side walls, and two pillars in the middle—all equally spaced. The facade is longer with four, six or eight equally-spaced pillars between the extreme pilasters and with three, five, or seven shrine-cells. The pillars are all massive, short, square in section at the base and top, with the middle third of the height octagonal in section. They carry massive corbels with bevelled or curved ends, sometimes with the faces carved as a series of rolls, the *taranga*, with a median flat band, the *patta*. A massive beam is cut above the corbels, but there is no well-formed cornice projection, or *kapota*, the rough rock brow itself acting as one. The faces of the square sections of the pillars are adorned with large, circular lotus medallions often inscribed inside a square. The *mandapa* may be divided by inner longitudinal row of pillars and pilasters into two sections, front and rear, indicating the *mukha-mandapa* and *ardha-mandapa* portions, though both may be of the same width and of the same type, corresponding to the facade row. Where there are no inner pillars, the differentiation is indicated by the varying floor-levels or ceiling heights.

A flight of about three rock-cut steps from the floor of the *mandapa* leads to the simple shrine entrance which is cut projecting a little into the *mandapa*. The shrine often shows a moulded pedestal, or *adhishthana,* and the wall is cantoned at its two front corners by four-sided flat pilasters with two more in between, each of the inner pairs flanking the shrine entrance. Often these two inner pilasters form also the two jambs of the simple doorway with a low lintel across and a sill cut at the top of the flight of steps below. The door-frame, if distinct, is again simple and unadorned. The pilasters carry in some cases distinct capital mouldings and corbels, or *potika*, on top. A beam and flexed overhanging cornice or *kapota* is cut on top. The *kapota* is adorned by semi-circular *kudu* ornaments, with a flat shovel-shaped finial above.

The shrine doors are generally guarded by relief sculptures of two armed *dvarapalas,* or gatekeepers, one on each side. In the earliest cave-temple where the shrines for the trinity—Brahma, Siva and Vishnu—are but deep plain niches cut into the rear wall, the two *dvarapalas* are found one on either side of the facade of the *mandapa*. The Vasantesvaram at Vallam, the Vishnu cave-temple of Mahendravadi and Mamandur and the Avanibhajanas cave-temple at Siyamangalam are examples of cave-temples with a single shrine-cell cut into the hind wall of the *mandapa*. The Rudravalisvaram of Mamandur and the Kalmandakam cave-temple at Kuranganilmuttam are examples with three shrine-cells, as at Mandagappattu. The four additional cells, two on each lateral wall of the *ardha-* and *mukha-mandapas* of the Kalmandakam temple, are later additions to the original scheme of three cells on the rear wall. The Pallavaram cave-temple has five shrine-cells, while the unfinished Vilappakkam cave-temple has seven shrine-cells. The similar unfinished Aragandanallur cave-temple, with four pillars and two pilasters on the facade and in the hind row, would indicate five shrine-cells on the rear wall still uncut. Thus the number and disposition of shrines on the rear wall would correspond to the pillars of the *mandapa* in front, each shrine-opening coming in between two equally-spaced pillars, or a pillar and a pilaster. This along with the equal inter-columniation would contrast with the arrangement of the wider central nave and the narrow lateral aisles of the earlier Buddhist examples followed by the contemporary and later examples of the Chalukya-Rashtrakuta series.

The facades as well as the shrines of the Kalmandakam, Rudravalisvaram, Vasantesvaram and the Vishnu cave-temples of Mahendravadi and Mamandur face almost east, while those at Mandagappattu, Vilappakkam and Siyamangalam face almost west. Pallavaram is the only example in the series where the *mandapa* facade and shrine-cells face south. The Lalitankura and Satrumalla cave-temples at Tiruchirapalli and Dalavanur are examples with the *mandapa* facing south and the shrine cut into the lateral wall—the eastern one at Tiruchirapalli and the western one at Dalavanur—so that the shrines face west and east respectively. In the Dalavanur cave-temple the larger *mandapa*, with a single row of pillars and pilaster on the facade, indicates an inner division of the front and rear portions of the *mandapa* by a difference in the floor levels. The shrine on the western wall of the *ardha-mandapa* part is cut with a small porch-like pillared *mandapa* in front of it. This too is rock-cut and stands on the floor of the *ardha-mandapa* on a distinct plinth at a still higher level. In the case of the Tiruchirapalli cave-temple, an inner row of pillars and pilasters is cut very close to the hind wall with a narrow passage in between it and the wall. The cell on the east faces west into the front part of the *mandapa* between the inner and outer rows of columns. This is a feature not quite Pallava, but rather reminiscent of the cave-temples in the Pandyan country, for example, the one at Tirup-parankunram. Incidentally, the Lalitankura Pallavesvaram cave-temple of Tiruchirapalli is the southernmost Pallava cave-temple nearer to the borders of the Pandya territory. The lotus medallions on the top and bottom cubical parts (*sadurams*) of the pillars, which are absent in the earlier cave-temples of this series like those at Mandagappattu, Pallavaram and Kuranganilmuttam, and the Siva caves at Mamandur and Vallam, are to be found in the later ones of the series as in the Vishnu cave-temples at Mahendravadi and Mamandur. The Siva cave-temples at Tiruchirapalli and Siyamangalam have, in addition, other motifs incised in side circular medallions, such as *makaras, kinnaris, matanganakras* (combination of an elephant and a *makara*) and *pushpa-lata* and *patra-lata* (scrolls of leaves and flowers). The Siyamangalam cave-temple has small relief panels of sculpture on top of the pilasters.

The shrine-cells, or *garbha-grihas*, in all these cases are empty and do not contain either a rock-cut *linga* or *linga-pitha*, as is common in the Pandya, Muttaraiyar and Chalukyan cave-temples. They do not have in fact any appropriate sculpture of the deity in worship—Siva, Vishnu or other gods—to whom the temple according to the inscription is known to be dedicated. Often there are traces of lime plaster with a painting over it on the hind wall indicating that the object of worship was a mural painting of the god. Sometimes one finds a slight relief of a pedestal cut at the base of the hind wall indicating that the deity was done in stucco, or lime mortar and painted, or was a wooden panel with a carving set into a sunk chase on the wall.

These Mahendra temples are noted also for the absence of other kinds of sculpture even in the *mandapa* part, except those of the *dvarapalas*. These *dvarapalas* are found at either end of the facade of the *mandapa* in the Mandagappattu cave-temple. In the Dalavanur and Siyamangalam cave-temples, the *dvarapalas* are found not only on either side of the *mandapa* facade but also on either side of the shrine entrance. In the case of the Vishnu cave at Mamandur and the cave-temple at Pallavaram, there are *dvarapalas* neither on the flanks of *mandapa* facade nor on the flanks of the shrine-cells. The *dvarapalas* either face full-front or are in semi-profile or half-turned towards the shrine door and stand resting on a massive club entwined by a serpent. In Siyamangalam the two outer *dvarapalas* are, however, depicted as warriors inside separate niches at either end of the *mandapa* facade, while the two flanking the shrine entrance are of the usual form. The Tiruchirapalli upper rock-cut cave-temple of Lalitankura is unique in that it has a large group sculpture forming a panel on the western wall of the *mandapa* directly opposite the shrine and depicting Siva as Gangadhara. The Siyamangalam cave-temple is unique even otherwise, in having small sculpture panels on top of the facade pillars and pilasters in place of the lotus medallion. The two panels on top of the two pilasters depict, respectively, a dancing form of Siva, or *tandava murti*—perhaps the earliest such representation in Pallava sculptures, and Siva and Uma standing with the bull behind them depicting the form called Vrishabhantikamurti.

Mahendra's son, Narasimhavarman Mamalla (630-68) and his lineal successors, Mahendravarman II (668-72), Paramesvara I (672-700), and Rajasimha (700-728) continued the tradition started by Mahendra I and excavated a number of cave-temples in the Mahendra style in the course of the century. They are the Orukal *mandapam* at Tirukkalukkunram, the Kotikal *mandapam* at Mahabalipuram, the Narasimha cave-temple at Singaperumal-kovil, the Ranganathan cave-temple at Singavaram, the Dharmaraja *mandapam* or Atyantakama Pallava's cave-temple at Mahabalipuram, and the Atiranachanda *mandapam* cave at Saluvankuppam, near Mahabalipuram—all in the Chingleput district of Tamil Nadu, except Singavaram which is in South Arcot.

The Singavaram and Singaperumalkovil cave-temples are dedicated to Vishnu, the Kotikal *mandapam* to Durga and the rest to Siva. While none of the Siva cave-temples contain a rock-cut *linga* in the sanctum, the two Vishnu cave-temples have in the sanctum stucco figures of the deities now modernized. The Kotikal *mandapam* of Durga has no sculpture of Durga inside the sanctum, though the dedication is indicated by the female *dvarapalikas* on either side of the shrine entrance as also by the name of the temple. The Atiranachanda *mandapam* of Rajasimha, the last of the series, alone contains a bas-relief panel of Siva as Somaskanda, with Uma and Skanda sitting beside him and Brahma and Vishnu standing on either side of the group behind. The carving of such a bas-relief in place of the earlier traditional

painting, or stucco-relief, or woodcarving of the principal god of
the sanctum appears to have been started in the time of
Paramesvaravarman I (672-700). Two more such Somaskanda
reliefs are found carved on the hind wall of the *mandapa* on either
side of the shrine entrance. It would appear that while
Mahendravarman I broke the tradition of the wooden and brick-
and-mortar temples and excavated temples in stone, he could not
go far enough to change the traditional material of which the
principal deity in the sanctum was made. This had to wait for a
few decades till Paramesvaravarman I, in the last quarter of the
seventh century, introduced for the first time among other innovations the carving of the principal deity as a relief on the back
wall of the shrine. In Rajasimha's cave-temple, the Atiranachanda
mandapam, a black polished, fluted or sixteen-sided stone *linga*
(*dhara-linga*) also came to be planted on the floor of the sanctum
in front of the Somaskanda relief on the hind wall. This indicated
the commencement in the Pallava territory with the installation
of the formless *linga* to represent Siva.

   In most respects this series of post-Mahendra cave-temples
resembles those of Mahendra in plan and design and other
general features. But one observes a tendency for the pillars and
pilasters to become thinner and taller, sometimes flatter, with an
oblong section. The space between them is equal but wider. The
kapota over the facade is still an undifferentiated, projecting rock-
ledge over the beam. All the cave-temples of the series have single
shrine-cells cut into the rear walls, with the frontage projecting
more into the *mandapa*. The only example with triple shrine-cells
is the Dharmaraja *mandapam* or Atyantakama Pallava's cave
temple where the two lateral shrine-cells are simple excavations,
which are perhaps later additions, without definite shrine front,
as is found in the case of the main central one. All these cave-
temples have only two pillars and two pilasters on the *mandapa*
facade, and a similar set behind, inside the *mandapa* wherever
there is such a demarcation of *ardha-* and *mukha-mandapas*, as in
the Ranganathan cave-temple, the Orukkal *mandapam*, and
Dharmaraja *mandapam*. The pillars have the top and bottom
sadurams and intervening *kattu*, while the pilasters are uniformly
four-sided as in Mahendravarman's cave-temples except that in
the Singavaram Ranganathan cave-temple the pilasters like the
pillars are demarcated and have lotus medallions on the *saduram*

faces. This cave-temple is the only example in the series which has an outer pair of *dvarapalas* at either end of the *mandapa* facade. The inner pair flanking the shrine entrance is in common with the rest.

There are generally no other sculptures in the *mandapa* beside the *dvarapalas*. In the Orukkal *mandapam*, however, there are relief sculptures of standing Brahma and Vishnu on the rear wall, one on either side of the shrine entrance and beyond the *dvarapalas*. In addition there are two fine, bold, life-size reliefs of *dvarapala*-like sculptures, one on either end wall of the *mukha-mandapa*. In the Singavaram cave-temple, as at Siyamangalam, there are small panel reliefs of two female devotees on top of the pilasters of the inner row.

The last series of Pallava temples dated after AD 730 are small and less interesting. They mark the decadent phase of this type of rock architecture in Tondaimandalam. The Kilmavilangai cave-temple is the only example in the Pallava kingdom of Tondaimandalam of a rock-cut cell without a rock-cut front *mandapa*, but such cell-shrines are more common in the Pandya and Muttaraiyar and Kerala areas, most of them contemporary with the late, post-700 AD Pallava period. The cell contains on its hind wall a flat bas-relief of standing Vishnu. The two smaller cave-temples at Vallam on the rock below Mahendra's Vasantesvaram cave-temple, one dedicated to Vishnu and the other to Siva, have very thin pillars carrying bevelled corbels on the *mandapa* facade, the *mandapa* itself being narrow and the shrine-cell behind very small. An inscription in script of the seventh century reading *Pa(l)lava-peraraisaru* meaning 'Pallava emperor' has since been found in the Vasantesvaram cave-temple in Vallam. This and the other almost similar excavation, both below the larger Mahendra cave-temple, are rather feeble attempts, considering the fact that they are rather crude, small in proportion and shallow in depth.

THE PALLAVA: MAMALLA STYLE CAVE-TEMPLES

Mahendra's great son and successor, Narasimhavarman I Mamalla (630-668), in addition to excavating some Mahendra style cave-temples like the Orukkal *mandapam* and the Kotikal *mandapam* described earlier, initiated a new and more ornate series of cut-in cave-temples. This was in addition to his unique invention of totally cut-out monolithic temple forms, or *vimanas*, the so-called *rathas*, and some open air bas-relief compositions of considerable size and superb quality, all confined to the great Pallava port-city of Mamallapuram or Mahabalipuram. These ornate cave-temples that Mamalla initiated were mostly completed in stages by his immediate successors for two generations, who also created a few monuments in the same style and at the same place. The oustanding development discernible in these is a fuller represen-tation of their *mandapa* facades, their interior decoration and the replacement of the square massive pillars and pilasters by typical pillars with ornate bases and full capitals and all the moulded members of the 'order', thus making the stone copies more true to their contemporary structural originals in brick and timber.

The *adhishthana*, or plinth, shows all the usual mouldings as could be seen in the finished examples. The *mandapa* facade has a fully represented entablature, or *prastara*, which constitutes all the architectural parts coming over the beam and including it, as against what is seen in the Mahendra-style cave-temples. The *prastara* is fully finished with a flexed *kapota*, or an eaves-like cornice projection, decorated by horseshoe-shaped *kudu* arches. The *prastara* has also a string of miniature shrines above it, all of oblong plan, often with a barrel-vaulted roof, the *sala*, while in the later examples, the *sala* string ends at either extremity in similar miniature shrine models of square plan with a four-sided domical roof, the *kuta*. The entire string constitutes what is called the *hara* with interconnecting lengths of cloister. The pillars generally conform to the wooden prototypes, but are taller and slenderer and have their bases often shaped into squatting lions. The top of the shaft has the variously moulded captial members such as the *malasthana*, the *padma bandha*, the *kalasa*, the *tadi*, the *kumbha*, the *pali* and the *phalaka* or abacus, the last-mentioned one omitted in some cases, and the topmost member carrying the corbel or *potika*, with curved profile and roll ornamentation, or *taranga*, with a median plain *patta*.

Their *mandapas* are often demarcated into front and rear sections by an inner row of pillars. The shrine fronts, one, three or five, are at the rear of the inner *mandapa*, project more into the *mandapa*, and have all the *angas* of a *vimana* front, namely, moulded *adhishthana*, pilasters, or *kudya-stambhas*, with capital components as detailed above and *prastara* with well-formed *kapota* and *kudu* decorations. The further superstructure of the *vimana* is not shown, as in a depiction of the interior aspect of a *mandapa* with the shrine behind, the upper parts of the *vimana* would not be visible. The *prastara* of the shrine front abuts on the *mandapa* ceiling.

There are eight such cave-temples in various stages of completion: the Koneri *mandapam*, the Varaha *mandapam*, the Mahishamardini *mandapam* (locally called Yamapuri *mandapam*), an unfinished cave-temple next to the Koneri *mandapam*, the Pancha-Pandava *mandapam*, the Adivaraha cave-temple called Paramesvara Mahavaraha Vishnu-*griha* in its inscriptions and the Ramanuja *mandapam*. Of these the Varaha and Ramanuja *mandapams* have undivided *mandapas* while the Koneri *mandapam* and the Adivaraha cave-temple have their *mandapas* divided into *ardha-* and *mukha-mandapas* by an inner line of pillars. The Mahishamardini *mandapam* is peculiar in that its principal central shrine is preceded by a square and a pillared portico projected into the larger *mandapa*, as in the case of the Dalavanur cave-temple. The Pancha Pandava *mandapam* records an attempt to cut a square central shrine with a surrounding cloister in the form of a *mandapa* having two rows of pillars running all round. The Varaha *mandapam* and the Adivaraha cave-temples have each a single shrine-cell while the Mahishamardini and the Rámanuja *mandapams* have three shrine-cells in them; the Koneri *mandapam* has five in a row behind the *mandapam*.

The Mamalla-style cave-temples show a marked advance over the Mahendra type in plastic decoration also, in having a wealth of large and fine sculptures in addition to the usual *dvarapala* sculptures. These are often synoptic, narrating important *Puranic* legends. The Varaha *mandapam*, which is the most complete cave-temple and has been preserved in all its parts, contains bas-relief compositions of Bhu-varaha and Trivikrama inside large panels on the side walls of its *mandapam*. Its back wall has two more—one on either side of the projected shrine entrance, carrying panels of Gajalakshmi and Durga. The front and side walls of the projected shrine front have niches with *dvarpala* sculptures. The manner in which the boar-head of Bhu-Varaha merges at the neck imperceptibly with the human body is a masterpiece of art not equalled by similar representation in the Gupta and other sculptures. The central shrine is now empty, but perhaps once contained painted or stucco representation of Narasimha. Almost identical, but more artistic and graceful delineations of Gajalakshmi and Durga are reproduced in almost the same positions on the rear wall panels on either side of the projected shrine entrance in the Adivaraha cave-temple. In addition, the front wall of the projected central shrine of the Adivaraha cave-temple has three niches, each on either side of the entrance containing other sculptures. The niches flanking the entrance contain *dvarapalas.* The two central wider niches, one on each side have sculptures of standing Vishnu and Harihara, respectively. The extreme ones on the north and south show a Nagaraja or Adisesha in human form with the five-headed serpent-hood and a portrait sculpture in graceful *tribhanga* posture. The south and north walls of the *mukha-mandapa* contain large reliefs of standing Brahma, and Siva as Gangadhara. Similar panels on the south and north walls of the *ardha-mandapa* have almost life-size royal portrait groups of the Pallava kings, Simhavishnu and Mahendra with their queens and consorts and with label inscriptions over them indicating their identity. The main sanctum contains a modern stucco form of Varaha *murti*. This temple is in use for worship while others are not. The bas-relief sculptures of Durga on the south and Gajalakshmi on the north side walls of the Ramanuja *mandapam* have been totally chiselled off in later times by the Vaishnava occupants as also the three shrine fronts and their *dvarapalas* of this original triple-celled Siva cave-temple. The back wall of the central shrine retains traces of a Somaskanda group. The Mahishamardini cave-temple contains on the two side walls of its *mandapa* two of the most celebrated and famous Pallava sculptures, namely, Durga as Mahishasuramardini, mounted on a leaping lion and battling with Mahishasura and his hordes on the north, and Vishnu as Anantasayin in yoga-*nidra*, or contemplative sleep, on a serpent-couch on the south. Besides the beauty, grace, vigour and agility depicted in Durga, the clever synthesis of the buffalo-head and human body of the demon Mahishasura would equal only that of the Varaha form mentioned above, not to speak of the defiance and haughtiness depicted by his stance and demeanour even in the animal face. All these sculptures would thus constitute some of the earliest extant representations of the respective forms and as such afford valuable material for a study of the development of early iconograpy in the south.

Recent research (by Lockwood, Siromoney and Dayanandan—*Mahabalipuram Studies*) has established that the *dvarapalas* of the Pallava cave-temples, Saivite and Vaishnavite, are really *ayudapurushas*, or deified personifications of the appropriate weapons of Siva (*sula* and *parasu*, i.e. trident and axe) or of Vishnu (*sanka* and *chakra,* i.e. conch and discus), which are shown on the headgear of the concerned *dvarapala*. Also it has been demonstrated that the original dedication of the Mahishamardini cave-temple was to Vishnu, subsequently made Saivite in the same century by the introduction of the large Somaskanda panel, on the lined wall of the shrine, in place of the original Vishnu that was perhaps a painted stucco. Appropriately enough the two *dvarapalas* wedged in a curious manner into the narrow spaces on either side of the shrine's door-jamb, were afterthoughts likewise, modified for the Saivite re-dedication as also the two flanking shrine-cells on either side in the *trimurti* pattern, Vishnu occupying the place of precedence in the central cella in the original scheme.

Though not strictly cave-temples like his Atiranachanda *mandapam*, other creations of Rajasimha Pallava (700-728) in the series of rock-carvings found in Mahabalipuram and neighbourhood are the Yali *mandapam* at Saluvankuppam, a hamlet to the north of Mahabalipuram, familiarly called 'tiger cave', and similar ornamental pavilions. These would stand apart from either group of cave-temples described above. The Yali *mandapam* is a small, oblong, shallow pavilion, or *mandapa*, excavated on the eastern face of a boulder facing the sea with its moulded *adhishthana* and a facade of flanking pillars, which are adorned at their bases by rearing lions or *vyalas*, cut over a lower platform reached by a flight of steps. The whole structure is surrounded by an arched frieze of eleven large *vyala* heads mistakenly called 'tiger heads'. To the south of the pavilion, and carved on the rock face, are reliefs of two elephant fronts with *howdahs* over their necks, a *dvajastambha* in between, and horse at the south extreme. The northern face of the rock is roughly carved out into a large squatting lion-front with a small square niche cut into in its bosom, enshrining a relief panel of Mahishamardini. The Yali *mandapam* obviously served as resting-place of the processional idols or the royalty during festivals.

This, even the name of the place—Tiruveluchchiyur—found in the inscriptions, would suggest. A smaller replica of the Yali *mandapam* is found on the surf-beaten boulder to the south of the Shore temple in Mahabalipuram. To the north of the temple is another larger rock called the Mahishamardini rock with a large lion face and Durga niche in its bosom.

In passing, mention may be made of the two celebrated open- air bas-relief compositions of large group sculptures on the face of the massive rocks in Mahabalipuram. They are Arjuna's penance and the Govardhana-Krishna scenes. The compositions are both synoptic and narrative of the respective themes. Arjuna's penance depicts the scene of Siva granting to Arjuna as a boon the desired weapon—*pasupata*—sought by the latter through the performance of a severe penance. The depiction is after the description of the scene in Bharavi's *Kiratarjuniya*. The Govardhana-Krishna scene depicts Krishna as holding up the hill to afford shelter to the displaced *gopas* and *gopis* with their children, cattle and other belongings, when they had to flee their homes as result of a great deluge of rain and stone brought down by the irate Indra. The depiction is quite powerful and realistic. A unique south Indian note is struck by the introduction of Krishna's favourite *gopi*, Nappinnai, huddling near him in the group and distinguished from the rest of the women in the scene by her dress, stance and attendant lady. The Krishna-Nappinnai theme is special to the earlier and contemporary Tamil literature and tradition.

PANDYA AND OTHER NON-PALLAVA
CAVE-TEMPLES OF THE SOUTH

In Pandimandalam farther south, comprising mainly the modern districts of Madurai, Ramanathapuram, Tirunelveli, Kanyakumari, Trivandrum and Quilon, and the southern parts of the Pudukkottai area now forming a district, the Pandya contemporaries of the Pallavas started rock architecture soon after the pioneers, that is to say, from after the middle of the seventh century. They continued the activity for over three centuries till they, like the Pallavas, were overthrown by the rising Cholas of Thanjavur. Their cave-temples in the southern half of Tamil Nadu and the adjoining Kerala area are far more numerous than those of the Pallavas.

The Muttaraiyar chieftains, who had their kingdom astride the Kaveri in the traditional Cholamandalam, viz. Tiruchirapalli, Thanjavur and the southern half of the South Arcot districts, and who owed allegiance alternately to the Pallavas and Pandyas, left in the latter part of the period, quite a few cave-temples in their area. These are found at Tiruvellarai, Narttamalai, Kunnandarkovil, Puvalaikkudi and other places, all in the Puduk-kottai and Tiruchirapalli districts. Their cave-temples too are a type of *mandapas* with simples shrine-cells and are much akin to the Pandya cave-temple in the same area. The Atiyaman, or Adigaiman chiefs, ruling in the Kongu area of Salem and Coimbatore districts, bordering on the Tiruchirapalli district, have excavated two fine cave-temples in Namakkal. They are dedicated to Vishnu and are noted for their fine sculptured panels.

These cave-temples, numbering about sixty in all, are like the Pallava examples, excavated into the hard, local rocks and are essentially similar to the Mahendra-style excavations in plan and design. But they also show certain characteristic features of their own, incorporating in the process a few features peculiar to the Chalukyan examples, particularly in respect of their sculptural make-up and iconography.

They, like the Mahendra-style cave-temples, consist of a *mandapa* with one or more shrine-cells cut often at the rear, but in some case excavated into the side walls of the *mandapa*, as in the lower rock-cut Pandya cave at Tiruchirapalli and the cave-temple at Tirup-parankunram, near Madurai, among others. They have massive pillars on the facades, essentially square in section at the base and top, with an octagonal middle section, carrying heavy *potikas* or corbels, usually with a straight bevel, resulting in an angular profile. There are, however, some examples with pillars of other types and corbels with a curved profile and *taranga* moulding. The cave-temples, all, lack a well-defined *kapota* in the architrave over their *mandapa* facades, as is also the case in the Mahendra-style cave-temples.

Some of the excavations are merely shrine-cells scooped directly into rock face, without a rock-cut *mandapa* in front. Such cave-temples are numerous in this region and very rare in Tondaimandalam.

The cave-temple at Malai-yadi-k-kurichi (Tirunelveli district) would appear to be the earliest known Pandya cave-temple of the *mandapa* type, with a single shrine-cell on the rear and containing a foundation inscription of the seventeenth year of Pandya Maran Sadaiyan in the second half of the seventh century. The inscription mentions the cave-temple significantly as *kal-tiru-k-koyil* or 'the sacred stone temple', echoing the pioneering idea for this region as found in Pallava Mahendravarman's inscription at Mandagappattu in Tondaimandalam. The rock-cut cave-temple at Pillaiyarpatti (Ramanathapuram district) with an inscription in an archaic script would also be one of the early Pandya cave-temples, as also Siva Cave-temple III at Kunnakkudi in the same district, which has another short inscription in the same script calling it Masilisvaram. The Vishnu (Narasimha) cave-temple at Anaimalai (Madurai district) has a foundation inscription giving the *Kali* year 3871 (AD 770) and referring to its excavation by a minister of Pandya Maran Sadaiyan, *alias* Parantaka. The large cave-temple at present famous as the Subrahmanya temple at Tirup-parankunram near Madurai was excavated earlier and later re-modelled by another Pandya minnister and his wife in the *Kali* year 3874 (AD 773), according to their foundation inscriptions there. There is a complex of four cave-temples on this northern face of the Tirup-parankunram rock and one of the above inscriptions mentions the excavation of a separated Jyeshtha cave-temple also, which is of the cave-cell type, without *mandapa* in front. The other two excavations on either side of the larger *mandapa*-type cave-temple and above the level of the Jyeshtha cave shrine should be of a somewhat later date. One of these contains a bas-relief of Gajalakshmi, and the other a group comprising *devi* as Bhuvanesvari and her attendants.

The well-known rock-cut cave-temple at Sittannavasal in the Pudukkottai area (Tiruchirapalli district), containing the celebrated early mural paintings in fresco, is an example of a Jain cave-temple of the eighth-ninth centuries. This, according to a long verse inscription associated with it, was re-embellished by a certain Ilan Gautaman *alias* Madurai Asiriyan and a structural *mukha-mandapa* added in front, all in the reign of Avanipa-sekhara Sri Vallabha Pandya (*c.* 815-862). This contains bas-relief Jain *tirthankara* sculptures on the hind wall of the shrine and in the niches on the lateral walls of the *mandapa* in front. This cave-temple is a typical Pandya version of a Mahendra-style cave-temple, with the facade pillars carrying *taranga* corbels.

The eastern cave-temple at Malai-yakkovil, the upper Siva cave-temple at Tirumayam, the cave-temple at Mangadu, the Malai-k-kolundisvaram near Rayavaram, the Jyeshtha, the Gajalakshmi and the Bhuvanesvari cave-temples in Tirup-parankunram, and the cave-temple at Vilinam (Vizhinam), among other, are examples of simple cave-shrines of the Pandya-Muttaraiyar-Ayvel vintage of the non-Pallava series.

Among the cave-temples that have the shrine-cell on one of the lateral walls of the *mandapa* may be mentioned the Satyagirisvara or Siva cave-temple at Tirumayam, the southern cave-temple at Malai-yakkovil, the Siva cave-temple at Tirumalapuram (Tirunelveli district), and the Umaiyandar cave-temple on the southern face of the rock at Tirup-parankunram. In the case of some cave-temples, like the Siva cave-temple at Malai-yadippatti, the cave-temple at Pillaiyarpatti, and the cave-temple in Muvaraivenran (Ramanathapuram district) the shrine part occupies, as it were, a corner of the oblong *mandapam*, which thus encloses it on two sides—in front and on one of the flanks, suggesting a partial copy of a model with a central shrine and a surrounding *mandapam* with a greater part of it in front. Such a plan is not to be found commonly in the Pallava examples except in the case of the Pancha Pandava *mandapam* of Mahabalipuram and the unfinished Cave-temple IV at Mamandur. The cave-temple at Trikkur, near Trichur in Kerala, is a large excavation of a square chamber with a *linga* at the centre. Cave-temples with shrine-cells cut into both the lateral walls of the *mandapa* are exemplified by the lower rock-cut cave-temple at Tiruchirapalli and also the larger cave-temple, called the Subrahmanya temple, on the north face of the hill at Tirup-parankunram. This has also a third shrine cut into the rear walls of the *mandapa*, in addition to the two thus excavated into either end walls of the *mandapam*.

While the *mandapa*-type facade pillar with a cubical base and top and an octagonal belt in between is the general rule, as in the Mahendra-style cave-temples, there are often variations. For example, in the Malai-yakkovil at Kudumiyamalai capital components like the *kalasa*, *kumbha*, etc. are cut on tops of the facade columns. In the Vishnu cave-temple at Malai-yadippatti the pillar bases are shaped into squatting lions. The corbels of the Malai-yadi-k-kurichi cave-temple are peculiar in that the *taranga* rolls are cut as incurved curls, a feature indicating Chalukyan inspiration.

What is more interesting in these cave-temples is their varied sculptural content and iconographic forms, some of which are the first to appear in the southern cave-temples of Tamil Nadu and Kerala. They are Ganesa, the Saptamatrika and Jyeshtha. The Ganesa and the Saptamatrika cults would thus appear to have come into the far south from the Chalukyan area through the Ganga region, before they penetrated the Tondaimandalam of the Pallavas. These two are not to be seen in any of the Pallava cave-temples, till they make their first appearance in the structural temples of Rajasimha Pallava (700-725) as, for example, in the Kailasanatha at Kanchi. In the far south, Ganesa is to be found in the cave-temples at Pillaiyarpatti, Kudumiyamalai, Malai-yakkovil (southern cave-temple), Tirugokarnam, Kunnandarkovil, Tiruvellarai (Siva cave-temple), Devarmalai, Tirukkalakkudi, Tiruchirapalli (lower cave-temple), Tirumalapuram, Kunnakkudi, Muvaraivenran, Tirup-parankunram (larger cave-temple), Sevilippatti, Kunnattur (Nilakanthesvara), Virasikhamani and Arittapatti. The Saptamatrika group is met with in the cave-temples at Tirugokarnam, Malai-yadippatti, Tirukkalakkudi and Kunnattur. While many of the cave-temples dedicated to Siva have a rock-cut *linga* with a *pitha* in the shrine, there are others where the iconic forms of Siva are represented as bas-reliefs on the rear wall of the sanctum. There is often a small cistern or pit cut into the floor of the sanctum below the projected channel-spout on the top of the *linga-pitha* or image pedestal to receive and collect the *abhisheka* water. This feature is unknown in the Pallava temples, whether cave, monolithic or structural, but is found in the Chalukyan area and in the far-off temples of the Dieng valley in Java (Indonesia). The *linga-pitha* is generally square, but octagonal in the eastern cave-temple, at Malai-yakkovil. In the Siva shrine of the Tirup-parankunram cave-temple, there is a Somaskanda panel on the rear wall, as in the Pallava cave-temples of the close of the seventh century and subsequent structural temples. In the cave-temples at Piranmalai and Tirumalai (Ramanathapuram district) it is only Siva and Parvati (Umasahitamurti) seated, without Skanda. The rear wall of the shrine of the Umaiyandar cave-temple at Tirup-parankunram contains a relief of Ardhanari-Siva while in the case of

Ladankovil cave-temples at Anaimalai, dedicated to Subrahmanya, he is shown with his consort in the central shrine.

But for the single exception of the eastern lateral shrine in the Subrahmanya cave-temple, Tirup-parankunram, containing a basrelief of Somaskanda on its rear wall after the familiar Pallava pattern, the reliefs of Umasahitamurti (Siva), without Skanda, in the Pandyan cave-temples is significant. Such icons found for example on the rear wall of the shrine in the cave-temples of Piranmalai and Tirumalai (Ramanathapuram district), and on the north wall of the rock-cut front *mandapa* of the Kunnandarkoil (Pudukkottai district) cave-temple are reminiscent of the Siva-Parvati wedlock, or *vaivahika* form of Minakshi-Sundaresvara, prevalent in that region.

In the lower rock-cut cave-temple at Tiruchirapalli (Pandya), while the two lateral shrine-cells are dedicated to Siva and Vishnu, the rear wall of the *mandapa* has five niches enclosed by pilasters, the central one with Brahma and the others with Ganesa, Subrahmanya, Surya and Durga. With Siva and Vishnu, these would form the gods of the Shanmata grouping which Sankaracharya is stated to have re-established after reformation of the extant ritual practices. Sankara is reputed to be the Shanmata *sthapanacharya*, the Shanmatas being Saiva, Vaishnava, Sakta, Kaumara, Saura and Ganapatya. The grouping in this cave-temple would indicate also a superimposition of the Shanmata deities on the pre-existing *trimurti* concept of Siva, Vishnu and Brahma, inaugurated by Mahendra Pallava in his first Mandagappattu cave-temple. The larger cave-temple at Tirup-parankunram takes in five out of the six deities, excluding Surya, for the two principal lateral shrines are dedicated to Siva and Vishnu, while a third, for Durga, has been cut out of the rear wall at its centre with the two recesses on either side having sculptures of Ganesa and Subrahmanya. In the comparatively fewer Vishnu cave-temples dedicated solely as such and in the Vishnu shrines of other cave-temples, the standing, seated and, more often, reclining forms are met with as the main sculptures. The standing form occurs in the Vishnu shrine of the Tiruchirapalli lower cave-temple, the sitting form in the Vishnu shrine of the larger Tirup-parankunram cave-temple, and reclining form in the Vishnu cave-temples at Tirumayam, Malai-yadippatti and Tiruttangal (Ramanathapuram district), and in the eastern or

Ranganathan cave-temple at Namakkal (Salem district). The other cave-temple at Namakkal has Narasimha in the sanctum.

The Malai-yakkovil Siva temple at Kudumiyamalai, the Satyagirisvara or Siva cave-temple at Tirumayam, the upper Siva cave-shrine in the same place, the Gokarnesvara cave-temple at Tirugokarnam and the eastern cave-shrine at Malai-yakkovil are associated with inscriptions on musical notations in what is called the *Pallava-grantha* script as also colophons in the old Tamil script, as indicated by the label *parivadini-e* inscribed on them. While the actual notations, or remnants of them, are to be seen in the first two cases, they have disappeared in the rest. The extant colophons indicate that the art of the *parivadini* (a stringed lute) called *Vidya-parivadini* was enunciated by a Gunasena, and the notations were got inscribed for the benefit of the votaries by a king who was a great Saiva or Paramamahesvara, and a disciple of Rudracharya. While the Satyagirisvara cave-temple at Tirumayam is thus connected by the presence of the musical inscriptions with the others above, it has besides, as one of its *dvarapalas* flanking the shrine entrance, a portrait sculpture of a king or chieftain which is found also in the cave-temples at Kunnandarkovil and Devarmalai within 48 km from it in the same district (Pudukkottai). What is more, it is also found in the Siva cave-temple at Virasikhamani in the far southern Tirunelveli district and in the cave-temple at Kaviyur, near Quilon in Kerala. These would indicate a similarity of origin, namely, Pandya, and a proximity of date. The cave-temple at Tirunandikkara with a south-facing *mandapa* facade and an east-facing shrine inside on the western wall of the *mandapa* is celebrated for the remains of ancient fresco paintings of the same period as Sittannavasal and Tirumalapuram of Pandya vintage.

The Siva cave-temple called Vagisvaram at Malai-yadippatti was excavated by Vidalvidugu Muttaraiyar in the sixteenth year of Pallava Dantivarman. The adjoining Vishnu cave-temple of a later date was also perhaps a Muttaraiyar excavation. The cave-shrine called Paliyilisvaram at Narttamalai, another Muttaraiyar excavation, dates a few years before the seventh year of Pallava Nripatunga in the late ninth century. The same may be said of the Puvalaikkudi cave-shrine, which was excavated by a certain Amarunri Muttaraiyar. The Vishnu cave-temple at Tirumayam, containing the reclining Vishnu group, is a natural cavern converted into a cave-temple with the addition of the facade pillars and other features by a queen of Perumbidugu Muttaraiyar and would date some time later than the Siva cave-temple of Satyagirisvara adjoining it. A few others like the Mangadu cave-shrine and Malai-k-kolundisvaram cave-shrine in the same area, as also the cave-temples at Tiruvellarai, can be attributed to the Muttaraiyars.

The cave-temples at Trikkur, Irunilamkodu, Kottukkal and other places in the northern Kerala region are of the times of the rulers of the Chera country, while those in the southern parts, in the Quilon and Trivandrum districts of Kerala, and the Kanyakumari district of Tamil Nadu, or Venadu and Nanjilnadu as they are called, are perhaps mostly of the Pandya affiliation. Because of lack of specific authentication and of the fact that Kerala was under more than one dynasty during the period from the middle of the seventh to the middle of the ninth centuries to which these cave-temples belong, it would be more correct to give them the regional nomenclature of Kerala than to call these all 'Chera'. The connected political history of the Cheras of the second period after the earlier *Sangam* epoch starts from the middle of the ninth century.

The two Vishnu cave-temples at Namakkal, one dedicated to Ranganathan or Anantasayin, and the other to Narasimha, are, according to their inscriptions, excavations by the Atiya king, Gunasila of the line of the Adigaimans known earlier from Tamil literature. They belong to the first half of the eighth century and contain some fine sculptures. The inscription in the Ranganathan cave calls it Atiyendra Vishnu-*griha* and is unique in that it gives an apt description of the various figures in the iconographic grouping round Anantasayin. The sculptures are noted for their sharp delineation and vigorous poses and flexions that are quite distinct from their Pallava compeers.

The Western Gangas of Talkad in south Mysore, following the Chalukya-Rashtrakuta idiom, have left two unfinished cave-temples in the hard rock at Melkote near Mysore.

In addition to the incorporation of the Chalukyan traits noted above, these southern cave-temples, essentially following the Pallava Mahendra-style and hard rock tradition, also reproduce many iconic forms that are found in the Pallava rock-cut and structural examples. The more important ones are the reproduction of Durga with a devotee cutting off his own head in sacrifice, a common Pallava form, reproduced near the Vishnu cave-temple of Tiruttangal, and the Mahishasuramardini group, as at Mahabalipuram and Saluvankuppam, reproduced with variations in the Vagisvaram cave-temple at Malai-yadippatti. The Bhu-Varaha and Gajalakshmi forms are found in the cave-temples at Tirup-parankunram and the Trivikrama form along with Bhu-Varaha in the cave-temple at Namakkal. The other iconographic forms so reproduced are Lingodbhava, Harihara, Subrahmanya, Vishnu with *garuda* in human form, Narasimha, and the *tandava* forms of Siva.

The Kerala cave-temples of a rather indeterminate authorship, however, form an important landmark in southern cave architecture combining as they do the features of the Pandya and the Adigaiman cave-temples of the adjoining territory and like them are essentially of the Pallava Mahendra-style model both in their granite rock material and the plan and technique of excavation, though with an import often of some Chalukyan motifs. The incomplete Branthanpara excavation demonstrates the familiar Pallava technique of rock excavation as at Mahabalipuram, followed in the Pandya-Muttaraiyar-Adigaiman areas, as at Narttamalai, Mangadu and other places. The cave at Vizhinam, of the rock-cell type without the front *mandapa* and characteristic of the Pandya-Muttaraiyar region, is unique in having on either rock flank of its door-opening, reliefs of Siva in *chatura tandava* with Parvati in attendance on one side, and Siva with bow as *kirata*, followed by a dwarf *gana* on the other. These bas-relief sculptures are more akin to the Pallava than to the neighbouring Pandya forms. At Irunilamkodu, another simple diminutive single-cell excavation without any facade or front porch, is a fine sculpture of Yoga Dakshinamurti in a majestic pose on the south wall, with an attendant *rishi* and disciples below, while the *linga* proper is placed in a small niche cut into the western wall over a platform. The other cave-temples are those at Tirunandikkara and Kaviyur. These are examples of typical cave-temple pattern with cell and front *mandapa*. Likewise there are those at Kallil, Trikkur, Kottukkal, Ailurpara, Tuvarangadu and Bhutapandi, the last two to the south of Vizhinam, near Kanyakumari. Some of these cave-temples are unconventional in so far as the relationship between the orientation of the temple and the placement of the *dvarapalas* and other attendant niche-deities are concerned. The Trikkur cave-temple, for example, has a north-facing facade with the only opening on that side; the corbels are of the double-volute type as in the Chalukyan style and the deity inside the shrine faces east as indicated by the water-spout of the *linga-pitha* projected on the north. The *dvarapalas* are cut almost in the round-out of the side walls on the eastern and western sides, a little behind the median east-west axial line. The *linga-pitha* is often a structural addition, though monolithic examples cut out of the same rock as the cave itself are known. At Kaviyur and Tirunandikkara the style is, as in early Pallava cave-temples, without the original rock-cut *linga* but with *lingas* planted into sockets of the shrine-cell. We have square sockets on the floor into which the square-sectioned lower part, or *brahmabhaga*, of the *linga* is inserted, and the *pitha* assembled round its exposed base, as is found to be the case in the Pallava cave-temples, a feature starting from about AD 700. In Ailurpara and Bhutapandi, the *linga* is an integral part of the cave and is rock-cut as in the Pandya-Muttaraiyar examples. The placement of Hanuman as one of the two *dvarapalas* in the cave-temple at Kottukkal recalls the similar feature found in the Pandya cave-temple at Kunnattur, near Madurai.

THE CHALUKYA AND RASHTRAKUTA
CAVE-TEMPLES OF THE DECCAN

The Chalukyas of Badami from the middle of the sixth century AD and the Rashtrakutas of Manyakheta who supplanted them effectively in the middle of the eighth century, together with the Eastern Chalukyas of Vengi have left a number of cave-temples in the region between the Tapti and the north Pennar rivers, extending from coast to coast. The Chalukyas of Vengi were a collateral line that had independently started ruling the Andhra coast from the commencement of the seventh century under Kubja Vishnuvardhana, the intrepid brother of Pulakesin II, and continued throughout the period. The cave-temples are to be found at Badami, Aihole, Ellora, Bhokardan, Elephanta, Jogeshvari, Poona, Arvelam (Goa), Mahur, Advi Somanpalli, Vijayawada, Mogulrajapuram, Undavalli, Sitaramapuram, Penamaga and Bhairavakonda. While the Chalukyas were mostly of Hindu persuasion, though they encouraged the Jain creed, the Rashtrakutas and many of the Western Gangas were votaries of Jainism. As such one could perceive a congruity of purpose, technique and the raw material chosen to stabilise Hinduism and foster Jainism and perpetuate their traditions at the cost of Buddhism which was having till then a greater hold on the rich, lay, agricultural and mercantile sections of the people.

The choice of all these dynasties was the local soft-stone formations, viz. sandstone, as in Badami and Aihole and in most other places, laterite, as at Aryelam on the extreme west coast, schist as at Bhairavakonda, and trap on the north-west Deccan and western India around Aurangabad, Poona and Bombay. The Western Gangas alone despite their Chalukyan affinities as stated before made a deviation in that they excavated into the hard local granite as at Melkote (Mysore).

The eastern branch of the Chalukyas, ruling from Vengi, though excavating into soft rocks, followed a different mode and design in their cave-temples, which took in what was prevalent in eastern Andhra and northern Tamil Nadu, or Tondaimandalam, with Pallava affinities, thus inaugurating what was to be a distinct Andhra tradition, as opposed to what the Badami Chalukyas did for Kannada tradition and culture.

The Chalukya-Rashtrakuta domination of the areas to the west resulted in the upper Deccan affiliations becoming quite distinct from what obtained in the lower Deccan, thus exhibiting two regional idioms. This was because the northern zone lay nearer the sites of the earlier Buddhist cave art and rock architecture. The skills and traditions that had prevailed for more than eight centuries among the local guilds of craftsmen thus continued in the generations that took up Hindu and Jain rock architecture and cave art. Rock architecture was also sustained longer as a mode in the northern zone. It developed more vigorously particularly under the Rashtrakutas as could be seen from their enormous output and such large-scale compositions as the caves at Elephanta, Dhumarlena and Jogeshvari, not to speak of the monolithic carvings of the Kailasa temple, and the Jain Chota Kailasa and the Jain *chaumukh* in the Indra Sabha complex. But rock architecture soon became a mere second to structural stone constructions in the southern zone of the Chalukyas as would be seen in the sequel. This was due to the fact that with the facility of quarrying the soft sandstone blocks, dressing and carving them more easily with the help of the skills acquired, coupled with the urge to construct stone temples on the models of brick-and-wood originals, the stone workers of the Badami-Aihole-Pattadkal area soon trained themselves into guilds of *sthapatis* that could build temples better instead of carving them out of rocks. The structural creations of the Rashtrakuta period are, however, less pretentious, of medium or small dimensions, and less well-finished as compared with their rock-cut monuments.

The lay-out plan of the cave-temples varied from the structural temples in the successive rise in floor levels of the axial *mandapas* and shrines, in the much raised level of the sanctum floor, though the ceiling level throughout remained the same. The development of these non-Buddhist cave-temples can be divided into five or six stages or patterns. In the first group would be those that follow the scheme generalized by the later Buddhists in that area, namely, the *vihara-chaitya* type, with a cella and a frontal-pillared hall. The second would be those with a triple cella at the rear and lateral dispositions, each with a pillared facade in the form of an *ardha-mandapa*, the whole fronted by a common larger hall, or *maha-mandapa*, and a narrower *agra-* or *mukha-mandapa*, again with a pillared facade. Thirdly, there would be those which show or tend to show the side shrines in the form of chambers containing panel sculptures and Saptamatrika shrines with a regular or principal sanctum at the rear, which is *sandhara* or one provided with a circumambulatory passage round it, with *ardha-* and *maha-mandapas* often having *vedi* parapets. A Nandi-*mandapa* is also to be seen in front in some cases as in the Lankesvara cave at Ellora (Kailasa complex). The fourth type is exemplified by the structures where the principal shrine has no circumambulatory passage, that is, *nirandhara*: the *ardha-mandapa* has sculpture panels on its side walls, and the large *maha-mandapa* is pillared and with or without side shrines. Often there is an additional *mukha-mandapa*. The Saptamatrika shrine, or niche, is cut independently outside the main cave-temple, usually on its left flank, while there is a Nandi-*mandapa* in front, as in Ellora Cave 22. The fifth group would be that where the *sandhara* pattern with circumambulation develops a *sarvatobhadra* sanctum cell, with door-openings on all the four sides, fronted by a series of two or three *mandapas*, and, in the most advanced type, having an additional *agra-mandapa* that contains sculpture panels of Ganesa, Durga and other forms on one side and the Saptamatrikas on the other side of the *agra-mandapa*. Lastly, there are the examples which, like the more southern forms, have in front the transversely oblong halls—the *ardha-* and *mukha-mandapas*, without any *vedi* parapet for the latter, and where the pillars carry the sculptures on their shaft portions instead of on the bracket region as female figures that are usual in other cases.

Thus the main varieties observed in the Chalukyan cave-temples are with individual variations: the *nirandhara* type where the shrine-cells are devoid of a circumambulatory passage as at Badami, the *sandhara* type with shrine-cells having a circumambulatory passage as at Ellora, Ramesvara, etc., the *trikuta* type with triple shrine-cells as at Aihole and Ellora, and the *sarvatobhadra* type with shrine-cells having door-openings on all the four sides as at Elephanta, Ellora and Jogeshvari. The *sandhara* and *sarvatobhadra* forms are the most outstanding. In the *sarvatobhadra* types, as seen in the Dhumarlena at Ellora, the principal cave at Elephanta, and in the cave at Jogeshvari, the outer *mandapa* cut out of the rock tends to have at least three open passages on the three sides, while the fourth at the rear forms the one ending in the parent rock.

The heaviness of the Chalukyan pillars as at Badami is apparently reduced by the flutings and carvings; the pillar and corbel shapes are various, but in their development they retain their individuality till the close of the Chalukyan period and do not recur in the Rashtrakuta creations. In the Rashtrakuta pillars the square-sectioned forms prevail and the corbel does not show the characteristic volute on the curved face of corbel arm, but for a weak roll at the upper end. The embellished median band, or *patta*, common in the Chalukyan corbels, is absent.

The most characteristic feature of the style is the door-frame of the cella with elaborate over-door components. In this respect at least a congruity is maintained among the Chalukyan and Rashtrakuta cave-temples, as also in the structural temples. The *sakhas*, or components of the over-door, range from three to many, the lintel-piece has a crest ornament—the *lalata bimba*, and a superstructure, or *uttaranga*. The basal part of the inner *sakhas* and the jamb carry panels with reliefs of the river goddesses, Ganga and Yamuna. In the Chalukyan cave-temples of the southern zone, the Kannada area, *dvarapala* forms along with the river goddesses are depicted in the same panels. This is in addition to the relatively larger *dvarapalas* in the niches flanking the outermost entrance of the front *mandapa*, or front porch of the cave-temple. On the other hand, the cave-temples of the northern zone in the Deccan, as at Ellora, Elephanta, Mahur and other places, have more than lifesize *dvarapala* pairs touching the ceiling in height. In Jogeshvari they flank the sanctum entrance, as also the outer *mandapa* entrance. This would indicate an earlier stage, while the other Rashtrakuta caves show a tendency to revert to the scheme of less-than-life-size *dvarapalas* on either side of the sanctum entrance. The *mandapa* ceilings show carvings of large lotus medallions, or scroll design, except in the case of Badami Cave III, where the ceiling medallion sculpture motif shows Brahma in the centre, anticipating similar ceiling sculptures in the structural temples where the scheme is the *ashtadikpala* grid with the central figure often conforming to the main deity of the temple.

In most cases there is a general provision for a stone image or symbol (*linga*) of the principal deity in worship in the sanctum, a thing which did not appear in the Pallava examples till the last quarter of the seventh century, though it occurs in the Pandyan examples where too, in the earliest cases, the preference was for a stone-imageless sanctum. The sanctum had a stucco panel or painting or a stone sculpture as a bas-relief on the rear wall, rather than on the floor at its centre. In the earliest examples of the cave-temples as at Badami, the sanctum, or *garbha-griha*, is relatively small and just enough for the *pitha* of the *linga* in the Siva cave-temples, and the image in others. The *pitha* in all cases is also rock-cut, or monolithic, and not a separate installation, and often the *linga* too is monolithic and of live rock. The invariably square *linga-pitha* has a projecting spout on its top to drain off the *abhisheka* water, and a cistern is cut into the rock floor below it to collect the same. In all early temples there is no further provision to drain it off along the floor and outside the shrine chamber. This is found again only in the Pandyan cave-temples of the farthest south, and not at all in the intervening Pallava cave-temples, or in the cave-temples of the north. As stated earlier, the cisterns on the floor of the sanctum are also found in the stone temples of the Dieng Valley in far-off Java (Indonesia). The spout projects invariably northwards irrespective of the direction of the sanctum. In cases where the sanctum itself faces north, the alternate *Agamic* injunction that it should be on the proper left is adhered to. This, among other things, would indicate the early enunciation of the *Agami*, or ritual principles, which were elaborated and re-codified in later times.

The *mandapa* in front of the early cave-temples has more bays laterally on the transverse axis and only one bay at either end of the long axis. In the Ajanta *viharas* on the other hand, the *mandapa* is a concentric scheme with one bay all round the central bay, which is often larger than the rest. While this *navaranga*, or concentric nine-bay pattern, is repeated in the main scheme in the structural temples of the Chalukyan series, later, the Badami cave, *mandapa*-type also finds its structural analogues particularly in temples of the south-west Deccan, west Mysore and the Konkan and Malabar coasts down to the times of the Ikkeri Nayaks of the seventeenth century. The provision of more aisles or bays parallel to the central nave with only one extreme bay at either end of the longitudinal axis finds its application in structural temples where the lateral bays, with pillars or walls of diminishing height from the centre, carry successively stepped down, slopy or flat roofs. Such early structural temples are the Ladkhan in Aihole and the Kallamatha in Badami. It would be evident that this feature in rock architecture is after the contemporary and earlier brick-and-timber structural models. The Ramesvara facade at Ellora would also indicate the prototype or archetype of *mandapa* of mediaeval structural temples. The projected porches have bench-like platforms with seats and lean-backs between the pillars, the *kakshasanas*, their exterior view being parapet-like with a *vedi* form and dwarf pillars and other decorations and sculptures. As a result the intercolumniation of the facade is not generally equal, the central pillars having a wider interspace than the lateral ones.

In Badami there are four cave-temples excavated at various heights on the vertical scarp of the sandstone rock. These are reached by a natural incline in front with steps. The earliest and largest one is Cave III excavated by Mangalesa in AD 578 and dedicated to Vishnu. It is cut at the most commanding height visible from the valley in front. Cave-temple I, which is of medium size and is Saiva, and the smallest Cave-temple II, which is Vaishnava, are cut at lower levels, the former being almost near ground level. Cave-temple IV, also small but Jain, cut near the top of the rock, came much later than the other three which belong to the last quarter of the sixth century. These cave-temples consist of a rectangular pillared *mukha-mandapa* preceding a more or less square-pillared *maha-mandapa* with a shrine-cell at the rear end. The *ardha-mandapa* that should intervene between the shrine and the *maha-mandapa* is not distinct, and is taken up by the rear bays of the *maha-mandapa*. The facade opening is wide and sufficiently high. The facade pillars are tall and massive, often of a square section, carrying corbels, or *potika*, supporting the beam. The massive overhanging ledge over the beam forms eaves or cornice, the *kapota*, with ribbing and cross-pieces imitating a frame-work carved on its curved underside. The beams over the *potika*, as also the underframe of the *kapota*, are often strutted, as it were, by bold caryatid-like supports of human, celestial or animal figures sculptured almost in the round. The inter-columniation between the two central pillars is wider than that between the others. The ceilings of the *mukha-mandapa* or *agra-mandapa* are sunk into regular four-sided coffers by thick cross-beams, that are filled with carved medallions in relief. The inner pillars, especially of the inner row of the *mukha-mandapa*, though square at the base, are of a circular section above, complete with the moulded capital components, viz. the vase-shaped *kalasa* and the cushion-shaped bulbous *kumbha*, to mention only the most prominent ones. The pillared *maha-mandapa*, as already stated, has a wider nave at the centre than the lateral aisles, and the inner pillars are polygonal in section. A functional division of the *mukha-mandapa* from the central hall is shown by the introduction of a screen wall stretching to about a fourth of the width from either end between the two *mandapas* with the front pillars and pilasters of the *maha-mandapa* fitted in the central gap. The higher floor-level of the central nave would suggest a central clerestory roof, rising above the roofs of the side aisles as could be seen in the structural examples referred to before, though in this rock-cut model the ceiling is of even height right through. Cave I has a monolithic *linga-pitha* and is slightly later in point of time. Cave II would be slightly later than Cave III which has only a monolithic *pitha* for the original Vishnu image. The recessed *kantha* of the plinth of the *mukha-mandapa* facade in Cave III shows paired pilasters interposed between the *gana* groups while in Caves I and II the *gana* friezes are continuous. There are no Vaishnava friezes on the ceiling in the front *mandapa* of Siva Cave I while they are present in the earlier Caves II and III, which are Vaishnava. The Jain cave-temple of a still later date is replete with Jain sculptures and cameos, while the other three are noted for some of their bold wall sculptures, mostly subsequent additions.

In respect of the sculpture panels, even in Cave III of Badami, the earliest of the series, it has been demonstrated (by A. Lippe) on the basis of technical and stylistic evidence that, they, barring the Vaikunthanatha (seated Vishnu) and Varaha *murti*, are not coeval with the cave excavation, but additions, made at a slightly later time, about the middle of the seventh century, possibly after the period of Pallava occupation of Badami by Mamalla.

Of the two rock-cut cave-temples at Aihole (Bijapur district) while the one called Ravalagudi is dedicated to Siva, dating about AD 700, the other one of a slightly later date is a Jain temple. Both are excavated into the low sandstone outcrops, and mark the latest of the early Chalukyan or Western Chalukyan series in their home districts. Though smaller than the Badami cave-temples, these are interesting from the point of view of plan, design and sculpture. The pillars are more slender and have the usual capital components of the 'order'. The Ravalagudi consists essentially of an almost square *mandapa* with a large principal cella of almost equal size on the rear, and two more, wide, lateral shrines, thus making a *trikuta* plan. While the rear shrine has a rock-cut *linga*, the lateral shrine on its right is dedicated to the Saptamatrikas and attendant deities, and the one on the left to other forms of Siva. The slightly projecting dividing wall-strips between the *mandapa* and rear shrine, leaving a wide entrance in between, carry the *dvarapala* sculptures. On the facade on either flank on the rock wall are niches containing the sculptures of the two *nidhis*—*Sankha* and *Padma*. The Jain cave-temple has a front *mandapa* which is more pronouncedly rectangular, and conforms to the typical *mandapa*-type cave-temple pattern.

The high trap-ridge at Ellora which had afforded the venue for a series of Buddhist excavations described earlier, now provided a scope for Hindu and Jain works. The Brahmanical cave-temples, occupying the central section of the hill and the parts higher up, belong to the period of the Chalukyas and their Rashtrakuta successors. The Hindu excavations, designated as

Caves 13 to 29, are mostly Saivite in character and fall into two distinct chronological series, the earlier series being more after the models of the preceding Buddhist excavations, characterized by the general absence of a rock-cut image or symbol like the *linga* in their sanctums. There are, of course, variations of plan and content in some. Cave 16 is the Kailasa complex, where the main part is the monolithic *vimana* temple of Kailasa with cave-temples on the scarp of the circumambulatory passage as in the case of the Lankesvara (16a). The later series are more after the models of the south and often contain an image in their sanctum, a rock-cut *linga* pedestal with sometimes a rock-cut Nandi also.

The pillars in these caves are of a varied nature and design and are square or octagonal in section, or, generally, of the *kumbha-valli* type with full vases and excrescent foliage at the middle height, or they have cushion-shaped *kumbha* mouldings in their capitals. The corbels, where present, are either simple or ornate. The cornice, or *kapota*, over the facades and shrines entrances is decorated by horseshoe-shaped *kudus* which are small *nasikas*. The door-frames have elaborate over-doors and carry, as the *uttaranga* on top, miniature representations of the southern *vimana*-type shrine or the northern *sikhara* or *prasada* shrines. The Ramesvara (Cave 21) would represent the earliest of this group. The facade of the rectangular *mukha-mandapa* has four short, bulky, ornate pillars, and two pilasters at either end rising above a highly decorated *vedi* parapet, or dwarf wall, interrupted in the middle between the two central pillars to provide the entrance doorway. The transverse length of the rectangular portico, or *mukha-mandapa*, which is carried across the entire front of the excavation has further extensions, one at either end in the form of a side shrine or chamber. Behind the *mukha-mandapa* is the pillared *maha-mandapa*, the two central rows of pillars wider apart forming the nave, with the *sandhara* sanctum at the rear, while the extreme ones, which are closer to the central ones, form the aisles leading to the circumambulatory passage round the sanctum. The sanctum entrance is guarded by huge *dvarapalas*. The pillars have the *kumbha* mouldings. In the matter of shrine location, even with the modifications effected, it is yet in keeping with the Mahayana Buddhist shrine already excavated at Ellora. The exhibition of the *bhuta gana* friezes in the facade dwarf wall and the bracket figures, on the other hand, would take this excavation closer to the Badami group, thereby indicating the first quarter of the seventh century as its date. Caves 20, 22, 23 and 24, adjacent to this, would also belong to about the same period.

The Ravana-ki-kai (Cave 14) is of a simpler plan, with a large pillared *mandapa* and a *sandhara* shrine at its rear. The doubling of the front row of columns affords a *mukha-mandapa*-like verandah in front of the nave leading to the shrine, the aisles continuing as the circumambulatory passage round the shrine. The pillars are of the *kumbha-valli* type. On either side of the shrine entrance, there are a number of carved images, including the two *dvarapalas*. On the *mandapa* walls, and carved in the recesses between the pilasters, are sculptural compositions, Saivite and Vaishnavite. The cella is rectangular and has provision for a platform on its rear with a socket in it for Vishnu or Durga, but not for Siva or a *linga*. This excavation in the pre-Rashtrakuta series can be dated near AD 700. Besides the above, others like Caves 17, 20, 21 and 26 are of the *sandhara* type and have their shrine chambers at the rear of the pillared *mandapa* cut out on all sides, resulting in a circumambulatory passage. Cave 17 should be nearer Ramesvara in point of time, i.e. the second quarter of the seventh century, and Cave 26 should approximate to the Rashtrakuta excavations.

The Dhumarlena, or Cave 29, is of greatest interest since it is the largest and most imposing of the caves at Ellora. Its *sandhara* and *chaumukh*, or *chaturmukha* shrine, is not only isolated but also contained within a group of *mandapas* arranged in a cruciform plan which is similar to that of the Elephanta and the Jogeshvari caves. The four doorways of the shrine are flanked by large *dvarapalas* and other accompanying sculptures. The long rectangular *maha-mandapa* or main hall that precedes the shrine and also partly surrounds it has a wide nave and aisles formed by a colonnade of five pillars on each side, of which the front encloses the main entrance. Additionally flanking the main hall are two lateral entrances through two portals or pillared transepts. The pillars are huge in size with *kumbhas* or cushion capitals, and the statutory inside is also ponderous and of large proportions. The shrine contains a *linga* on a monolithic *pitha*. The cave-temple can be dated to the middle of the seventh century in the Chalukyan period.

Cave 27, or the Milkmaid's cave (Gopilena), is an interesting example with triple shrines on the rear and side walls of the *mandapa*. Cave 25, or the Kumbharvada, has multiple shrine-cells as in Bhokardan and has lateral galleries attached to the ante-chamber. While Cave 27 may be of the transitional period be-tween the Chalukyas and Rashtrakutas, Cave 25 should be earlier, datable to the second half of the seventh century.

The Dasavatara, or Cave 15, is an odd example in as much as it is the only two-storeyed cave-temple or cave-complex of a very large size. It is apparently a case of reconditioning of what all was prepared and cut out for Buddhistic requirements. It would mark the earliest example of Rashtrakuta work at Ellora. Its front pavilion carries the inscription of Dantidurga (*c.* 752-756) and is an accomplished piece of contemporary rock architecture. The cave-temple will have to be placed in the mid-eighth century. The detached Nandi-*mandapa* is four-pillared with flights of steps at the front and the rear. The facade of the temple that rises beyond has its two storeys with two rows of pillars, one above the other, the pillars being square and reminiscent of the arrangement in the Tin-tal cave of Ajanta. The groundfloor is a compartment with fourteen square pillars and the upper floor has the plan of a large pillared *mandapa* with central nave and lateral aisles and a shrine with a *linga* at the rear. The *linga-pitha* is circular. The pillars are arranged in six rows of nine each with two additional ones at the far end of the nave forming a vestibule in front of the shrine. The two pillars at the front of the vestibule are elaborately carved while the rest of the pillars are plain, square in section. The pilasters along the walls enclose between them large sunk panels with fine group sculptures. Cave 16 is another example having a circular *linga-pitha* in its shrine.

The Lankesvara cave at the upper level, to the right of the Kailasa monolith, is again a Rashtrakuta excavation, showing a reversion to the type with a *sandhara* shrine-cell at the rear of a pillared *mandapa*. It is compact and has a terminal Nandi pavilion and contains a very rich grouping of sculptures of great icono-graphic value.

The Ganeshlena constitutes over a score of cave-temples forming a group collectively numbered as Cave 21. Each unit consists of a *mandapa* having simple pillars and pilasters of square section with corbels of the Chalukyan type on the facade, and the shrine chamber at the rear. The rear wall of the shrine has a relief of Mahesamurti. In most cases there is a *linga* inserted into a monolithic circular *pitha* on the floor, and in one case there is a rock-cut *linga* as well. The shrine doorways have over-doors. These may be placed just about AD 750, in the early years of the Rashtrakuta rule in Ellora. The Mahesamurti reliefs here are quite different in treatment and finish from the celebrated one at Elephanta and, unlike Elephanta, they are placed on the wall behind the Rashtrakuta *linga* in the main shrine.

The Jain excavations (Caves 30 to 34) mark the last phase of activity in Ellora commencing from about AD 800 and continuing into the next century. They follow mostly the earlier Hindu examples in plan and design, differing only in their sculpture and iconography. The Indra Sabha (Cave 32) and the Jagannath Sabha (Cave 33) standing close together, are both two-storeyed excavations. The Indra Sabha has in its open forecourt the *chaumukh* Jain monolithic temple. The rock faces on the sides of the open front quadrangle are profusely sculptured and have elaborately carved *kapota* entablatures, one separating the lower from the upper storey with a lion and elephant series in the frieze, and the other, on top of the upper storey, with a series of shrines depicting *tirthankara* forms. The lower storey of the cave is an unfinished hall, mostly with simple pillars, some of them moulded. There are attempts to cut cells into the walls. The upper storey is again a *navaranga-mandapa* with twelve pillars, the central bay having a raised platform for a Jain *chaumukh* with the ceiling showing an elaborate lotus carving. The hall has a pillared portico, and there are two side shrines projecting on either side of the front.

The Jagannath Sabha, though of the same type, lacks the regularity of the plan. The groundfloor is a complex of three asymmetrically disposed sanctuaries, each a complete unit, consisting of *agra-* and *maha-mandapas*. The rear shrines open into the courtyard which has crumbled away. The upper floor has the *navaranga* hall with twelve outer pillars as in the Indra Sabha, but there is also a shrine at the rear. From one corner of the *mandapa* and disposed at an angle is an additional unit similar in proportions and character to those of the groundfloor, but complete and richly carved.

In Elephanta, a tiny island off Bombay, the cave-temple is distinguished by the exceptional quality of its sculptures of which the great Mahesamurti is the most well known. With the main east-west linear axis of the excavation parallel to the length of the rock, its plan consists of a large *mandapa* supported by twenty pillars on its periphery, eight ranged on each of the longer sides and two each on the front and the rear, between the corner pillars. There are flights of steps in front of the shorter or front and rear sides, leading out into open courts on the respective sides, which are formed by cuttings that more or less isolate the section of the rock with its excavated cave-temple from the rest of the mass. In the eastern court on its floor is a circular rock-cut pedestal, perhaps for Nandi. The northern side of the main *maha-mandapa* has two pillars and pilasters on its facades; the *mukha-mandapa* is longer than the former by the addition of one more bay at either end. These two are designed as the northern lateral extensions of the *maha-mandapa* with an entrance on the open side, while the corresponding lateral extension of the same plan on the south, dug into the parent rock, contains the niches of Mahesamurti and other sculptures. Towards the rear end of the *maha-mandapa* is a *sandhara*, *chaturmukha* shrine, square, and with doors framed by elaborate over-doors on the four sides. Inside there is a large rock-cut *linga* pedestal, with its spout on the north, and with an inserted *linga*. In front of the shrine there is an inner *pradakshina-mandapa* between two rows of four pillars each, forming part of the circumambulatory passage round the shrine. A cutting into the rock on the east, beyond the northern portico, leads to the eastern forecourt and the main entrance to the temple. On the southern side of this court, a smaller cave-temple for Durga is excavated into the scarp. A similar cutting at the western end beyond the northern portico leads into the court behind the main temple into the western scarp. Into this a smaller Siva cave-temple is cut, consisting of a square shrine with a *mandapa* in front. This cave-temple may have to be placed in the middle of the second quarter of the seventh century, while Ellora Cave 29 (Dhumarlena), which is to a large extent its copy, should be placed in the beginning of the last quarter of the same century.

The Jogeshvari cave-temple in Salsette, near Bombay, which is excavated into an almost underground low trap outcrop, is larger in area than the Elephanta cave, but is essentially of the same type. Trenching on three sides all round a marked area into the rock outcrop isolated a large rectangular mass on which the scarps for the excavation were prepared. At the eastern and longer end a large gateway or *mahadvara* is carved with a central passage and flanking *mandapas* on either side, one of them enshrining Ganesa. The *mahadvara* leads into an open court and the eastern facade, which is an *agra-mandapa* with a higher floor-level. The main part of the temple beyond consists of a square *chaturmukha* shrine surrounded by a pillared cloister with six pillars on each side, counting the corner ones too. This is surrounded again by an outer astylar cloister, or *mandapa*, with a lower floor-level enclosed by the rock walls on all sides except for an entrance each on the east and the west, and for three on the south. The shrine here occupies a central position and its doorways are framed by elaborate over-doors. On the western side there is another *agra-mandapa*, similar to the one on the east, which leads out and up through a narrow tunnel to the road beyond. On the southern side, the main *mandapa* leads through its three openings, with a fine over-door frame round the central one flanked by two intermediate windows, to an extension on this side, which is in the form of an outer open *mandapa* with a row of ten pillars and two pilasters on its southern facade. Outside this is a narrow open court. The rock wall beyond has incomplete or abandoned excavations of a smaller size, of which the one at the extreme end is dedicated to Siva. This has interesting pillars with caryatids on its facade. The original dedication of the main sanctum was to Siva, though the temple now enshrines a modern idol of a goddess.

The Patalesvara (or Panchalesvar) cave on Jangli Maharaj Road in Poona, cut into a low trap rock, is unique in that it has a triple-shrine with common *pradakshina* round it, a circular front pavilion for Nandi, and a side shrine for Durga. The three shrine-cells were perhaps dedicated to the Hindu trinity, the central one to Siva and the lateral ones to Brahma and Vishnu. All these features would point to the second half of the eighth century as its date in the Rashtrakuta times.

The Hindu cave at Mahur (Nander district) in Maharashtra has a *sandhara*-type of sanctum with two smaller transverse corridors in front and two smaller subsidiary shrines on the flanks. This is apparently a late plan after the model of Caves 17 and 21 of Ellora, and datable to the first quarter of the eighth century. It was perhaps a provincial contemporary of Dhumarlena of Ellora. There is an unfinished excavation by the side of the Siva cave.

The cave at Bhokardan near Aurangabad has five shrine-cells in a line behind the pillared rectangular *mandapa* at the rear of an open cutting in a low outcropping trap rock on the left bank of the Kelna river-bed. Each cell has a door-opening. The *mandapa* has two bays, at the front and the rear, forming *mukha-* and *ardha-mandapas*. The side walls of the *mandapa* are scooped into shallow curves with large figure sculptures. The *dvarapalas* are large-sized, and there are sculptures of Anantasayin, Surya, Balarama, Mahishamardini, etc. It is not clear if this cave is of Western or Eastern Chalukyan authorship; it could even have been of mixed tradition. The nature of the sculpture and other evidence indicate an Eastern Chalukyan authorship in the mid-seventh century AD.

The group of two adjacent cave-temples at Arvelam in Goa is a rare instance of excavation into the local laterite of the west coast overlooking a stream. Both are of simple features. One of them, the southern cave-temple, is a triple-celled unit containing in each unit a *linga* mounted on a rock-cut *pitha*. The *linga* forms in their symbolic aspect differ from one another and represent three different deities. The central *linga* is the normal Chalukyan-type *sivalinga*; the one in the southern cella is a *linga* shaft surmounted by a solar disc representing Surya or the sun-god, with an inscription below the disc specifically mentioning it as a Surya form. The *linga* shaft in the northern cell is surmounted by a flat spear-head, or *sakti*, indicating that it represents Kumara or Kartikeya. It is an interesting instance of Vishnu of the trinity being replaced by Surya according to the Surya-Narayana concept, and Brahma by Brahmanya or Karitkeya, as in the *trimurti* cave-temple at Mahabalipuram.

The most outstanding feature of the rock-cut cave art has been, from the Buddhist times, the dominance of sculpture over architecture. This was facilitated largely by the softness of the stone material and the urge to exploit spaces, as on the pillars, on the walls between pilasters, and even on the ceiling. The same tendency resulted in large-scale paintings, as at Ajanta, Ellora and Badami.

The different god-forms sculptured are depicted often in the narrative or synoptic panels. They vary in size from very large-sized individual figures, as the *dvarapalas*, Mahesamurti, etc. to almost the size of cameos. In the earlier Western Chalukyan caves as at Badami, Vishnu and Siva sculptures occur indiscriminately, while in the later ones they are well-nigh separated. The former type of caves show among the female deities only Durga, while the latter have the Saptamatrikas, Sarasvati, Gajalakshmi and Parvati. The latter category is also to be found in the Rashtrakuta caves along with a relapse to the admixture of Vaishnavite carvings, though to a lesser extent. While the Western Chalukyan sculpture is noted for clarity in form, pose and expression, the Rashtrakuta phase is characterized by crowded ornamentation with less emphasis on pose and expression and, what is more, a tendency to depict *Puranic* episodes, either in a synoptic or narrative form. The profusion of such didactic depictions compensates richly for the diminution of the aesthetic trends of the earlier phase. In the Saiva temples at least, tendencies of cult domination and the prescriptions of *Agama* are noticed. While the Western Chalukyan *linga-pithas* are mostly square, the Rashtrakuta *linga-pithas*, as in Ellora Caves 15 and 16, and the Ganeshlena caves are circular. They are monolithic and form part of the live rock of the excavation. These contrast with the absence of *linga-pithas* in the Pallava cave-temples where the advent of *lingas* of the prismatic *dharalinga* type inserted into sockets in the floor, or of even uniform circular section over the square lower part that goes into the socket, is of a later date than the cave-temple. The Chalukya-Rashtrakuta *lingas* are of a different type. It is only in the monolithic *linga-pitha* and *linga* of the Pandyan temples that we find square, circular, and even octagonal *linga-pithas*.

While the *linga* symbolizing Siva in his aniconic aspect with the characteristic *linga-pitha*, called *avudaiyar*, is absent as organically rock-cut with the cave itself in the earlier stages of the Pallava cave-temples, they appear as integral rock-cut forms of the Pandya-Muttaraiyar series, coinciding chronologically with the later Pallava structural phase. But in the north of the Tamil country, in the Chalukya-Rashtrakuta cave-temples, the presence of the rock-cut *linga-pitha*, though not always along with the *linga* on it, would suggest a continuity with the earlier prevailing trends in that area. For after the unique example of the *urdhvalinga* (phallic) form in Gudimallam (Chittoor district), *lingas*, many of them of the *arsha* (or naturally occurring type), inserted into sockets of *linga-pithas* have been found in the course of excavations of the river-side area in Nagarjunakonda of the Ikshivaku times, followed by the recent finds of *lingas* in *linga-pithas* in the

salvaged area of the river-valley projects in the Kurnool and
Mahbubnagar districts of Andhra Pradesh. These linked up with
such finds of an earlier period from Karvan (Kayarohana), associated with Lakulisa—the founder of the *pasupata* creed, would
indicate the gradual spread of the *linga* cult southwards during
the centuries, reaching Tamil Nadu in the beginning of the eighth
century AD.

The iconographic forms noticed in the Badami group include,
among Vaishnava forms, Varaha, Trivikrama, Narasimha,
Anantasayin, Vaikunthanatha, Vishnu, and Vaishnavite legends
and Krishna-*lila* in friezes. The Siva forms are *tandava murti*,
Harihara, and Ardhanari. Among the others are Ganesa, Kartikeya,
Durga and Mahishamardini. At Aihole (Ravalapudi or
Ravalagudi), we have Varaha, Harihara, Ardhanari, Gangadhara,
Saptamatrikas, Mahishamardini and the two *nidhis*.

In the Chalukyan phase at Ellora are to be seen Ganesa,
Kartikeya, Sarasvati, Gajalakshmi, Saptamatrikas, Siva-Parvati
legends in synoptic forms, Parvati's penance, Kailasa-*tolana*,
Akshakridamurti, Kalyanasundara, Andhakari, Siva-*tandavas*,
Lakulisa, Siva-Lakulisa, Krishna, Balarama, Subhadra, Surya,
Anantasayin and Brahma. The Rashtrakuta phase in the same
place is noted for such sculptures as Durga, Mahishamardini,
Parvati-*tapas*, Kalyanasundara, the Kailasa scene, Ardhanari Siva,
Govardhanandhari, Kaliyadamana, Varaha, Narasimha, Lakshmi,
Sarasvati, Ganesa and Kartikeya. The Ganesalena at Ellora de-
picts also the Shanmata or six-fold cult of Surya, Vishnu, Siva,
Kartikeya, Ganesa and Durga.

The Elephanta sculptures are almost the same as those in
Dhumarlena (Ellora), with some additions, such as the
Mahesamurti and Sivayogi; Jogeshvari has Kartikeya, Lakshmi,
Ganesa, Saptamatrikas, Lakulisa and Kalyanasundara. The
Patalesvara at Poona has Gajalakshmi, Tripurantaka, Anantasayin,
Lingodbhava and Andhakari. Mahur depicts Ardhanari,
Gangadhara, Tripurantaka, Ganesa, Kartikeya and Surya.

THE EASTERN CHALUKYAN CAVE-TEMPLES
OF COASTAL ANDHRA

In the Andhra coastal region, excavated into the softer rocks on
either bank of the Krishna in the territory of the Eastern Chalukyas

of Vengi, there are over a dozen cave-temples. They are to be found in the hills of Vijayawada and Mogulrajapuram on the north bank, all in Krishna district, and in the hills of Undavalli, Penamaga, and Sitaramapuram on the south bank in Guntur district. These cave-temples of Eastern Chalukyan authorship show individualistic characters in their lay-out, iconography and the scheme of the cella. They partake in some respects of the neighbouring Pallava modes, apart from their parental Chalukyan and northern inheritance. The remarkable feature of this series of cave-temples is the occurrence of a rock-cut pedestal socket at the base of the rear wall of the cella, denoting the object of worship, whether it be the *linga* form of Siva, or a sculptured stele bearing the image of other gods inserted into the socket. In Bhairavakonda, the socket is cut in a sunken recess on the wall over the pedestal to take in the *linga*, or image. In respect of the cave temples of the Eastern Chalukyas, the absence of Vishnu carvings is notable as against what is found in the Western Chalukyan-Rashtrakuta group. Practically all the cave-temples are Saiva, or are dedicated to other deities of the Saiva pantheon. The only exception is the aberrant Undavalli cave-temple which is dedicated to Vishnu. The Nandi in Saiva cave-temples is rock-cut as in the Pandyan examples farther south. In point of time the Akkanna-Madanna cave at Vijayawada in its present form comes first. It is ascribable to the middle of the seventh century, and is closely followed by Caves I to IV of Mogalrajapuram, the lower cave-temple at Vijayawada, the Undavalli and other caves in a series, ending with the Bhairavakonda group datable to the middle of the eighth century. The last, if not of direct Eastern Chalukyan vintage, can at best be of Telugu-Chola authorship.

These cave-temples essentially consist of a rock-cut hall, or *mandapa*, with one or more, often three, shrine-cells behind. The multiple shrines are in a row at the rear. The *mandapa* is in some cases astylar and in others multi-pillared, or demarcated into front and rear sections by two rows of pillars and pilasters—the usual facade row and the parallel inner row. The pillars are usually simple, thick-set, short and square in section throughout, or have their middle height bevelled at the corners. This results in the middle section being octagonal, while the basal and apical sections are square in plan. The cornice of the facade, the *kapota*, is decorated by *kudu*, or *nasika* arches. The doorways of the shrines are simple like those in the southern cave-temples and unlike the Western Chalukyan-Rashtrakuta types with elaborate over-doors. The doorway is often enclosed by two flanking pilasters carrying a *torana* festoon above. While most of the cave-temples are dedicated to Siva, two are definitely dedicated to Durga, and a few to Vishnu. The sculptural content is very meagre compared to the examples at Badami, Aihole, Ellora, etc. Among the few sculptures, mention may be made of *tandava* Siva. The Anantasayanagudi cave-temple at Undavalli is the largest of the group and is a three-storeyed structure akin to the Ellora Buddhist Caves 11 and 12, the Do-tal and Tin-tal. It belongs to the seventh century if not earlier, and was perhaps intended originally for the Buddhist creed, but was adopted later for a Vishnu temple, the principal deity being a recumbent Vishnu, or Anantasayin.

The Bhairavakonda cave-temples are excavated into a soft schist intrusion in the hills at Kottapalle in Nellore district, a rock material different from the Krishna-Guntur group. Interposed between them, along with two rock sculptures of dancing Siva and Harihara, are small niches or memorial shrines with *lingas* cut inside them, with dedicatory or other inscriptions of the eighth century.

The eight larger cave-temples fall into two groups. The first four, starting from the northern end of the horseshoe valley or ravine, are simple shrine excavations without a front *mandapa* and lack the elaborately decorated *kapota* cornice and its *kudu* ornaments. The cave-temples of the second group are of the regular type having an outer *mandapa* with a facade row of two pillars and two pilasters and a rear shrine-cell. The *mandapa* facade has on top a fully formed *kapota* with *kudus* as in the Mamalla-style cave-temples of the Pallavas. The pillars are square in section and of the Chalukyan pattern as found in the cave-temples on the banks of the Krishna. In some, the pillars have lion caryatids on top and are also lion-based, with capital components above as in the Mamalla-style cave-temples. The shrine entrances are plain and without any over-door. These mixed characters and other features, as also the presence of relief sculptures of Brahma and Vishnu in the *mandapa*, provision for a *linga* in the shrine, and the presence of other sculptures like Chandesa and Ganesa, and the rock-cut Nandi, would indicate their non-Pallava origin and their date as being the middle of the eighth century.

Pandava *ratha*: Rockcut chariot, Mahabalipuram

Shore temple (Shiva), Mahabalipuram

Sculpture on Halebid temple walls, Halebid

Ramesvaram temple corridor, Ramesvaram

Manjunath temple, Mangalore

Minakshi temple, Madurai

Minakshi temple gate, Madurai

sanctum. The main doorway is framed by a fine *torana* as also the three *devakoshthas* which also enshrine standing relief sculptures of Durga on the three side walls. On either side of the doorway are flanking *dvarapalikas*, one on either side in the niche between the corner plaster and the *torana* pilaster framing the entrance. This *ratha* lacks a *mukha-* or *ardha-mandapa*, unlike the other *rathas*, as also the *nasikas* projected from the *sikhara*.

A *dvitala* and hence *ashtanga*, or *ashtavarga vimana* of the same *Nagara* order, square from base to apex is illustrated in the incomplete Valaiyankuttai *ratha* facing east. It has a small *ardha-mandapa* and the *aditala* has a single wall, hence it is *nirandhara*. The *prastaras* of both the *talas* carry *arpita haras*, applique on the *harmya* of the second *tala* and on the *griva* above, and made up of four *karnakutas* at the corners and four *salas* in between them on each side over each face. There are *nasikas* on the four sides of the *griva sikhara* region. The *hara* at the *aditala* level is extended also over the top of the *ardha-mandapa*, a feature of all early *vimanas*. The *kutas* and *salas* over the *mandapa* are of a smaller size than those over the *aditala* as usual. This is an example of the elaboration of the *talachchanda* by the addition of one storey over the *ekatala* form of six *angas* illustrated by the bas-relief *vimanas* which are depicted in Arjuna's penance sculpture and again at either end of the facade of the Ramanuja *mandapam* cave-temple. The northern *ratha* of the twin Pidari *rathas*, facing north with its *ardha-mandapa*, is of the pure *Nagara* order, with only this difference that there is no *hara* over the second *tala*—an advanced feature—making it out as the last of the series in Mahabalipuram and anticipating in this respect the later *vimanas* of the eighth century. The *griva sikhara* faces are provided with projected *nasikas*. Both the *rathas* lack sculptures on their *aditala* walls and are incomplete.

The incomplete southern Pidari *ratha* facing east and the more complete Arjuna *ratha* are likewise double-storeyed, square in section in both the *talas* and carrying applique *haras* of four *karnakutas* and four *salas* at both levels. The *griva* and *sikhara* are, however, octagonal in section, making them both *ashtanga*, *nirandhara vimanas* of the *Dravida* order of the composite variety. There are four *nasikas* projected from the four cardinal sides of the *griva sikhara*. The *ardha-mandapa* in both the *vimanas* carries *haras* of *kutas* and *salas* of a smaller size than those over the *aditala*.

There are no sculptures on the walls of the northern Pidari *ratha*, while in the Arjuna *ratha* the faces of the *aditala* from *adhishthana* to *prastara* are offset thrice, at the two corners and in the middle, and the reliefs contain plain niches carrying fine figure sculpture. The second *tala* too has sculpture on its walls inside the corner pilasters of each face that are exposed to view on either side of the central *sala* of the *hara* in front. The two pillars and two pilasters of the *mandapa* facade are *vyala*-based. As in all the above cases, the *hara* is extended over the *mandapa*.

The Dharmaraja *ratha* is three-storeyed, square in its *talas* and octagonal in the *griva sikhara* region; but all the three storeys are intended to be functional. Thus the *vimana* is designed to have three superposed *garbha-grihas*, as against the non-functional but symbolic upper *talas* in the other *rathas* and most of the later structural examples. This is achieved by a cellular mode of construction with three concentric walled squares of increasing height, rising one inside the other to the successive heights of the respective *talas*, thus leaving interspaces in between. The outermost wall rising to the height of the *aditala prastara* is, however, present in sections only round the four corners, the intervening open sides having each a facade of two pillars and two pilasters, all *vyala*-based. The *haras* over the *prastara* of the three *talas* are thus detached from the *tala* walls, and hence *anarpita*. The small *mukha-mandapa* on the west in front of the *aditala* carries a *hara* which in its composition includes for the first time the apsidal *nida* or *panjara* along with the *kutas* and *salas*. The octagonal *griva sikhara* region has four projected *nasikas* on the four cardinal sides. While the lower *talas* remain unfinished but for their exterior, the topmost *tala* has a sanctum excavated into it that enshrines a Somaskanda form of Siva, with Vishnu and Brahma in attendance carved on its rear wall. In addition to *dvarapalas* on either side of the entrance, this *tala*, like the two lower *tala* walls, contains in its niches fine sculptures of various gods illustrating varied features of early Pallava iconography. This was perhaps commenced by Mamalla, as indicated by the label inscribed on the eastern side of the second *tala*, and was brought to its present stage of completion with the consecration of the top *tala* by Paramesvaravarman, as the labels on the top *tala* would denote.

In the Dharmaraja *ratha* what apparently looks like the outer wall of the *aditala* cantoning the corners leaving open–pillared entrances on the four cardinals, in between, is really the wall of an outer, narrow peripheral *mandapa* investing the *aditala* or groundfloor shrine. The pattern is really one where the wall of the *aditala garbha-griha* or cella rises up as the outer wall of the second *tala* sanctum which is render *sandhara* with an inner wall, in addition, that rises up higher as the wall of the third *tala* of lesser linear dimensions than the ones below. Thus the Dharmaraja *ratha* is only pseudo-*sandhara* on its groundfloor or *aditala*.

The Bhima and Ganesa *rathas* illustrate the oblong or *ayatasra vimanas* of the *koshtha-* or *sala*-type, with wagon-top roofs (*sala sikharas*) carrying a row of *stupis*, or finials over the ridge as opposed to the *kuta* or convergent type of *sikhara* with a single finial in the others. The incomplete Bhima *ratha* appears to be pseudo-*sandhara*, like the Dharmaraja *ratha*, in that its oblong *aditala* is surrounded by a narrow *mandapa* with walls round the corners and intervening open facades of two pillars and two pilasters on the long and short sides, the pillars and pilasters being *vyala*-based. The *mandapa* carries above its *prastara* a *hara* of *kutas* at the four corners and *sala* in between, over the sides. The oblong sanctum facing west was perhaps intended for a reclining form of Vishnu with his head to the south and legs to the north. The oblong *griva*, which rises as an upper continuation of the *garbha-griha* walls, is rather tall. On each of the two long sides of the *griva sikhara* are five well-projected *nasikas* in three sizes, the central one being the largest, the extreme ones middling, and the intermediate one being the smallest. The three larger ones represent full *nasikas* with the *prastara* element in their composition. The two smallest ones lack the *prastara* part. The *harantara* parts between the *kutas* and *salas* of the *hara* circuit have still smaller *nasikas* than are usual in all the other *rathas*. Thus this *ratha* alone would illustrate the various forms of *nasikas* as described in the texts. The two-storeyed Ganesa *ratha* is *nirandhara*, single-walled, and with a narrow *mukha-mandapa* in front and of the same length as the *aditala*. The *mandapa* is walled on its shorter sides and round the front corners leaving an open facade in front, with *vyala*-based pillars and pilasters. The *hara* over both the *talas* as also that over the *mandapa* contains the *kutas* and *salas* alone. There are three projected *nasikas* on the two longer sides of the *griva sikhara* region of which the central one is larger with the *prastara* element in its make-up and the two lateral ones smaller without that element. The *stupis* are integral and cut out at the completion of the *vimana* from the mass left over the ridge unlike in the other *rathas* where they are separate insertions. The crest of the two end-arches of the *sikharas* carry, in addition, a *trisula* finial each, which is the head of a three-horned *sula deva* represented by the face only. Similar *sula deva* finials, like the *stupis* were inserted in the case of the Bhima *ratha*. Except the *dvarapalas* there are no other sculptures in this *ratha*. In the facade of this *ratha*, besides the two *vyala*-based pillars, the pilasters of the facade are different, in that another type of mythical animal, a *vyala*-like form with beaked face, is introduced in the pilaster base. The *ratha* according to its inscription was originally dedicated to Siva; the Ganesa idol, now found planted in the cella, is an introduction of very recent times.

The *dvitala* and wholly apsidal and *nirandhara* Nakula-Sahadeva *ratha* well illustrates the *dvayasra* (two-sided with apse end) or *chapa* (bow-curve) form also called *gaja-* or *hastiprishtha*, in that it resembles the rear of a standing elephant, a large sculpture of which is carved by the side as if to emphasize the resemblance. The *chapa* form of the Nakula-Sahadeva *ratha* derives its architectural nomenclature *chapa* from the fact that the shape of the *vimana* on plan resembles the U-shaped curve of a fully drawn bow or *chapa*. Because of its elliptical shape, though truncated at the front end, this is also classified as of the *Vesara* order. It has a small open *mukha-mandapa* in front, of almost the same width as the *aditala*. The two front pillars are *vyala*-based and the two rear pilasters are elephant-based. The *prastara* over the *aditala* has a *hara* with two *karnakutas* at the two front corners, while over the sides and round the rear apse there is a row of *salas*. The *hara* on the *mandapa* too has only *kutas* and *salas*. The *hara* of the second *tala*, however, shows two *nidas* or *panjaras* (which are *ekatala* miniatures of the main *vimana*) between the two *karnakutas* on the front face, while the rest of the *hara* on the sides and round the curve is made up of *salas*. The innovation, namely, the addition of the third element, the *panjara* or *nida*, in the composition of the *hara* seems to have been made for the first time here, as over the *mukha-mandapa* of the Dharmaraja *ratha*, the stage of completion of which should have been at about the same time as this apsidal *ratha*. This *ratha* has no sculpture either inside the sanctum, or on the walls of the *talas* between the pilasters.

The Pallava vogue of creating cut-out monolithic temple forms was soon caught up, as it were, not only by the neighbours of the Pallavas in south India, but also by others much beyond, and quite a few monolithic temples of the southern and northern types were created in various parts of India, from the Tirunelveli district at the far southern tip of the peninsula to the Kangra district in the foot-hills of the Himalayas in the north; from Bihar in the east to Mandsaur in the west and Gwalior in central India— all within the two succeeding centuries.[1]

Following this pioneering work of the Pallavas, a few attempts at the cutting out of monolithic *vimana* forms in the same or succeeding centuries are noticeable in the Eastern Chalukyan region north of the Pallava territory of Tondaimandalam. At Undavalli, immediately to the west of the well-known four-storeyed cave-temple, the Anantasayanagudi, a projecting section of the rock is cut into a temple form with *vimana* and front *mandapas*, the latter fully cut out and the former presented externally in front elevation. The tiered superstructure rises on the main hill-face over the top line of the front *mandapas*. Internally, the work presents the full aspect of an excavated cave-temple with front halls and a shrine-cell behind. The *mandapa* facade has two pillars and two pilasters, all of the plain type. There is a well-defined *kapota* on its architrave decorated by *kudu* arches. The lateral wall of the *mukha-mandapa* inside has *devakoshthas*, now empty. Similar niches surmounted by *toranas* are to be found on the rear wall of the *ardha-mandapa* on either side of the shrine entrance. The shrine-cell is empty. In the adjoining rock faces bas-relief *vimana* miniatures are cut, six in number, of varying sizes

---

[1] Beyond the confines of the peninsula, the spread of this mode of carving down monolithic temples, though of the northern *rekha-prasada* type, is indicated in the west by the example of the Vaishnavite temple complex with seven *parivara* shrines, entrenched in the laterite hills of Dhamnar (Mandsaur district) of the eighth-ninth centuries. In the north there is the complex with *parivara* shrines of monolithic temples at Masrur (Kangra district) cut out of the over-ground sandstone rock and attributable to the ninth century. In central India there is the Chaturbhujaji temple with *prasada* and *mukha-mandapa* on the sandstone Gwalior hill assignable to the Pratiharas of the ninth century, and also the incomplete monolithic temple of the tenth century carved out of a granite boulder near the summit of a rocky island in the Ganga at Colgong (Bhagalpur district) on the east. It has a *sala sikhara* (with *prastara* and *griva*) with architectural wall-reliefs in the fashion of Orissan temples.

and much resembling the model bas-reliefs seen in Arjuna's penance composition and on either side of the Ramanuja *mandapam* at Mahabalipuram. They are replicas of *ekatala Nagara vimanas*, square in section from base to apex.

The much damaged remains of a monolithic *vimana* are to be found in Vijayawada, in front of the upper cave-temple of the Akkanna-Madanna group. In the precincts of the apsidal brick temple of Kapotesvara at Chejerla (Guntur district) are to be found a number of miniature shrine models, monolithic in character, evidently of a votive nature. These would also recall similar models found in the temple precincts at Satyavolu, Mahanandi and Alampur in the adjoining Kurnool district. One of the Chejerla models is interesting: in that it shows a completely free-standing pair of pillars for the shrine front.

While the contemporary Western Chalukyas of Badami, who were forging ahead with their structural stone temples, did not take up the carved-out monolithic mode of the Pallavas, the Rashtrakutas, who soon replaced the Chalukyas in their own territory, took it up with zest and, among others, created at Ellora the greatest and largest monolithic version of a southern temple complex that is familiarly known as the Kailasa.

This creation of Rashtrakuta Krishna I (756-775) is rather unique. By trenching vertically down into the sloping hill on all sides of a chosen area at right angles up to the base of the rock, an oblong central mass (about 60m × 30m) was isolated and in front of it, beyond the wider front trench, a further trench isolated a narrower transversely oblong mass stretching across like a wall. The larger oblong mass, longer from front to rear than from side to side, afforded the material for carving out the complex of the main *vimana* and its axial *mandapas*, as also two tall and stout free-standing monolithic pillars on either side in front surrounded by an open courtyard formed by trenches on all the sides. The forecourt on the front, measuring 90m × 60m, was cut wider than on the sides and it is on the two sides of this that the two monolithic free-standing pillars are found carved. The much narrower, transversely oblong mass in front afforded the material for the carving out of a front *gopura* entrance, with the two wings of *prakara* walls on either side. The *gopura* is double-storeyed with a *sala sikhara* on top and a passage cut through its lower part to provide access to the forecourt in front and the circumambulatory passage round the base of the main *vimana* complex. The upper storey is connected with the floor of the Nandi-*mandapa*. This is likewise conceived as a two-storeyed structure with the lower storey solid and non-functional and serving only as a raised platform, despite the external markings of all the architectural features of an *aditala*, and the upper functional, containing Nandi inside. The main part of the temple beyond consists essentially of a *vimana* containing the sanctum with an *antrala*, or *ardha-mandapa*, and a closed *maha-mandapa* axially in front. The whole axial series is raised over a highly ornate plinth with its top platform supported, as it were, over a frieze of boldly carved fronts of elephants, lions and a number of mythological animals. The *maha-mandapa* is cantoned at its two rear corners by *dvitala vimanas* of the *kuta*-type, and has three projected porch-openings on the middle of its south, west and north sides, which are superposed by larger and more raised *salas* to simulate *gopuram*-like entrances. The top of the *mandapa* is more or less flat with a large multi-petalled lotus surrounding the base of the finial cut over its centre. Behind the *maha-mandapa* and the *antarala* stands the principal *vimana*, its moulded square *adhishthana* of lesser sides than those of the platform below, occupying the centre of the *upapitha*, while five detached sub-shrines are cut at intervals over the edge of the platform. The three lesser *vimanas* on the three cardinal sides of the *upa-pitha* are *dvitala sala vimanas*, while the two at the rear corners are *tritala kuta vimanas*. These five together with the two dummy *dvitala kuta vimanas* embracing the hind corners of the *maha-mandapa*, and the Nandi shrine in front, would complete the full complement of the *ashta parivara* or shrines of the eight subsidiary deities round the principal *vimana*, a concept already evolved in the structural temples of the far south. The principal *vimana* is four-storeyed (*chatushtala*). The lowermost *tala* of the superstructure over the *aditala* with sanctum is projected in front over the *antarala* to form a gable-like projection called *sukanasika*, a characteristic of the southern temples of the Chalukyan series as well as of all their northern *prasada* temples. Though the *talas* are square, the *griva* and *sikhara* are octagonal, making the *vimana* conform to the *Dravida* class of the mixed type. The *stupi*, now missing, was not part of the monolith. On the four corners of the topmost *tala* , which is devoid of a *hara*, are placed four bulls, the cognizant *lanchanas*. The structure is replete with sculptures of varied iconography. Behind this on the hill are the remains of an unfinished *sala*-type edifice, monolithic likewise and akin to the Bhima and Ganesa *rathas* of the Pallavas.

The monolithic Nandi-*mandapa* in front of Cave 15 at Ellora with an inscription of Rashtrakuta Dantidurga is perhaps a slightly earlier carved-out monolith in this region.

The smaller and much later Jain monolith version of the Kailasa *vimana*, also of the Rashtrakuta period at Ellora, is popularly called the Chota Kailasa. There is another *chaumukh* standing in the forecourt of Cave 33. It is a *tritala vimana* with square *talas* and with the *aditala* having projected, porch-like entrances on the four cardinal sides. The stele is placed at the centre of the sanctum floor and is visible through the doors from all four sides. The top of the porch projections carry *panjara*-like *nasika* fronts instead of the usual *salas* of the *hara*. There are the usual *karnakutas* at the corners. The second *tala* has few cardinal-ly projected *nasikas* and no *karnakutas*. The top *tala* has no *hara*, but has four lions, the cognizant *lanchanas* at the corners. The *griva* and *sikhara* are octagonal, making the cave *vimana Dravida* of the mixed variety. The monolithic temple complex, called the Chota Kailasa, is not the monolithic *chaumukh vimana*, in the Indra Sabha forecourt. The Chota Kailasa stands farther away and higher up. It is a Jain replica of the Kailasa (Siva temple complex), with a *dvitala vimana* having an octagonal *sikhara*, the *sukanasa*, leading to an upper shrine in the second *tala* over the *aditala*. The *tala prastara* is provided with a *hara* of *kutas* and *salas* and the axial extensions in front of the *vimana* constitute *mukha-* and *maha-mandapas* with a triple entrance, and a *dvara-mandapa* with sculptures at the entrances leading into the entrenched court.

As against these Pallava and Rashtrakuta creations, the contribution by the contemporary Pandyas of the far south to this series is the exquisitely carved Vettuvankovil monolith at Kalugumalai (Tirunelveli district). It can be dated about AD 800, if not slightly earlier. Unlike the Pallava technique of free cutting or carving down of segmented parts of standing rocks or free-standing boulders of hard rocks, the Pandyas, though they always followed the Pallava tradition of rock architecture in hard stones, adopted in the creation of this monolith the trenching technique of the Rashtrakutas as at Ellora. Both the *dvitala vimana* and its *ardha-mandapa* cut out of the entrenched mass on the hill slope are incomplete, but the finished upper parts reveal a high degree of workmanship and art and contain some outstanding sculptures. The *talas* are square on plan and the *griva* and *sikhara* are octagonal. Thus this would be an example in the *Dravida* order of the *misra* type. The four Nandis on the corners of the top *tala* round the base of the *griva* indicate the date and the dedication of the temple to Siva. The dating is further indicated by the sculptures of Dakshinamurti, Vishnu, Brahma and Siva on the south, west, north and east *nasika* fronts, respectively, on the faces of the *griva sikhara*, a feature that became constant from the ninth century onwards.

6

STRUCTURAL STONE TEMPLES:
THE EARLY PHASE

THE PALLAVA-PANDYA SERIES

While with the Chalukyas of Badami, the construction of stone temples started almost simultaneously, if not as a sequel to their cut-in-cave-temples, with the Pallavas of Kanchi, it may be said that the structural vogue started after their cut-out monoliths from the time of Narasimhavarman II Rajasimha (700-728). In the keen competition with their Chalukyan rivals, that had all along motivated the urge for unique achievements in architecture and faced with the comparatively greater difficulty in the quarrying and sizing of such very hard native rocks as granite, gneiss and charnockite—as against the soft standstone exploited with ease and advantage by the Chalukyas—Rajasimha Pallava experimented, as it were, with the different kinds of stones from the rocks of Tondaimandalam. Furthermore, 'rock architecture' implied the creation of temples only in places where there were hills or rocks. Such temples could not be created elsewhere, for instance, in the Pallava capital of Kanchi. His experiments with different kinds of stones could be seen from the blackish hard variety of leptinite used in the Shore temple, the hard reddish gneiss in the Mukundanayanar temple, and the somewhat softer greyish-white granite employed in the Olakkannesvara temple, all in Mahabalipuram, and the hard pinkish gneiss of the Talagirisvara temple at Panamalai. Finding that construction in these hard stones was difficult and time-consuming, and in order to step up the tempo and keep pace with, if not outstrip, his rivals, Rajasimha ultimately resorted to the softstone tradition and had to employ the coarse, friable, local standstones of a not very commendable quality for the temples in his capital city. Even in such standstone constructions the use of hardstone, a tradition inaugurated by his forbears, was not totally abandoned. It was used as slabs and as the bottom and top courses of the basement or *adhishthana*, namely, the *upana* and *pattika* components. The great Kailasanatha temple in Kanchi and others in the same place are of this kind. However much the Pallavas lagged behind the Chalukyas in this respect, their monolithic or cut-out *ratha* interlude did confer definite advantages, for it gave them better ideas of form, proportion and design that helped them in making their structural edifices more elegant and better composed and dimensioned than the Chalukyan structural creations.

The Shore temple at Mahabalipuram is a complex of three shrines with accessory *mandapas*, *prakara* enclosures and *gopura* entrances. Of the three, the larger *vimana* facing the sea on the east, called Kshatriyasimhesvara, and the smaller *vimana* at its rear facing the village on the west called Rajasimhesvara, are both dedicated to Siva and have wedged in between them a rectangular *mandapa*-shrine without a superstructure—called Narapatisimha Pallava Vishnu-*griha*. This is built over a previously existing recumbent Vishnu carved on a low rocky outcrop. These names inscribed on the structure are all titles of Rajasimha, the builder of the complex. The axial *mandapa* and *gopuras* are built in front of the smaller *vimana*, and the whole is enclosed by a common *prakara* wall. The larger eastern *vimana* has an additional *prakara* of its own, closely investing it on the east, south and north, and leaving the west open. The smaller *vimana* is threestoreyed, all square on plan, but with octagonal *griva* and *sikhara* and *stupi* on top. While the *aditala* is devoid of the *hara* elements on top, it has, like the top *tala*, four seated *bhutas* placed at the corners blowing conches. The *hara* elements are found over the second *tala* on all the four sides, and again over the *ardha-mandapa* in front of the *aditala*. The *bhuta* forms take the place of Nandis or bulls to be invariably found on the top *tala* of the later Siva temples. The *talas* are proportionately tall, the top *tala* rising high and clear over the *hara* elements of the *tala* below, the *stupi* over the octagonal *griva* and *sikhara* being made of polished black basalt. The pilasters on the walls have rearing lion bases, as is characteristic of the Rajasimha temples. The four-storeyed eastern *vimana* is also of square plan up to the *griva* which with the *sikhara* and basalt *stupi* above is octagonal. The *hara* of *kutas* and *salas* are restricted to the tops of the second and third *talas,* as also to the top of the *ardha-mandapa* in front of the *aditala,* which carries instead figures of squatting lions at the four corners. The top *tala* has four squatting *bhutas* blowing conches, symbolizing a Siva temple, as in the case of the smaller *vimana.* The very closely set *prakara* that is special to this *vimana* is of a lesser height than the *aditala,* and carries *karnakutas* at the corners and *salas* over the lengths of the sides. The gap at the rear on the west is partially filled by the *hara* elements on top of the Vishnu *mandapa* at the same level. The central *sala* over the seaward entrance on the eastern length of this *prakara* is made larger than the rest in order to simulate a *dvarasala* or lesser *gopura* scheme. The proportionately tall storeys and the elimination of the *hara* elements over the lowest and topmost *talas* lend a grace and charm to this attenuated structure, while the close-set *prakara* of a lesser height surrounding the *aditala,* with *hara* elements over its coping, gives externally the appearance of an additional *tala.* It apparently enlarges its basal area in apt proportion to the total height. The usual Somaskanda relief panels are found on the rear walls of both the *vimana* sanctums in addition to a sixteen-sided, fluted, polished, basalt *linga,* planted without the usual pedestal on the centre of the floor of the *garbha-griha.* Though the sculptures on the walls of this temple complex are much eroded by the moist and saline winds from the sea, the architectural proportions and make-up, and the natural setting on the sea make the edifice one of the finest monuments in India. Besides the usual rearing lion-based pilasters, the larger *vimana* shows on its own walls and those of its *prakara,* other types which have the elephant, ram, *naga, nagadeva,* and *bhuta* forms for their bases.

The Olakkannesvara structure on top of the light-house hill, devoid of its original superstructural *talas* and with the outer shell of its *aditala* and *ardha-mandapa* alone extant (owing to its earlier conversion and use as a light-house before the present one was constructed in 1900) retains the sculptures, niches and pilasters of the outer walls. Its most interesting feature is the occurrence of the Dakshinamurti icon in the central niche on the southern side, heralding this usual feature of the southern *vimanas* which followed. An important feature that enables one to assign the Olakkannesvara temple to Rajasimha Pallava is the presence of rearing *vyala*-based pilasters cantoning the outer corners of the shrine and *ardha-mandapa*.

The Talagirisvara temple on the Panamalai rock (South Arcot district) of the same pinkish-red hard granite has an interesting plan. It is essentially square on its base and *talas*, but its east-facing *aditala* has smaller oblong shrines with cells attached to the middle of its south, west and northern sides over corresponding offset extensions of the *adhishthana*. The corresponding oblong attachment on the east, with the passage through it, forms the *antarala* entrance to the main sanctum. The two lateral shrines facing east as also the rear shrine facing west are like the main sanctum, dedicated to Siva. The main sanctum has a Somaskanda relief panel inside a special niche high upon its rear wall and visible above the top of the fluted *linga* stele, planted without a *pitha* on the sanctum floor, unlike the other Rajasimha temples where the *linga* more or less hides the Somaskanda panel, set at the centre of the rear wall. The *vimana* is four-storeyed, and the *sala* superstructures of the two-storeyed oblong side shrines are dexterously made to merge into the *hara* of *karnakuta* and other elements of the *aditala*. The *hara* is found again on the upper storeys except the topmost. The *griva* and *sikhara* which are modern restorations in brick and mortar are, as per the original plan, octagonal. The corners of the walls of the *aditala* and of the attached shrines are cantoned by bold rearing *vyala* pilasters characteristic of Rajasimha temples. The top *tala* carries *bhuta* forms at the corners. Otherwise the walls lack sculpture as in the Mukundanayanar temple, evidently because of the hard material of construction. There are only the *dvarapalas* and the Brahma and Vishnu sculptures on the inner walls of the *antarala* that maintain the original *trimurti* concept, but with Brahma and Vishnu relegated to lesser positions. The northern outer shrine contains remnants of a Pallava mural painting depicting a dancing Siva with Parvati.

The Mukundanayanar temple in Mahabalipuram, also built of a reddish granite, is a more plain and severe structure, with a *dvitala vimana*, square below but with octagonal *griva sikhara*, and is hence *Dravida*. It consists of the *vimana* and *mandapa* in front. The upper parts of the *sikhara* and the *stupi* are lost. The walls are plain, the pilasters simple, crudely shaped and devoid of *vyala* bases. It contains a Somaskanda relief as the main deity on the back wall of the sanctum.

The Kailasanatha complex at Kanchi is a joint venture of Rajasimha and his son Mahendra III. The main *vimana*, Rajasimhesvara (now called Kailasanatha) facing east is four-storeyed, and is essentially a square structure up to the *griva*, which and the *sikhara* above are octagonal. The *aditala* is double-walled and its moulded base is prominently offset on all the four sides and four corners—for they carry over them smaller shrines with cella in them, abutting on and incorporated with the outer wall of the main *aditala*. This is an elaboration of the feature found in the Panamalai temple. While the *adhishthana* offsets at the four corners are square and carry smaller two-storeyed *vimanas* of square plan with four-sided *kuta sikharas*, those on the four sides are oblong and carry smaller *dvitala vimanas* of the oblong plan, with *sala sikharas* on the south, west and north. The corresponding one on the east is also oblong with the *sala* superstructure having a passage through in place of a cella and functioning as the *antarala* passage to the main sanctum. The *kuta* and *sala sikharas* of the abutting shrines are cleverly incorporated into the *hara* scheme over the *prastara* of the outer wall of the *aditala* as in Panamalai. The cells of these abutting *vimanas* in their ground storeys enshrine forms of Siva. The abutting *vimanas* on the south-east, south, north and north-east face east like the main sanctum, while those on the south-west, west and north-west face west. The main sanctum has a large fluted, sixteen-faceted, polished, basalt *linga* with an immense circular *linga-pitha* occupying almost the entire floor of the sanctum. On the rear wall, in a special niche, is carved the usual Somaskanda panel, with Siva and Uma seated with little Skanda on Uma's lap and Brahma and Vishnu standing behind on either side. The inner wall of the *garbha-griha* is plain and square, while the outer wall, visible in parts between the abutting *vimanas*, is profusely sculptured with reliefs of gods and goddesses, as also are the walls of the abutting structures. In between the two walls internally is a narrow, covered, circumambulatory passage. The superstructural *talas* are built over a bridge of slabs spanning the tops of the two massive walls of the *aditala*. The double-walling and the additional buttressing by smaller *vimanas* on the sides and corners are evidently expedients to support the mass of the superstructure of this *vimana*, which is the largest one of the period, and at the same time to provide a pleasing base to the height ratio and a balanced proportion to the edifice. While the *panjaras* are absent among the *hara* elements over the *aditala prastara* which, in addition to the corner *kuta* and the lateral *sala sikharas* of the abutting shrines, carries *salas* over the intervening parts of the *aditala* outer wall; the *hara* of the second *tala* has the full complement of *kutas, salas,* and *panjaras*. The third storey has again a *hara* of *kutas* and *salas* above, and the fourth carries only four Nandis on the four corners at its top. The pilasters cantoning the *aditala* wall and those of the abutting shrines have rearing *vyala* bases, peculiar to the Rajasimha temples. There is a detached multi-pillared oblong *mandapa* in front, longer on its north-south axis and with its cantoning pilasters *vyala*-based while the rest are of the plainer type with basal and apical square sections and intervening octagonal belts. The whole is surrounded by a *prakara* with a gap on the middle of its east side and enclosing an open court all around. The large eastern opening is occupied by a fair-sized oblong *dvitala sala*-type *vimana*, with its *ardha-mandapa*, the *vimana* itself appearing like a *gopura* when viewed from a distance. Both its *talas* are devoid of the *hara*. This *vimana*, called Mahendravarmesvara after Rajasimha's son, contains in its sanctum the usual fluted *linga* and Somaskanda panels, besides Brahma and Vishnu sculptures on the inner wall of the *ardha-mandapa*, as also other sculptures on its outer wall and in the *devakoshthas*. The cantoning pilasters are rearing *vyala* based. The *prakara* has another entrance on the west at the middle, which is a real *gopura* entrance with a *sala* superstructure; it is smaller in magnitude. All round the inner face of the *prakara* is built an array of fifty-eight small *dvitala vimanas*, all except two being square and of the *kuta* type. They are all dedicated to Siva except the two which are oblong and come opposite the north and south of the main Rajasimhesvara sanctum and contain groups of Vishnu and Brahma sculptures facing south and north, respectively. But among the *kuta vimanas* of the *malika* of *parivara* shrines, those along the east face west, those along the west face east, while those on the north and south both face east. The cells of many of these contain traces of old paintings on plain walls or painted stucco over reliefs. The external walls of these *parivara* shrines of the *malika* contain a variety of sculptures, both Saivite and Vaishnavite, of varied iconography, thus making this temple complex a veritable museum of iconography and plastic art. The sculptures include the *dikpalas* and Ganesa, who makes his first appearance in Pallava temples, as also the Saptamatrika group, Chandesa and other *parivara* deities. The Mahendravarmesvara has a smaller enclosure with a small *gopura* or *dvarasala* in front and two lateral entrances in addition near the two front corners. Inside there are two lateral oblong shrines in the centre on the north and south. In front of the whole complex stands a row of eight small *dvitala* square *kuta vimanas* with octagonal *griva* and *sikhara*, all of them memorial shrines, and, like the Mahendravarmesvara and the *parivara* shrines of the inner *malika*, devoid of the *hara* elements over their *talas*. All of them contain Somaskanda panels on their hind walls and varied sculpture on their external walls.

The remnants of fresco paintings found inside the various cloister shrines around the Rajasimhesvara of the Kailasanatha complex in Kanchipuram cannot, all of them, be coeval with the date of the main shrine and Pallava. While some are undoubtedly Pallava, painted over the plaster ground laid over the coarse sandstone surface, which expedient was found necessary (as at Ajanta) to smoothen and protect the stone surface even at the outset, there are undeniable evidences of the renewal of the plaster and the paintings over them in subsequent periods. For example, in one of the cellas on the north-east corner of the *malika*, the extant plaster was found by the present writer to overlie an inscription on the stone below of Rajasimha himself. This alone would denote that the plastering was at best an afterthought in the times of the founder himself or immediately thereafter. For, an inscription would not be incised on a surface if it was to be covered over by plaster. Likewise the present writer again found in another cell, on the southern row, the painted plaster revealing beyond its broken edges, parts of a later Chola inscription of Kulottunga I (*Accn.* AD 1070) indicating that the stone face was bare at that time and that the plaster was laid after that time. Thus the painting over it could only be after the above date. From other evidences it is known that the temple, which was flourishing in Pallava and early Chola times, fell into disuse in the times of the later Cholas (after Kulottunga I) till the times of the rise of the Vijayanagar dynasty. Prince Kampana is known from inscriptions to have repaired the damages wrought by the Muslim incursions and restored worship in the temple.

This accounts for fragmentary paintings of the Vijayanagar period too. The temple saw bad times again subsequently till it became a protected monument and came to be attended to. Thus the Panamalai temple painted fragment, mentioned earlier, would alone be the earliest Pallava painting extant as found so far.

The Vaikunthaperumal temple in Kanchi built by Nandivarman Pallavamalla (AD 731-796) and dedicated to Vishnu is another Pallava structure of the larger variety facing west and built in sandstone with an admixture of granite in the top and bottom courses of its *adhishthana*. It has a square four-storeyed main *vimana* with all the *talas* except the topmost, containing the superposed *garbha-griha*, to enshrine the three forms of Vishnu, standing (*sthanaka*), sitting (*asana*), and reclining (*sayana*). It is thus a forerunner of many such Vishnu temples that came later even till recent times, e.g. the Sundaravaradaperumal temple at Uttiramerur, the Chitrakuta at Madurai, and the Vishnu temple at Mannarkovil, to mention only a few. The triple storey has been achieved by a system of three concentric walls forming three concentric squares, one inside the other with ambulatory passages in between in the *sandhara* mode. They are set on top of a boldly moulded *adhishthana*, the innermost wall rising to the height of the three storeys, enclosing the three tiers of cells, the intermediate wall rising to the terrace level of the second storey, and the outermost stopping short of the terrace level of the first storey. The *aditala* has thus its sanctum surrounded by two covered circumambulatory passages, the outer one functioning as such while the inner one provides access to the second *tala*. There is a flight of steps on the north and south, for ascent and descent, providing access to and exit from the second *tala*, terminating in an opening on the centre of the west outer wall. The open outer ambulatory of the second *tala* is surrounded by the parapet on top of the outermost wall formed by a *hara* of *kutas*, *salas* and *panjaras*; the inner covered ambulatory lies at the heads of the two flight of steps from below. This *hara* is extended over the top of the pillared *ardha-mandapa* in front of the *aditala*. The intermediate wall extending up to the top of the second *tala* and enclosing the closed ambulatory carries on top a similar *hara* forming the parapet edging for the open circumambulatory passage round the third-tier cella. The innermost wall reaching to the top of the third-tier cella has, likewise, a *hara* of *kutas* and *salas*. The *kutas*, *salas* and *panjaras* of each tier crown the correspondingly relieved bays and recesses of the walls. The fourth *tala*, which is a smaller square, is closed on all sides and carries the octagonal *griva* and *sikhara* with a metal *stupi* on top, and four lions originally (now replaced by *garuda* figures in stucco) at its four corners. The central bays of the *aditala* outer wall have small door-openings, while the lateral ones have *devakoshthas* with figure sculpture, the intermediate recesses having perforated windows. The bays and recesses of the upper *tala* outer walls have similar sculpture, all Vaishnavite. The lowermost storey and the *ardha-mandapa* in front are surrounded by an open narrow circuit at the level of the base of the *adhishthana*. The whole is again surrounded by a pillared cloister running all round on a raised platform with *vyala*-based pillars on the edge facing the central edifice and a wall on the outer edge that carries on its top a string of *kutas* and *salas*, at a level slightly lower than that of the *aditala*. This arrangement when viewed from outside would simulate a *pancha-tala* appearance, as in the case of the Shore temple described earlier. In addition to the numerous divine sculptures on the *vimana* and *ardha-mandapa* and contemporary inscriptions, the most interesting part of this temple would be a series of panelled sculptures narrating the history of the Pallavas from their legendary ancestors down to the time of Nandivarman II Pallavamalla, the builder of the temple—a unique feature rarely met with elsewhere.

The other temples of this period to be found in Kanchi, though smaller in proportions, are interesting for their architecture and iconography. They are the Muktesvara, Matangesvara, Airavatesvara, Valisvara, Iravatanesvara and Piravatanesvara temples, built mainly of sandstone with granite slabs forming the base and top of the *adhishthana*, and the *upa-pitha* platform below it in cases where it is added to raise the stature of the edifice. All of them are composite varieties of the square *vimana* with varying numbers of *talas*, the upper storeys non-functional and closely invested by the *hara* over the *prastara* of the storey below, and with different plans in the *griva sikhara* part. The Iravatanesvara and Tripurantakesvara are *dvitala*, square throughout, including the *griva* and *sikhara*, and hence are *Nagara*. The Matangesvara and Muktesvara temples which are *tritala* have likewise square *talas*, but carry circular *griva* and *sikhara* conforming to the *Vesara*. The Piravatanesvara and Valisvara are two- and three-storeyed respectively, their *talas* square, but the *griva* and *sikhara* octagonal, making them *Dravida*. The superstructure of the Airavatesvara is lost. The Kailasanatha at Tiruppattur (Tiruchirapalli district) is a larger *vimana* in sandstone and is much like the Kailasanatha of Kanchi. It is of the late eighth century and is an example of the provincial variety of the Pallava *vimana*.

But soon after the middle of the long reign of Nandivarman II Pallava, in the later part of the eighth century, temples came to be built entirely of granite blocks, cut, moulded, carved and sculptured, as seen in some of the smaller temples and in the granite *adhishthanas* of the large brick temples of Vaikunthaperumal and Sundaravaradaperumal at Uttiramerur (Chingelput district) of the time of his successor, Dantivarman. In the former, the niches were meant to contain stucco figures and in the latter, slab reliefs. The extant three-storeyed brick structure of Sundaravaradaperumal over its stone *adhishthana* is unique again in having all the three storeys functional with the cellas dedicated to the standing, seated and reclining forms of Vishnu, while the abutting smaller shrines on the three sides of its two lower *talas* south, west and north, contain the six other principal forms of Vishnu—Satya, Achyuta, Anirudha, Naranarayana, Narasimha, and Varsha—thus incorporating the nine forms or *navamurtis* in accordance with the *Vaikhanasa Agama*. These two temples and the large and fine renovated brick temple at Tiruvadigai (South Arcot district) on a stone *adhishthana* corroborate the fact that brick and timber continued to remain in use in spite of the advent of stone, and skills in their use in large constructions were fostered and maintained.

The Virattanesvara temple at Tiruttani (Chingleput district) affords a very good example of a single-storeyed *vimana* square in its *adhishthana* and *aditala* that carries an apsidal *griva sikhara* superstructure. It was built of hard black stone in the ninth century in the time of Pallava Aparajitavarman, one of the last rulers of the dynasty. It contains some good bas-reliefs in its wall niches which exemplify the definite polarisation of the deities in the *vimana* and *ardha-mandapa devakoshthas*, namely, Ganesa and Durga respectively, in the southern and northern outer wall niches of the *ardha-mandapa* and Dakshinamurti, Vishnu and Brahma respectively, in the south, west and north outer wall niches of the *aditala* wall. The introduction of a projected gargoyle-like water-outlet, the *pranala*, from the northern side of the *garbha-griha* floor to drain off the *abhisheka* water, till now not noticed in earlier temples, is another noteworthy feature. The *pranala* becomes an invariable component of all the temples built later.

The credit of constructing fine *vimanas* of hardstone, though small, and perfecting the same would, however, go to the contemporary Pandyas of the south who, following their rock-cut temples and the single carved-out monolithic *vimana*—the Vettuvankovil at Kalugumalai (AD 800), built a series of small *karralis*, or all-stone temples, in the southern districts. The contemporary Western Gangas of the Talkad in the south Mysore area, and the Muttaraiyar, the Irukkuvel and other chiefs on either bank of the Kaveri, is the dividing border line between the Pallava and Pandya empires, followed by the early Cholas (who till then in hibernation had risen at the close of the ninth century to imperial power with their capital at Thanjavur, and soon spread over the Pallava and Pandya territories) have likewise left a number of fine temples in granite dating before AD 1000.

The series of small and elegant all-stone temples at Kaliyapatti, Tiruppur, Visalur and Panangudi (Pudukkottai district) have square *ekatala vimanas* with simple moulded *adhishthanas*, less than 2 metre square at the base, carrying on top over the cella a square *griva* and *sikhara*. In addition to the *vimana koshtha devatas* in the prescribed order as mentioned above, in the context of the Tiruttani Virattanesvara, they have eight smaller sub-shrines, the *ashta parivara*, dedicated to the ancillary deities located on the corners and sides and inside the *prakara* wall that surrounds the nuclear *vimana* and its axial adjuncts. While all the rest of the eight sub-shrines are square on plan like the main *vimana*, the one on the middle of the south side, dedicated to the Saptamatrikas, is rendered oblong with an appropriate *sala sikhara* as exemplified in the typical temple complex of the Sundaresvara at Tirukkattalai (Pudukkottai district). Such oblong or elliptical shrines of the linear pattern are prescribed for and found employed in cases where the deity is reclining, or where more than one deity (as the Saptamatrikas) is installed in a row, or a deity is with consorts (like Sri and Bhu *devis* for Vishnu), and attendants are enshrined in the sanctum. The oblong form with *sala sikhara* became the invariable rule, according to prescription and practice, for all the *devi* shrines. Occasionally also, one or more of the other seven *parivara* shrines deviate in form, as, for example, the apsidal or *gaja-prishtha* (elephant back) sub-shrine for Gajanana or Ganesa found in the Sundaresvara temple at Nangavaram (Tiruchirapalli district). The cult of Chandesa as the *mulabhritya*, or chief seneschal of a Siva temple, which had its emergence even in the time of Rajasimha Pallava as seen in his Kailasanatha at Kanchi, had now become crystallized and one of the *ashta parivara* sub-shrines on the north was assigned to him till about AD 1000. Subsequently in the temples of the imperial Chola period he, like Nandi of earlier times and the other equal associate of Siva, Chandesa came to have a more honoured place by coming into closer proximity with the main *vimana* just to the north of the *pranala* which had by now emerged on the northern side of the main *vimana*. These form the peculiar features of the southern temples, particularly of the temples of Tamil Nadu.

The Balasubrahmanya temple at Kannanur and the Siva temple at Viralur (both in Pudukkottai district) are examples of the kind where the *griva* and *sikhara* are circular in section, mounted over the square body of the *ekatala vimana*. The former carries on the four corners of its *aditala* four elephant figures as symbols for Subrahmanya Kartikeya, instead of the later and usual peacock forms.

The *dvitala* Talinatha temple at Tiruppattur (Ramanathapuram district) and the similar Siva temple in Tiruvalisvaram (Tirunelveli district) are slightly larger examples. The former has four *karnakuta* miniature shrines at the corners of the topmost *tala* in place of the Nandis. The latter is noted for its fine sculptures and cameos in relief on its walls and superstructure, amongst which is to be found the well-known *ananda-tandava* of Siva Nataraja, perhaps the earliest depiction of this characteristically crystallized and sublimated concept of Tamil Nadu and its unique contribution to Indian and world art.

The celebrated icon of Nataraja in the characteristic *ananda-tandava* pose, depicting, esoterically, the *pancha kritya* of Siva of Tamilian *Saiva Siddhanta*, as ably described and interpreted by Coomaraswamy, makes its advent late in the ninth century. The

Saiva saint, Manikkavachakar is the first among the Nayanmars
to refer to this form and aspect of Siva's dance and the small
Tiruvalisvaram panel (*c.* AD 890) is perhaps the first to capture the
imagery in stone. The concept was perhaps first revealed in
copper or bronze, in the casting of which the Tamilian artisan had
achieved skill and excellence, primarily to serve as a processional
deity, that came to be translated into stone subsequently. Such
early stone representations are to be met with again, in miniature
mostly, as the crest figure in a niche *torana* arch in the early Chola
temple in Punjai (Thanjavur district) of the time of Parantaka I
(*Accn.* AD 907), and on a pillar in the temple in Turaiyur
(Tiruchirapalli district) of about AD 940. The other early miniatures are found in the Koranganatha temple, Srinivasanallur in
the same district, and also in a niche *torana* in the Tirumiyachur
temple (Thanjavur district). It occurs as a niche sculpture in stone,
perhaps for the first time, in the *devakoshtha* of the south wall of
the *ardha-mandapa* in the temple at Konerirajapuram (Thanjavur
district) and becomes a usual feature in that position in the other
early Chola temples.

The Vijayalaya Cholisvaram in Narttamalai (Pudukkottai
district), though so called after the founder of the Chola line of
Thanjavur, is an interesting and fine Muttaraiyar example. The
sandhara aditala of this *tritala* structure is square on plan externally
with an almost equal-sized closed *mandapa* in front, while its
inner wall enclosing the sanctum is circular, leaving an intervening passage all round. The second *tala* rising over the inner
circular wall is square, while the third, as also the *griva* and
sikhara above, is circular in section. The *aditala hara*, extended
over the top of the front *mandapa*, also shows a series of dance
sculptures. But for these and the *dvarapalas* at the *mandapa*
entrance, the sculptures on the four faces at the top and the
cylindrical *linga* with circular *pitha* in the sanctum, there are not
many sculptures. The west-facing complex is surrounded by the
ashta parivara and a *prakara* with a small *gopura* entrance on the
east located near the north-east corner at the top of a slopy ascent
on the rock over which the temple is built.

The Muvarkovil at Kodumbalur (Tiruchirapalli district) is of
Irukkuvel origin and has three equal-sized *dvitala vimanas* square
from base to *sikhara* with their *ardha-mandapa* standing in a north-
south row facing west, with a common large and oblong *maha-*

mandapa in front. Two of these are complete and the third is represented by its extant basement only. The whole was surrounded by sixteen sub-shrines and a *prakara*, with the small entrance *gopuram* on the west. This temple is another important landmark in the line of the great south Indian temples. It is built of fine-grained and neatly-dressed granite, and is noted for its exquisite sculptures—particularly Vinadhara, Dakshinamurti, Kalari Siva, and some feminine forms.

Likewise, the early Chola temples of Koranganatha at Srinivasanallur (Tiruchirapalli district), Nagesvaram in Kumbhakonam, Naltunai Isvara at Punjai and Brahmapurisvara in Pullamangai are other early all-stone temples famous for their sculpture of quality and grace including what appear to be portrait sculptures of men and women. Hundreds of such stone temples were being built in Tamil Nadu in the centuries before and after AD 1000, in replacement of earlier brick-and-timber structures, and in places hallowed by the memory of the Saiva and Vaishnava saints—the Nayanmars and the Alvars.

Similar activity, though on a lesser scale, is to be found in the southern Mysore country, where the Western Gangas of Talkad have left a few contemporary hardstone temples. The earliest would be the twin *ekatala vimanas* of a small size forming an adjunct to the later Jain temple on the Chandragiri hill in Sravana Belagola (Hassan district). But the more impressive Jain temple on the same hill would be the Chamundaraya *basti* (c. 982-985), with a three-storeyed east-facing *vimana* and closed *mandapa* and open porch in front. Its two square lower *talas* of the superposed sanctum type, with a double-walled square *sandhara aditala* leaving a passage in between the walls are functional and have *tirthankara* forms enshrined in their sanctums. The third *tala*, also square, is non-functional, and the *griva* and *sikhara* are octagonal. The *hara* of the *aditala* over the top of the outer wall, consisting of *kuta*, *sala* and *panjara* elements, is continued over the top edges of the front *mandapas*. The second storey has thus an open ambulatory round it. The *hara* contains a series of fine sculptures.

But the most interesting monument in Sravana Belagola is the hypaethral temple of the Gommatesvara colossus, 17.5 metres high, carved in the roundout of a standing tor on top of the Indragiri hill. This was the work of Chavundaraya, the minister of Ganga Rachamalla (974-984). Being a free-standing image of fine proportions and polished granite, it is even more interesting than the colossus of Ramses II at Abu Simbel in Egypt. The base of the colossus is surrounded by a *malika* of granite, built by Gangaraya, the minister of Hoysala Vishnuvardhana (1110-1152), and the *mandapa* abutting the lower part of the colossus from behind was built by another minister, Baladeva, in the twelfth century.

The Ganga temple at Kambadahalli near Sravana Belagola, also Jain, is interesting on account of the fact that its three principal *vimanas* of moderate dimensions and built wholly of granite open into the three sides of a common *mandapa*, the fourth side of which on the north affords the common outer entrance— a grouping called *trikuta*. The three square-based *vimanas* have square, octagonal and circular *griva sikharas* respectively, denoting the *Nagara-Dravida-Vesara* types as described in the *Silpa* texts. To this complex have been added two more lateral *vimanas* in front of the common *mandapa* of the *trikuta* nucleus. The whole is surrounded by a *prakara* with a small *gopura* entrance on the north. This complex called Panchakuta *basti* (Jain temple) in Kambadahalli (Hassan district), besides being a unique combination of units illustrating the ternary classification of the southern *vimanas* as *Nagara*, *Dravida* and *Vesara*, is interesting in its other aspects too. Particularly may be mentioned the variety of niche *toranas* framing the *devakoshthas*, that depict the different forms of *toranas* described in the texts and inscriptions, such as the *patra torana*, *chitra torana*, *makara torana*, *vidyadhara torana*, etc. This temple complex in thus exemplifying the various features of the *vimana* form as enumerated and codified in the *Silpa* and *Agama* texts of the period, can be said to be a perfect text-book illustration or specimen to be studied in comparison with the texts.

The granite temples of Nandi (Kolar district), the capital of the Banas, are of Ganga-Nolamba extraction. The small and earlier Yoganandisvara on top of the hill is not architecturally impressive, while the larger twin temples of Bhoganandisvara and Arunachalesvara, both of the square type, at the foot of hill are. This nuclear twin is enlarged with the addition of later axial *mandapas* and peripheral structures into a complex with *prakara* and *gopura* on the east. The Bhoganandisvara, earlier of the two, is evidently a renovation of a pre-existing structure, and is noted for the fineness of its structure and beauty of its sculptures. The Arunachalesvara would appear to be almost a later copy of the Bhoganandisvara. The ruined softstone-built temples at Hemavati (Anantapur district), noted for their fine sculpture, are examples of pure Nolamba architecture and art.

THE CHALUKYA-RASHTRAKUTA SERIES

The structural experiments of the early Chalukyas are found confined to their capital Vatapi (Badami), the adjacent Mahakutesvar, and the twin mercantile cities of Aihole and Pattadkal (all in Bijapur district). In all of them the native soft sandstone of fine grain and quality which was most easily tractable has been used. This alone was responsible for the larger-sized structures using massive blocks in the construction and richness of figure sculpture.

Before considering the well-known and typical *vimana* and *prasada* forms of temples of this series, it would be good to consider briefly the few *mandapa*-type temples that came early in the series and were made after the early cave-temple model. They are the small temples in the Jyotirlinga group—the Ladkhan, the Kontgudi and the Meguti temples of Aihole. The two temples of the Jyotirlinga group are hardly more than mere *mandapas* with closed walls and flat terrace-tops, with an outer Nandi-*mandapa* of a similar size.

The Ladkhan is a ponderous construction, essentially a large *mandapa* standing on a moulded *adhishthana* with four central pillars, surrounded by two concentric rows of successively lesser height, so that the flat roof over the centre is a raised clerestory, with the slab roofs sloping down on all the four sides over the outer rings of the shorter pillars. The inter-spaces between the outermost row of pillars, on the edge of the plinth are closed by slab screen walls, some of them with perforated window pattern, the walls extending on the front on either side with a central door-opening. The central bay at the rear end with a slopy roof is converted into a shrine chamber with a plinth and slab walls. Over the central clerestory has been constructed an upper cell of heavy slabs with flat roof. To the whole is added later, open pillared *mukha-mandapa* transversely oblong, with carved pillars of the *mandapa* type, their bases connected by a seat having a lean back-rest over its rear edge—the *kakshasana* typical of Chalukyan temples and their derivatives. Thus it would appear to be no more than a large assembly hall converted into a temple with a shrine inside at the rear. The large *mandapa* of the Ladkhan temple with its improvised shrine at the rear with an unconventional slopy roof standing on an *adhishthana* of its own was rightly suspected to have been originally the hall of the village moot (Percy Brown). Such assembly halls for the village elders to meet and transact business relating to local, social, administrative, judicial and religious matters were not uncommon, judging from the evidence of many inscriptions. A case in point will be what is nowadays called the Vaikunthaperumal temple in Uttiramerur (Chingleput district), a later Pallava structure, which we have not noticed in our preceding account of temples of the period. What is extant of this *sabha-mandapa* or grand assembly hall of Uttirameru-Chaturvedi *mangalam*, constructed, evidently for the village *sabha* or assembly, is only the magnificent, stone-built plinth, the *upa-pitha* and the *adhishthana*, the columned super-structure that stood over it having been lost. The extant moulded basement is in hard granite stone. The superstructure was per-haps walled on all three sides with lion or *vyala*-based hardstone pillars carrying moulded capitals of softstone (chloritic schist) on the facade over the front *sopana*. An inscription of the twenty-fourth year of Pallava Nandivarman III, on the extant structure itself calls it a *mandapa*, not a temple (*vimana*). The structure is of the time of Dantivarman (AD 796-846). Incidentally it carries the famous inscription of the twelfth and fourteenth years of Parantaka I Chola (AD 919-921), laying down the rules and conditions for eligibility in elections to and the manner of the constitution of the village assembly—perhaps the earliest inscrip-tion known as relating to elections to the village administrative bodies. Thus it was a village moot hall, a *santhagara*, even as the Ladkhan in Aihole was. It originally, like the Ladkhan, had a small shrine at the rear, now replaced by a much later one called Vaikuntha-perumal. This contained the deity before which oaths were taken, deliberations made and decisions arrived at, the deity standing as the divine witness or *sakshi bhuta*. Such *sabha-mandapas* associated with a Vishnu shrine are mentioned in the *Silpa* texts, such as *Maya mata* (9.73). The presence of a shrine for

Vishnu, on the *mandapa* of the Vaikunthaperumal is referred to in an inscription of Pallava Kampavarman. The other *mandapas* of the large mercantile city of Aihole can be deemed to have served a similar purpose.

The Kontgudi likewise, has a shrine at the rear wall of the hall and with the superstructural scheme added later since the roof shrine has the features of a more evolved Chalukyan *vimana* roof.

The Meguti of Jain dedication with an inscription dated AD 634 is better evolved. It is essentially a closed *mandapa* on a raised and moulded plinth with four central pillars and peripheral walls on all sides over the edge of the plinth and enclosing nine bays, one central and eight peripheral. The walled central bay forms the main sanctum and also carries the roof shrine over it. The rear bays on either side, close to the hind wall corners, provide for the two lateral shrines of the groundfloor with the two lateral bays in front on the median axial line having flat roofs like the central cell, thus forming their respective *ardha-mandapas*. The three front bays form a transversely oblong *mukha-mandapa* for all the three shrines. The three *mukha-mandapa* bays in front as also the corresponding three at the rear have slopy roofs. The outer walls are relieved with three recesses, by pilasters, the relieved parts carrying *devakoshtha* niches. Some of the recesses have perforated windows. The inscription of AD 634 may not relate to the stone structure of Meguti as has come down to us, but to an earlier structure, perhaps of brickwork, to which the inscribed stone stele was attached, or, in front of which it stood. For, judging by the components of the *adhishthana* and the wall pilasters and their developed mouldings one can only attribute them, on comparison with what obtains in other cases in Aihole, Pattadkal and Badami, to a date posterior to the first half the seventh century. A parallel case will be that of the extant Mahakutesvar temple, Mahakuta, which, as a wholly stone-built structure, can only be posterior to the date of the free-standing Mahakuta pillar, or one that at best could have gone into the composition of a *mandapa* and not of a *vimana*. The present stone temple, of a later date than the pillar, could have replaced an earlier brick structure that had the inscribed pillar in front of it.

The plan and design of these odd-looking temples do, however, anticipate similar temples of later times on the west coast, where owing to high rainfall slopy roofs were immensely suitable. As such, temples of this type became common there. The shrine located in the central bay had a raised roof and slopy side roofs all round. The central shrine was often of the *chaturmukha* type as at the *chaturmukha* Jain temple at Karkala. For other temples of such derivation, one has only to look at the many examples found in the region between Goa and Mangalore, if not further south, exemplified by the Ketapi Narayana temple at Bhatkal, or the Vaital temple at Keri in Goa.

Coming to the typical *vimana* temples of the Chalukyas of Badami, we find that the earliest essays were confined to the outskirts of the capital Badami and adjoining Mahakutesvar.

The Makutesvara temple, the main temple in the group formed of northern and southern-type temples enclosed by a wall in Mahakutesvar, was in fact existing from the time of Mangalesa—at the close of the sixth century—according to an inscription on a loose pillar (*vijayastambha*) that stood in front of it and is now kept in the Bijapur Museum. The temple has been apparently redone in stone and later renovated, but it still retains much of the earlier characters. The *aditala* of the *vimana* is double-walled with a closed ambulatory in between. The external wall as also the *adhishthana* below are relieved on the centre of each side into bays with *devakoshthas*. The recesses on each side are provided with perforated windows set inside a frame of lateral pilasters and a top cornice or *kapota* of a *prastara* carrying miniature shrine elements as found in the *hara* of either the southern *vimana* type or they are of the northern *prasada* type, a rather advanced feature as again found in the *devakoshthas* of the Durga temple at Aihole. The square *aditala* outer wall carries on top over its *prastara* four *karnakutas* at the corners and four *salas* in between over the central bays of the wall. The *adhishthana* below is extended forward and widened to form the base of the wider square *mandapa* in front. The central bays of its walls have *devakoshthas* for sculptures of Siva, as on the *vimana* wall, and the recesses have perforated windows. The second *tala* rising as an upward extension of the inner *aditala* wall is high and carries a similar *hara* of four *karnakutas* and four *salas*, while the octagonal *griva* and *sikhara* above have four large prominent *kuta* appliques on the diagonal faces and concealing much of them, while the intervening cardinal faces have *nasika* fronts.

Standing at the south end of the Mahakutesvara enclosure and also facing east is the Mallikarjuna temple with a *sandhara vimana, dvitala,* of the same type as the Makutesvara, except for some minor variations of architectural detail and sculptural content. The *griva* and *sikhara* of this otherwise square *vimana* are octagonal. Both these temples show some advanced features such as the elaborately carved over-door of the shrine entrance in addition to the niche decoration already noticed, and in having a water-chute, or channel, on the floor of the shrine with an outlet opening on the northern side.

The Malegitti Sivalaya standing on an outer crag among the hills of Badami is the simplest structure consisting of a ponderously built single-walled *nirandhara vimana* composed of large blocks of sandstone, with a closed *mandapa* almost of the same width in front of it, preceded by an open four-pillared porch of a lesser width, all standing over a common moulded *adhishthana*. The *hara* of four *karnakutas* and four *salas* of the *aditala* of the *vimana* is extended over the *mandapa* in front, the two front *vimana karnakutas* being also the rear *karnakutas* of the *mandapa*. The second *tala* of the *vimana* has a similar *hara* of four *kutas* and four *salas*. Four more large *karnakutas* closely adhere to the *griva sikhara* and conceal the corner faces of the octagonal *griva*, partially over-topping the squat dome of the octagonal *sikhara* and thereby lending a peculiar appearance to this *vimana*. The cardinal faces of the *griva* have four *nasikas* of equal size. The three bays on the *vimana* wall on each of its faces correspond, respectively, to the two extreme *karnakutas* and central *sala*, with plain rectangular niches for sculptures of deities. Likewise, the two lateral walls of the *mandapa* are relieved five times, corresponding to the *hara* elements, the central one on each side being a *devakoshtha* which is again found on either wing of the front eastern wall on either side of the shrine entrance. The extreme recesses on the north and south of each lateral face of the *mandapa* wall have perforated windows.

The Lower Sivalaya (so called for want of any other name) in Badami fort, which was perhaps originally dedicated to Vishnu, is differing from it in one important respect, namely, that its *aditala* is double-walled, or *sandhara*. The *hara* elements are present over all the *talas* and the *griva* and *sikhara* are octagonal with applique *kutas*.

The Upper Sivalaya, a little higher up on the hill within the fort at Badami, has a *sandhara vimana* square on plan, with the outer wall of the *vimana aditala* extended forwards over the similarly extended *adhishthana* to enclose a large *mandapa*. The *mandapa* is closed and pillared inside, with a central nave under a flat roof of the same width as the shrine behind. Two lateral aisles form the forward continuation of the circumambulatory passage between the double walls of the *vimana aditala*, with slopy roofs, as in the case of the ambulatory passage also. The external wall of the *aditala* and front *mandapa* are alternately relieved and recessed and the bays are cantoned by pilasters, to correspond with the widely spaced *hara* elements on top of their *prastara*. The recesses have shorter pilasters, topped by the *kudu* arches of the cornice of the *prastara*. The second *tala* is tall, rising as an upward extension of the *aditala* inner wall. It does not carry the *hara* over its top. The third *tala* of a lesser height over it is also devoid of the *hara* elements. The *griva* and *sikhara* are square, like the rest of the *vimana* below, and are not encumbered by applique *kutas*, as in the other cases.

In contrast with this group of earlier *vimana* forms showing different stages of development during the seventh century, we have the full-fledged *vimana* forms in the temples of Sangamesvara, Virupaksha, and Mallikarjuna in Pattadkal, reflecting to a great extent the *vimana* features as crystallized in the contemporary Pallava structural temples and their earlier monolithic *rathas*. The Sangamesvara is the earliest of the three and was built by Chalukya Vijayaditya (AD 697-733) and is nearer the Pallava form than any other, in that it has no *sukanasika* or gable-like projecting appendage from the front of the upper *talas* and *griva sikhara* region of the *vimana* over the top of the *antarala* or *ardha-mandapa* fronting the shrine below. The other two, namely, the Virupaksha built by the queen of Vikramaditya II (AD 733-746), and the Mallikarjuna built by another queen soon after, have the *sukanasika* forming the earliest of the Chalukyan *vimana* series that possess this characteristic architectural member, as does the later Kailasa monolith at Ellora. The Sangamesvara and the Virupaksha are both similar to each other in having a square plan from the base to the apex, and are hence of the *Nagara* order. The Mallikarjuna has a circular *griva* and *sikhara* over-topping the square *talas*, and is hence of the *Vesara* order.

The Sangamesvara *vimana*, which is *tritala*, has a double-walled *sandhara aditala*, with the outer-wall extended forward to form the *ardha-mandapa* over the similarly extended *adhishthana* and widening beyond to form the closed *maha-mandapa* with four rows of five pillars each inside. An open-pillared porch is attached to the middle of the northern side of the *maha-mandapa*. The exterior of this wall relieved and recessed alternately has a series of *devakoshthas* in the bays containing sculptures of deities of varied iconography. The *prastara* over this outer wall of the *vimana* and its forward *mandapa* wall extension carries a *hara* of *karnakutas* and *salas* corresponding to the relieved bays below. At the centre of each side the *hara* is pierced by water-outlets of the terrace. Over them the *hara* part carries incipient *panjaras*, perhaps the first appearance of this third characteristic member in the *vimanas* of the Chalukyas and their derivatives. The second *tala* too, which is an upward projection of the inner wall of the *aditala*, carries a *hara* of four *karnakutas* and four *salas*, while the third *tala* has four *salas* only on the cardinal sides, coming in front of the *nasika* projections of the *griva* and *sikhara* region. The absence of the *karnakutas* in the *hara* of the top *tala* marks the first step towards the elimination of the *hara* itself, and the placement of the *vahanas* and *lanchanas* of the main deity at the corners in its place. This is a significant change that occurred almost at the same time, if not slightly earlier, in the Pallava temples as in the Shore temple and the Kailasanatha of Kanchi. The Sangamesvara establishes another landmark in that it has in its scheme two side shrines in the *ardha-mandapa* at its two ends, on either side of the sanctum entrance dedicated to Durga and Ganapati.

The Virupaksha is the largest structural temple complex of the early Chalukyas consisting of a tall four-storeyed *vimana* with axial *mandapas* and peripheral two-storeyed *parivara* sub-shrines of the *kuta* and *sala* type round the court, the whole enclosed by a *prakara* wall with *gopura* entrances in front and behind on the east and west, which are again the earliest in the Chalukyan series. The square *vimana* has a *sandhara aditala*, the outer wall of which, as also the *adhishthana* below, is thrown out into five bays and four recesses on each side. They are of varying widths corresponding to their corner *karnakutas*, central *salas*, and intervening *panjaras* of the *hara* over the *prastara* of that side. The *mandapa* is multi-pillared with massive sculptured columns and has three openings with projected pillared porches on its three sides—east, north and south. The *salas* of the *hara* on top of the *mandapa prastara* that come over these three entrances, as in the Kailasa of Ellora, are rendered larger in dimensions than the rest of the *hara* elements in order to simulate miniature *gopuradvaras*. The *devakoshtha* niches accommodated between pilasters cantoning the relieved bays have varied sculptures set inside for *kuta*, *panjara* or *torana* frames. The *ardha-mandapa* has shrines inside for Durga and Ganesa. The second *tala* carries four *karnakutas* and three *salas* over its *prastara* on three sides. The third smaller storey of lesser height likewise has four *karnakutas* and three *salas*, the front of both *talas* projected over the *antarala* as the tiered *sukanasika* which in design is of the form of a multi-storeyed apsidal shrine with an appropriate front. The fourth storey, still smaller, carries only four *karnakutas* in its *hara* from which the four *salas* have been eliminated, as in the Pandya Talinatha temple in Tirupattur, exposing to full view the four *nasikas* of the *griva sikhara* region. The *prakara* wall has over its coping a series of *kutas* and *salas*, as over the *prakara* of the larger *vimana* of the Pallava Shore temple.

The Mallikarjuna built close to the Virupaksha is a smaller temple with a four-storeyed *vimana* square in all its *talas*. The *griva* and *sikhara* above are circular. It has also a prominent *sukanasika* projected forward from its upper *talas*. The topmost *tala* has no *hara* at all, marking the stage of the total elimination of this element, and heralding the advent of the characteristic *vahanas*, or symbols appropriate to the dedication of the main sanctum.

The Durga temple at Aihole is essentially of the southern variety of the apsidal or *gajaprishtha* form with an odd, clumsily-fitted northern-type square *sikhara* which would be aberrant if of original design or incongruous and inapt if a later addition. The shrine and its axial *mandapas* stand raised with their *adhishthana* built over a sub-base, a feature not common in the earlier temples considered above, but usual in later temples of both Chalukyan and Pallava-Pandya derivation. The moulded *upa-pitha* is apsidal in plan and carries a peripheral row of heavy *mandapa*-type pillars on its edge that surround the moulded *adhishthana* and the outer wall of the apsidal *sandhara aditala* of the *vimana* proper and its forward projection, as the closed *antarala mandapa* of equal width,

Stupa slab, Amaravati

Dharmaraja *ratha*, Mahabalipuram

Kailasa *vimana* superstructure, Ellora

Shore temple, Mahabalipuram

Vaikunthaperumal temple, Kanchipuram

Valisvara temple, Tiruvalisvaram

Vijayalaya Cholisvaram, Narttamalai

Chamundaraya *basti*, Sravana Belagola

Panchakuta *basti*, Kambadahalli

Bhoga Nandisvara temple, Nandi

Malegitti Sivalaya, Badami

Mallikarjuna temple, Pattadakal

Brihadisvara *vimana*, Thanjavur

Airavatesvara *vimana*, Darasuram

Gopurams of the Nataraja temple, Chidambaram

Kasi Visvesvara temple, Lakkundi

Gopuram of Arunachala temple, Tiruvannamalai

Mandapa of Vithala temple, Hampi

Kalyana *mandapa* of Jalakanthesvara temple, Vellore

Mandapa of Ranganath temple, Srirangam

Main *gropuram* of Vatapatrasayi temple, Srivilliputur

Subrahmanya temple, Thanjavur

Aghoresvara temple, Ikkeri

Visva Brahma temple, Alampur

Vadakkunnathan temple, Trichur

and also the frontal *agra-mandapa* on the forward extension of the same *adhishthana* at which region it narrows. Thus, the platform on top of the *upa-pitha* forms a covered outer ambulatory with a slopy roof, spanning the gap between the outer wall of the *vimana* and axial *mandapas* on one side and the pillars set on the edge on the other. The *upa-pitha* terminates in front as a still narrower landing platform with lateral flights of steps and a frontal banister. These peripheral pillars of the front *mandapa* section and those at the front or eastern end on either side of the inner edge of the landing have large statutory carved on them, while the rest are devoid of such embellishment. They are all interconnected by *kakshasanas* or seats with lean-back rests, as is common in Chalukyan structures. The *adhishthana*, as also the outer wall over it, are thrown out at intervals into eleven bays, three on each linear side walls, three more round the rear apse end, and two in front, where the wall turns in to embrace the front doorway of the *antarala-mandapa* flanking the entrance. These eleven bays carry *devakoshthas*, the niches of which are framed by shrine fronts of all patterns of southern-style *vimanas* and northern-style *prasadas*—such as the *kuta, sala* or *koshtha, panjara, udgama* (coalesced *kudu-like arches*), and *torana*, and containing bold sculptures of gods. This much-developed feature is coupled with the presence of a prominently projecting *pranala* or gargoyle-like water-spout over the *adhishthana* level on the northern side at the apse end of the outer wall. This is in continuation of the water-channel leading from the floor of the cella and passing through the base of the inner wall and the *sandhara* ambulatory. All this indicates a later date for this temple than is usually assumed, not to speak of other advanced features like the diverse corbel forms, the style of sculpture, the presence of the *upa-pitha*, etc. These and the presence of an inscription of Chalukya Vikramaditya II (AD 733-746) on the ruined outer *gopura* at the south-eastern part of the *prakara* indicate a date early in the first quarter of the eighth century. The inner wall of a typical short apse or *chapa* form encloses the cella. In forward alignment with its two linear side walls are two rows of four pillars each inside the *antarala-mandapa* dividing the space into a central nave with a raised flat clerestory roof and two lateral aisles with lower slopy slab roofs projected over the still lower slopy roof of the outer circuit. The *chapa* ends of the inner wall of the *aditala* are turned in to form the narrow front entrance of the *antarala-mandapa*. The *agra-mandapa* has four pillars set on the edge of the forward end of the *adhishthana* with a raised clerestory roof in continuation of the one at its rear. The aisles of the *antarala* are continuous with the inner circumambulatory between the two walls round the sanctum. The sanctum is empty for a circular *pitha*. Its original dedication is uncertain. The name Durga for the temple is misleading since it was evidently not dedicated to that goddess. This may be due to the fact that till the earlier part of the last century, the temple formed part of a fortification (*durga* or *durgam*) with a rubble defence work on top of the temple, probably of the Marathas. If the incongruous superstructure of the northern *prasada*-type is not original, the sanctum might have been either flat-roofed or might have had an apsidal roof of the pattern of Ter and Chejerla apsidal temples.

Coming to the Rashtrakuta phase of this early period commencing with the last quarter of the eighth century, we have, as a good example, the ruined Jain *vimana* temple standing on the outskirts of Pattadkal. It is essentially a three-storeyed *sandhara vimana*, square on plan from its base to *sikhara*, the two lower storeys being functional. The *kudu* motifs on the cornice or *kapota* tier of the *adhishthana* have lost their original *nasika* shape and have become flat triangular reliefs, precursors of the dentil reliefs of the later Chalukyan and Hoysala temples. The pillar capitals too have lost their original shape and robustness and are transformed into mere conventional shapes found in the later Chalukyan temples. The *navaranga-mandapa* in front of the *aditala* and connected with it by a short *antarala* shows on its walls seven bays with six intervening recesses, adorned with *nasika* forms containing the seated Jinas and other figures. The *prastara* carries a *hara* of *kutas*, *salas* and *panjaras*. The second *tala* has a sanctum enclosed by the upward extension of the inner wall of the *aditala*. Its *antarala* front is masked by the basal part of the *sukanasika*, while the *prastara* on the other three sides carries four *karnakutas* and three *salas*, there being no scope for a *sala* on the front side because of the *sukanasika*. The third storey of some lesser width is relieved on its sides except on the front or *sukanasika* side. The bays contain *udgama* motifs as in northern-style temples. The square *sikhara* following the same scheme of offsetting simulates a twelve-ribbed member heralding similar modifications in 'the later Chalukyan temples. In front of the *navaranga* is the open multi-pillared *mukha-mandapa*, the peripheral row having interposed *kakshasanas*. Except the two innermost pillars of peripheral series abutting on the *navaranga* front, all others, as well as the four central ones, though in sandstone, are partially lathe-turned heralding the more completely lathe-turned pillars of schist or soapstone of the later Chalukyas and their successors.

The Eastern Chalukyas of Vengi, a collateral branch of the early Chalukyas of Badami, however, have left a series of structural temples in sandstone which are more akin in their style to the Pallava style of Tondaimandalam to their south. Among these, the temples at Biccavolu (east Godavari district) are characteristic. The Biccavolu series falls into two groups. The earlier one comprises the temples called Kansaragudi, Nakkalagudi and a third having no local name, all built, perhaps in the time of Gunaga Vijayaditya (848-891) and his successors. They are all square on plan, three-storeyed *tritala Nagara vimanas* with four *karanakutas* and four *salas* intervening on the *aditala* and second *tala prastaras*, without *panjaras* and devoid of the *sukanasika*. These features indicate affinity and proximity to the Pallava type, though their distinct regional and parental Chalukyan traits would be evident from the other features and the general stature of the *vimana* form. The *makara toranas* show great emphasis in their detail, particularly by the addition of a pair of *makara* heads at the apex of the arch on either side of the finial. The pilasters are four-sided as usual in all early temples, with full capitals of the 'order'. The *kudus* in the flexed cornice, or *kapota*, are horseshoe-shaped as in the Pallava and early Chalukyan examples. The other three temples inside the village—the Golingesvara, the Chandrasekhara, and the Rajarajesvara—would belong to the second and later group (c. 950-1050), and the last perhaps to the time of Rajaraja Narendra (1019-1060). They are also two- or three-storeyed *Nagara vimanas*, square on plan, but with their superstructures entirely or partially restored in later times and heavily plastered over, obscuring many original diagnostic features. These temples have all a typically Chalukyan plinth form, with *nirandhara* or single-walled *aditala* and with a narrower *ardha-mandapa* in front. The niche sculptures are all Saivite. The *sikhara* is square as also the *griva*. In some cases, as in the

Rajarajesvara, the *talas* are devoid of the *hara* over the *prastara*, a feature that became common in the later temples of the Andhra coast. The *sikhara* form of the earlier group shows affinity to the Upper Sivalaya form at Badami.

7

STRUCTURAL STONE TEMPLES: THE MIDDLE PHASE

By about AD 1000, imperial Chola power had reached its zenith, its authority having spread over the entire Tamil region and Kerala, parts of south Mysore and coastal Andhra, and even overseas to Sri Lanka, the Andamans, the Laccadives and the Maldives. The contemporary rival power, the Rashtrakutas in the Deccan, soon gave way to the resurgent Chalukyas of Kalyani, the Western Chalukyas or later Chalukyas, as they are often called. With the experience and knowhow acquired in stone construction, technique and design, and with the forms and norms crystallized into codified *Agama* and *Silpa* manuals, the period that followed witnessed great activity in the construction of temples, particularly the great ones of south India and Sri Lanka. A great number of new temples were built by the Chola emperor, Rajaraja Chola I the Great (985-1014), his elder sister, queens and vassal chiefs, and some more still by the dowager queen, Sembiyan Mahadevi, the queen of the pious Gandaraditya Chola, the grand uncle of Rajaraja I.

THE CHOLA AND THE LATER PANDYA SERIES

The Brihadisvara temple at Thanjavur closely followed by the Brihadisvara at Gangaikondacholapuram (Tiruchirapalli district) mark the acme of the southern *vimana* architecture—in magnitude, quality of design, technique and embellishment. The great temple at Thanjavur, appropriately called the Brihadisvara, or the Rajarajesvara after its builder Rajaraja I, conceived as a whole complex on a grand scale and completed by the founder, constitutes the most ambitious undertaking and achievement of the Tamilian architect. It combines all that is best in temple-building

tradition—architecture, sculpture, painting and allied arts. It is a
large complex with an enormous monolithic Nandi recumbent on
a high pedestal in front of the *vimana* and its coeval axial *mandapa*,
but now sheltered in a *mandapa* of a much later date. It has the
loftiest known or achieved *vimana*, 66m high, standing over a
basal square, one side of which is about 28m in length and which,
in due proportion to the elevation, forms an appropriately broad,
high and amply moulded *upa-pitha* platform, on which the boldly
moulded *adhishthana* of the east-facing pyramidal *vimana* rests.
The same *upa-pitha* and *adhishthana* are extended forward as basal
structures of the axially placed *ardha-, maha-* and *mukha-mandapas*,
connected to the main *vimana* by a north-south transept across the
ardha-mandapa, reached from either side by flights of steps over
the heights of the *upa-pitha* and *adhishthana*. The pillard *maha-* and
mukha-mandapas are closed on their sides, the rows of pillars
inside forming a central nave and lateral aisles which, in the
maha-mandapa part, are raised as a continuous platform on either
side of the central passage formed by the nave. The structure of
pillars and roof over the frontal landing, constituting an open
porch, or *agra-mandapa*, are later replacements over the original
adhishthana and *upa-pitha* with a flight of steps added in front in
addition to the two original ones on the sides. While the transversely designed *mukha-mandapa* as also the connecting transept
rise in four storeys, the *maha-mandapa* was originally three-
storeyed. The top storey was evidently an open terrace, with a
row of Nandis placed on the coping of its walls.

The basal part of the *vimana* enclosing the *garbha-griha* is of
two *talas* and is double-walled in the *sandhara* mode, each of the
walls, outer and inner, of the same thickness and very massive.
The outer wall rising vertically to a height of about 15m is marked
externally into two storeys, lower and upper, by a dividing
prastara line marked horizontally by the bold cornice and the
centrally-placed additional doorways, complete with jambs, lintel and sill on each of the visible sides, south, west and north, the
vimana being an east-facing one. These two walls enclose inner
circumambulatories in two tiers, since the inner wall of the
sanctum too rises vertically to the same height of two storeys, in
order to accommodate the colossal *linga*, and its equally immense
linga-pitha in the sanctum. The outer wall, like the *adhishthana*
below, is externally relieved into five bays on each face, the

central ones on the south, west and north having the large door-openings in two tiers, one over the other, for both storeys of the inner circumambulatory. These along with the two superimposed larger or main doorways on the east make the *vimana* a *chaumukh* or *chaturmukha* structure, described as *sarvatobhadra* in the texts. In front on the east, the massiveness of the walls pierced behind the main doorway provides the *antarala* passage across the *sandhara* circuit, leading to the inner doorway of the sanctum. In front of this *antarala* is laid the north-south transept with flights of steps at either end, north and south, described above.

The outer doorway is flanked by two colossal *dvarapalas* as are the outer entrances too. The central bays of the outer walls, which are the widest with door-openings, have, at the top, over the *prastara* of the second *tala*, the largest central *sala* of the *hara* of that side. The extreme bays forming the respective corners and of middling width have on top the *karnakutas*. The intermediate bays of least width have the *panjaras* at their top, thus constituting the full *hara* of aedicules over the second *tala prastara*. The *hara* over the *aditala* is thus eliminated. The bays on either side of the central one with a door-opening are full-fledged *devakoshthas* containing fine and bold sculptures, inside, of various deities. The *Puranic* legend associated with the iconography of each niche figure is indicated by small cameos in a synoptic manner on the jambs on either side of the main sculpture, an innovation seen for the first time during the early Chola period. The four intervening recesses, or wall spaces, are each filled up by the 'decorative pilaster' motif which is a short pilaster, carrying a shrine motif—*panjara* front—on top, a motif characteristic of the period. The main pilasters containing the corners of the bays and their angles with the walls are square in section with full capitals. The abacus, or *phalaka*, as in earlier Pallava capitals, is large, massive and square, but the corbel or *potika* arms are bevelled with a central triangular tenon on the bevelled face.

The inner wall of the lower storey has on its three sides, in the recesses between immense pilasters and opposite to the outer wall openings, more than life-size sculptures of Siva seated on the south, dancing on the west, and of *devi* seated on the north. This lower ambulatory contains, over the rest of the inner wall and over the pilasters and ceilings and also over the inner face of the outer wall, extensive mural paintings of the Chola period,

overlaid by later palimpsests of the Nayaka period in the seventeenth century. The Chola layer has been exposed wherever
extant by peeling off the damaged Nayaka layer to reveal its
richness. The most important themes occupying almost entire
wings of the inner wall space are the panel representing Siva as
Tripurantaka (setting out for his fight with the Tripura demons),
the panel narrating the story of the Saiva saint Sundaramurti
Nayanar, and the panel representing the Chera king worshipping
at the shrine of Nataraja of Chidambaram, along with his queens
and his retinue. Other paintings of dancers, musicians, birds,
animals, etc. are interesting. After the earlier paintings of an
extensive nature in the Buddhist caves at Ajanta and the smaller
area of paintings in the Jain cave-temple at Sittannavasal, these
are the only other extensive series of quality forming an important landmark in the history of Indian mural painting. The second
tala circumambulatory is equally interesting, for on its inner wall
face at its middle height are blocked out one hundred and eight
square panels running as a belt right round, all except the last
twenty-seven with complete reliefs showing Siva, four-armed,
demonstrating the various *karanas*, or dance poses, as enumerated in Bharata's *Natyashastra*.

By a system of inward corbelling or offsetting of the successive inner courses of the two opposing faces of the two walls, or
kadalika karana—a system commonly adopted in Indian architecture to bridge spaces as an alternative to true arching or vault-
ing—the two walls are made to meet at the top level of the third
storey, from which point rises the rest of the pyramidal superstructure of the eleven further gradually receding *talas* of this
soaring *vimana* in all of sixteen stages from the *upa-pitha*, almost
the traditional maximum. Each *tala* carries over its *prastara* a *hara*
of *kutas*, *salas* and *panjaras*. The topmost *tala* has instead four
Nandis placed at the four corners with the octagonal *griva* and
sikhara rising up from the midst. The topmost stones closing the
ultimate gap alone is estimated from their size to weigh 80 tons
(81.3 metric tonnes). The *stupi*, as originally intended by Rajaraja,
and as stated in his inscription in the temple, is of copper, gilt
with gold and is 3.82m high. The entire interior of the pyramid
from its base to apex is rendered hollow by the gradual inward
offsetting of the successive courses of masonry in the *kadalika*
karana mode. On the front side the storeys up to the level of the

fifth *tala* are slightly extended forward over the *antarala* of the two lowermost vertical *talas*, in the form of what is called a *mukha sala*, or *mukha bhadra*, in order to take in these passages also in the organic scheme of the *vimana*, which is the largest *mukhya vimana* of the *Dravida* order.

From the top of the *adhishthana* at about the middle of the northern side, an immense and carved water-spout is projected which discharges the *abhisheka* water flowing out of the sanctum floor. The water goes along the chutes running through the bases of the two walls and along the floor of the *sandhara* circumambulatory in between. The lengthy *pranala*, or spout, is supported on the head of a *bhuta* squatting over the *upa-pitha* platform, blowing a conch. Opposite to this *pranala* and a little to the east is built the coeval square *vimana* for Chandikesvara, the seneschal of the Siva temple. This position located by Rajaraja in his great temple became the norm for all Siva temples of subsequent periods.

Enclosing the wide open court around the *vimana* and its axial *mandapas*, including the Nandi pavilion, is a two-tiered *prakara* wall of the same period. The tiers are demarcated externally by a horizontal *kapota* running at middle height, while both the tiers are sectioned by carved pilasters at intervals. On the middle of the eastern side the *prakara* has a massive *gopura* built entirely of stone. Ranged inside the *prakara* wall and built against it is a continuous double-storeyed cloister, or *malika*, with a third open terrace on top, interrupted at the four corners and the middle of the three sides by seven square *tritala vimanas* with octagonal *griva sikhara*. These are dedicated to the eight *dikpalas*, or guardians of the quarters: Agni, Yama, Niruti, Varuna, Vayu, Soma and Isana, from the south-east round to the north-east. The shrine for the eighth *dikpala*, Indra, and also another for Surya, merge into the inner face of the vertical base of the *gopura* on the east. For the rest, the cloister is divided by a row of pillars aligned behind the facade columns into a frontal continuous corridor and a rear section stringing a series of thirty-six, two- and three-storeyed shrines, all except those of the *dikpalas* with flat roofs of the *mandapa* type. On top of the *prakara* wall are ranged a row of Nandis. In front of the *gopura* and at some distance away from it is a second outer and larger *gopura*, perhaps going with an outer *prakara* wall originally, but now incorporated into the defensive fort-wall of much later times. In addition to the inner *gopura*, the *prakara* wall is pierced by three additional smaller entrances of the *torana* gate variety, placed opposite the centre of the south, west and north sides of the main *vimana*. These are framed by simple over-doors with *sakhas* and crowned by horizontal lintels.

The Brihadisvara, truly great in all respects, as its devout and victorious royal builder conceived it to be, is thus a repository of every branch of art—architecture, sculpture in stone and copper, iconography, painting, dance and music, jewellery, lapidary, etc. The numerous Sanskrit and Tamil epigraphs inscribed on it are in fine calligraphy. Some of them relate to the dedication of metal images of various deities with details of their forms and appearances, their measurements and weights. Some of these images are extant. Others describe the various ornaments, with details of weights of gold and gems, their variety and quality, the manner of their setting, the weight of lac and the strings used. The measurements of lands endowed are given to the fraction of units. All these would only show how meticulous the emperor was in matters relating to his great temple.

The other structures inside the court of this temple are the south-facing Amman temple, or the *devi* shrine unit of Brihannayaki, the consort of Brihadisvara, located to the north of Nandi, with the *vimana* having *sala sikhara* and axial *mandapas*, the adjoining *sabha-mandapa* for Nataraja also facing south, and the east-facing Ganesa and Subrahmanya-temple units on the south-west and north-west of the court. All these are later additions to this complex, the last one pertaining to the Nayaka period.

This *magnum opus* of the Cholas started in 1003, and still incomplete in a few of its details, was closely followed, within about twenty years, by another magnificent Chola structure, also called the Brihadisvara, built almost on the same plan and design by Rajendra I Chola (1012-1014), the great son and worthy successor of Rajaraja. The venue of this great temple was chosen in the newly found capital of Gangaikondacholapuram (Tiruchirapalli district), so named after the title of the king, signifying his conquests and successful expedition up to the Ganga. This temple complex had only two entrances, a *gopura* (now shattered) on the east and a plain double-storeyed *torana* gate on the north. While a great part of the stone enclosure wall, *gopura*, two-storeyed *malika*, and sub-shrines and *mandapas* were blasted and pulled down in the last century to supply stones for constructing a river dam in the neighbourhood, the main *vimana* and its axial *mandapa,* and two or three lesser *vimana* units in the court have fortunately been spared and are even now almost intact. The *vimana* is of a lesser height and smaller dimensions than its predecessor and model at Thanjavur, but the sculpture on the wall niches, bold and almost cut-out in the round, is perhaps of greater excellence. The square *vimana* with a boldly moulded *adhishthana* over a high *upa-pitha* is likewise *sandhara* in its two vertical lower *talas.* The Brihadisvara *vimana* of Gangaikonda-cholapuram differs from its predecessor and supposed model of the same name in Thanjavur in one important respect. It has only a single entrance on the east on both the functional lower storeys and is not *chaturmukha* or *sarvatobhadra* as the Thanjavur temple is. The tapering superstructure of further *talas* resting on the third *tala,* rendered in a similar *kadalika karana* mode, assumes an embowed outline at the corners in contrast to the severely straight corner lines of the Thanjavur *vimana.* This is an aesthetic achievement, resulting from the clever interposition of octagonal *kutas* in the *hara* elements of the upper *talas* as *karnakutas* at the corners. Externally this *vimana* may be said to excel its predecessor in the matter of quality, fineness and variety of bold sculpture, as also the more aesthetic design of its superstructure. Internally, however, it lacks the other embellishments, namely, the paintings and depiction of dances. The smaller temple units, called the Uttara Kailasa and Dakshina Kailasa on either side of the main *vimana,* also belong to about the same period.

The wholly apsidal and multi-storeyed main *vimana,* built of blackstone of the Tiruvorriyur temple near Madras, is another fine temple, though it is a smaller structure of Rajendra I Chola. The foundation inscription is interesting in that it defines the type of stone used as *krishna-sila* (blackstone), gives an account of the *angas* or parts of the *vimana* by which it was embellished, and also the name of the architect-designer. Following this, a number of wholly apsidal temples or temples with four-sided *aditala* and apsidal superstructure and *griva sikhara* continued to be built in this part of Tamil Nadu—Tondaimandalam in later Chola times and succeeding periods. Such temples are rather rare in the Chola and Pandimandalams further south.

The Rajarajesvara, now called Airavatesvara, at Darasuram,

built by Chola Rajaraja II (1146-1173), and the Kampaharesvara at Tribhuvanam, built by Chola Kulottunga III (1178-1223) (both in Thanjavur district) are the last great temples of the later Cholas with all-stone *vimanas* that were built before the later Pandyas supplanted them by the middle of the thirteenth century. These two are essentially lesser versions of the two Brihadisvara *vimanas*, but incorporate in their design some variations and innovations revealing an amount of Chalukya-Rashtrakuta influence. The Airavatesvara exhibits in its five-*tala vimana* superstructure, a clever variation of the corner elements in the *tala haras* which are square, octagonal and circular *karnakutas* conforming to the *Nagara*, *Dravida* and *Vesara* types; besides, there are also *panjaras* of the apsidal *Vesara* type, turned sideways in one of the lower *tala* corners. The topmost *tala* carries four square *karnakutas*, again flanked by a pair of recumbent Nandis, one on either side. This feature is an innovation made by Chola Rajendra I in his later temples. It persisted for about a century in some temples and disappeared, as before, leaving the place for Nandis alone. But at the same time this temple of Rajaraja II heralds the idea of placing paired Nandis or similar *vahanas* or *lanchanas* appropriate in other temples—which in later times were placed back to back, or coalescent with single neck and head—at the corner, with two independent bodies along the two sides. Another feature found abandoned in the post-Pallava temples and earlier Chola temples, but persisting throughout in the Chalukyan series of temples, and found again in this temple, is the extension of the *hara* of *kutas*, *salas* and *panjaras* over the tops of the axial *mandapas* beyond the transept in front of the *aditala*. The main axial complex of *vimana* and *mandapas* is similar to the plan in the Brihadisvara. Though it is lesser in dimensions, it is more ornate with bold and round sculpture in the niches and cameos of *Puranic* scenes formed by miniature panels. The one forming a belt round the base of the *vimana* walls is noteworthy in that it narrates synoptically the stories of the lives of the sixty-three Saiva Nayanmars according to the work called *Periyapuranam*. The larger loose sculptures set in the wall niches and in the *malika* corridors are in a new medium, namely, a black, polished basalt-like stone, as against the granite of the structure. They are all sculptures of a fine quality and most of them are now removed and exhibited in the Thanjavur Art Gallery. The closed *maha-mandapa* of this east-facing complex has an open porch-like *agra-mandapa* on its south, with ornately carved pillars having panel sculptures. The porch *mandapa* itself is designed to simulate a chariot on wheels drawn by horses, while the flights of steps, fore and aft, have balustrades guarded by elephants.

On the northern side of the *maha-mandapa* is the improved Amman shrine for the *devi*, consort of the presiding deity. The whole is surrounded by a *prakara* with a storeyed *malika* corridor running round inside and a storeyed *gopura* in front. Outside this *gopura* is the ornate but small Nandi-*mandapa*. Beyond is another outer *gopura* that fronted a now non-existent outer *prakara*.

The Deivanayaki Amman temple in a separate enclosure with a front *gopura* on the north of the Airavatesvara complex is also coeval, and the storeyed superstructure of the *vimana* carries a *sala sikhara* appropriate to *devi* temples. The pilasters cantoning the walls of the *aditala* are *vyala*-based, as in the Rajasimha Pallava temples of much earlier times.

The Kampaharesvara is much similar to the Airavatesvara, including its wheeled porch-*mandapa*, an extension of the *hara* elements over the axial *mandapas* in front of the *vimana aditala*, and the Amman or *devi* and Chandikesvara *vimanas* being coeval with each other. This temple too is a veritable museum of sculptures of varied iconography that include some fine dance poses. Of the coeval main *gopuras*, the inner one in front and the rear ones are ruined on top, and the taller outer-front *gopura* has the characteristic squat shape of the period.

The series of temples of this later Chola and later Pandya periods, terminated by the disruption brought about by the brief Muslim invasion and revival under the Vijayanagar empire of the south, often revert to the system of brick-building for the super-structural *talas* over the stone body of the *vimanas* and *gopuras*, the *mandapas* alone being wholly of stone. The temples of this and subsequent periods incorporate in the original plan and compo-sition of the temple complex—the new and significant addition brought into vogue late in the time of Rajendra I Chola, namely, the *Tirukkamakottam*, or Amman shrine as it is called in Saiva temples, or *Tayarasannidhi* in Vaishnava temples, that formed the unique feature of all temples of Tamil Nadu and of Tamilian-built temples elsewhere. For example, there is a Visalakshi temple built by the Tamils for the consort of Lord Visvesvara at Kasi-Varanasi.

These also came to be built in the precincts of, or adjoining to, earlier built temples that originally did not possess them, as, for example, the Thanjavur Brihadisvara. Assigned a definite location in the complex, it is a separate *vimana* with a *sala sikhara* dedicated to *devi* as the divine consort of the presiding deity in the main *vimana*, receiving equal importance in the rituals of worship and in the festivals. Thus, in accordance with the local names for the main deity, the *devi* consort has an appropriate name, e.g. Brihadisvara-Brihannayaki, Sundaresvara-Minakshi, etc.

The *gopuras* of the temple complex, in front and in rear, as also often on the sides of the multiple *prakaras*, become more prominent by their greater size, often overtopping the main *vimana* in height. The *gopuras* added to already existing temples by the later Cholas, the later Pandyas, and the contemporary Pallavaraya chieftains and others are many. The Hoysalas too, when they came to occupy a part of Tamil Nadu in the last days of the later Cholas left some significant *gopuras*, as, for example, the Ballala *gopura* at Tiruvannamalai. The Pallavara *gopuras* of Ko-Perunjinga at Chidambaram, Vridhdhachalam and other places are noted for their sculptures, particularly for the depiction of the hundred and eight dance poses with appropriate verses from the *Natyashastra* inscribed as labels. The decorative pilaster motif, which is essentially a pilaster carrying a shrine motif, often a *nasika* front, on top that adorned the recesses of the walls of *vimana aditalas*, *mandapas* and *gopuras*, came to have a *purna ghata* or *purna kumbha* base, appearing as though the pilaster emerges out of a full pot or pitcher of plenty signified by foliage flowing out of its mouth. These *kumbha panjaras* became a common feature. The corbel shapes also change, and the central tenon of the simple bevelled corbel of the earlier Chola temples assumes more or less the form of a bell-shaped pendentive, which gradually becomes floral and extended, anticipating the incipient *madalai*, or curved stalk of the characteristic *pushpa potika* of the Vijayanagar times and after. The abacus of the pillar and pilaster capitals becomes thinner, smaller, and polygonal in contrast with the large, thick and square forms of the Pallava and earlier Chola times. The octagonal *griva* and *sikhara* of the southern style, which were more common in earlier times become from now on the more general norm of the southern temples, though the square and circular shapes are occasionally, and the apsidal style still more rarely, seen.

Mandapas like the Airavatesvara porch-*mandapa* in the form of a chariot on wheels drawn by horses or elephants or both added to the front of the *mukha-mandapa*, or to one of its sides forming the main entrance, become rather common. These are found in the Sarangapani and Nagesvara temples in Kumbhakonam (Thanjavur district) where in the case of the Nagesvara it fronts the *sabha-mandapa* of Nataraja, which again is another feature added to the temples from the later Chola times. They are also to be found in Tiruvarur, Kudumiyamalai, Vridhdhachalam, Chidambaram and many other places. This provided inspiration to the Eastern Ganga king, Narasimha, for constructing such a *mandapa* in his Simhachalam temple in north coastal Andhra, and more so for his great Sun temple at Konark.

The addition of the *devi* temple brought into more common vogue the *kalyana utsava*, or annual ceremonial marriage festival of the god and goddess, for which special *kalyana dolotsava* (swing festival) *mandapas* with attached *yaga-mandapas* were built. The advent of the special Nataraja shrine as part of the *sabha-mandapas* or *nritta-mandapas* in Siva temples has already been mentioned earlier. The other types are the *utsava-mandapas* for various periodical festivals where the *utsava murtis* were decorated, worshipped and taken out in procession. *Snapana-* or *abhisheka-mandapas* (halls for ceremonial bathing rituals), *vyakarana-mandapas* (halls for exposition and educational purposes), *ranga-* and *natyasalas* for dance and music, and even *atura salas* (hospital *mandapas*) came to be added to the temple complex. All these made the medieval temple of the Tamil land the hub not only of the religious but also of the social, economic and other temporal activities of the community which always centred round the temple.

THE LATER (WESTERN) CHALUKYA-HOYSALA SERIES

The Rashtrakutas, whose two important temples, the Kailasa monolith at Ellora and the Jain temples on the outskirts of Pattadkal, have been considered earlier, were replaced in the Deccan by the resurgent Western Chalukyas of Kalyana who became the most important power between the eleventh and the thirteenth centuries. They continued the Chalukya-Rashtrakuta traditions with a gradual introduction of significant modifications of their own. Their earlier temples such as the Navalinga group and the Kallesvara at Kukkanur near Gadag (Dharwar district), assignable to the latter half of the tenth century, are perhaps the last among the structures that were built of sandstone, and mark the end of the sandstone-trap rock tradition. They adopted different soft stones, such as the chloritic schist, for their temples during the middle of their period.

The fine cluster of nine temples in a group called the Navalinga temple consists of nine two- or three-storeyed square *vimanas*, single-walled, and built round the sides and ends of a linear row of three *mandapas*, all of poor quality sandstone. In general appearance, but for the characteristic *sukanasikas*, they resemble the Biccavolu temples of the Eastern Chalukyas. The top *talas* are devoid of the *hara*, the top *sikhara* has a prominently splayed out brim or lip, and the sides are offset repeatedly. The *kudus* still retain their arched shapes. The *hara* elements too retain their characteristic shapes, and the projected bays of the *aditala* wall have *devakoshtha* niches framed by *kuta* fronts mounted on shorter pilaster pairs, or by *makara toranas*. The door lintels too are elaborate *makara toranas*, often with a Gajalakshmi crest as the *lalata bimba*. The *mandapa* pillars are partially lathe-turned in respect of their capitals, while the shaft is square and angular, marking the beginnings of the characteristic and almost wholly lathe-turned pillars of the later periods. Standing a little away from the group is the Mahamayi temple with an oblong shrine appropriate to Devi *vimanas*, and two front *mandapas*, also oblong. Another oblong shrine with narrow front *mandapa* stands next to the Navalinga cluster. It has a tank at one corner. The other ruined structures are all enclosed by a *prakara* with two openings on two of the four sides. The mention of goddesses like Ganga, Kalika, Sarasvati and Mahamayi in the associated inscriptions indicates a strong *devi* cult in this centre.

The Kallesvara has a square three-storeyed *nirandhara vimana* fronted by an *antarala* and a closed *mandapa* in the axial line over which also the *hara* of the *aditala* level is extended. The top *tala* is bereft of the *hara; a sukanasika* projects from the upper *tala* over the *antarala*. The storeys, however, are not boldly marked off as in the earlier type, and the square *sikhara* with offset sides has a well splayed out brim. The *kudus* on the cornices are beginning to lose their horseshoe shape and have become flat facets or ante-fixes. The wall spaces between the relieved bays of the *aditala* are adorned by reliefs of shrine frontals with superstructures of the southern *vimana* patterns, or of the northern *prasada* patterns. The square-based pillars of the *mandapa* are partially lathe-turned, particularly the capitals below the *phalaka*, showing some advance in this respect over the earlier Navalinga examples. There are two rectangular shrines facing the four central pillars of the *mandapa*, perhaps originally dedicated to Ganapati and Durga. The recesses of the *mandapa* wall have perforated windows. But what is more interesting from the constructional point of view is the fact that the walls, though of usual thickness, are built of smaller blocks of stone, a tendency to approximate to brickwork, in contrast to the large-sized blocks used in the earlier cyclopean or near-cyclopean constructions of the Chalukyas and the Rashtrakutas.

Turning to the temples of Lakkundi, also near Gadag, one comes across temples in the construction of which sandstone, till then usual, is totally abandoned in favour of a fine-textured, soft, chloritic schist stone that is quarried naturally in lesser thicknesses. The new material, because of its less thick quarry size and the greater ease with which it can be cut, naturally reacted upon workmanship, resulting in the reduced size of the masonry courses and increased volume of fine and delicate carvings on such tempting soft and smooth material. Of the many interesting temples of such material in this place, the Jain temple is the largest and most prominent which might have been built in the latter half of the eleventh century. It has a square five-storeyed *nirandhara vimana*, with a square *griva* and *sikhara*. It had originally a closed *navaranga-mandapa* in front, though an open *mandapa* was added later on. The central bay of the *navaranga* included within the four central pillars is a square larger than the eight surrounding peripheral bays. The single *aditala* wall is made thick and massive to carry the *hara* and the functional *tala* with a shrine over it (as in the Jain temple at Pattadkal which, however, is *sandhara*) and is also provided externally on its sides, with repeatedly offset projections. In addition, it has four supporting pillars at the four inner corners of the *garbha-griha*. The *aditala hara* is extended as usual over the *antarala* and the larger *navaranga*.

The upper *talas*, of a considerably lesser height and a gradually diminishing width, have the *hara* over them, except the topmost one. The *griva* too is very short and the prominent squattish *sikhara* has a well splayed out brim. The *kudus* on the cornice, though flat, retain their arched shape, and have *simha-mukha* finials. The pilasters on the walls are slender with capitals that have lost their robust shapes. The proportionate sizes of their components are lost and the abacus, or *phalaka*, is small and thin. In the spaces between the paired pilasters on the walls are inset *nasika* front motifs. In the recesses between the bays of the wall occurs the 'decorative pilaster'—a pilaster carrying a shrine front or pavilion on top, as is to be found in the Chola temples of the eleventh century at Thanjavur and Gangaikondacholapuram. The decorative pilaster is framed inside a *torana* over two shorter pilaster supports. The tall functional second *tala* and the five-storeyed elevation lend stature to this fine *vimana*.

The Kasi-Visvesvara temple at Lakkundi, and the Mahadeva temple at Ittagi, also not far from Gadag, mark among others the zenith of architecture and art in this area under the Western Chalukyas. The date of the latter temple is precisely indicated by its inscription as AD 1112. The main *vimana*, extant only up to the *griva*, the *sikhara* and *stupi* having been lost, is a square five-storeyed structure standing on an elaborately moulded *adhishthana* with a *sukanasika* projected from the level of the fourth *tala* over the *antarala* roof. The entire *vimana* on each side is thrown out into five prominent bays, the central one being the most projected, with four narrower recesses in between, the bays again offset repeatedly, so that the plan is apparently a scalloped one. The *hara* on each side of the *tala* in correspondence with the width of the bays is made of two *karnakutas*, one at either end, a central *sala*, and two intervening *panjaras*. The most projected central bay of each side of the *aditala* with *sala* superstructure embraces deep and broad niches forming miniature sanctums, making the whole appear like lesser *vimanas*, with their pillars, *prastara* and super-structure clustering round the base of the central one, while the corner ones, corresponding to the *karnakutas*, have narrower and shallower fronts. The *navaranga* forms a larger square in front, its outer walls and *adhishthana* similarly relieved and recessed, and with similar external ornamentation. What is more interesting is its highly ornate and raised central ceiling, and the fine carvings on its tier slabs, particularly those cutting the corners of the ceiling of square bays. This *mandapa* is provided with three entrances, east, south and north, with pillared porches, the front one connecting it with an open multi-pillared *agra-mandapa* axially in front, which again has three porches on its three sides. The excessive decorative elements of this temple, as also the plan and other features, indicate its proximity in time to the typical temples of the Hoysalas and Kakatiyas who came after them to power in this region in the late twelfth and early thirteenth centuries.

The temples built by or under the patronage of the Hoysalas in south Deccan and Mysore are of the very tractable, dense and fine-grained, soft chloritic schist or talc which permits fine and minute carving. The temple unit in general consists of a *vimana* connected by its short *antarala* to a closed *navaranga* which may often be proceeded by another *mandapa*. It is not also unusual for the temple unit to have three main *vimanas* on three sides of a common *navaranga*, each opening into it by the connecting *antaralas*, the fourth side of the *navaranga* being provided with the main entrance, or porch. This is termed *trikutachala*. The whole complex is raised over a common wider terrace, or *upa-pitha*, providing an open circumambulatory round the entire unit over its top platform. By the repeated offsetting not only of the sides but also of the angles, the resulting plan becomes star-shaped, the same plan as would result by rotating a square pivoted at its centre so that its corners, or the ends of its diagonals, touch sixteen or thirty-two or more points on a circle circumscribed round it. This star-shaped external configuration is made to extend from the *upa-pitha* to the apex of the *vimana* superstructure. This, incidentally, provided a larger surface area for the execution of the cloyingly prolific sculpture and carving for which the Hoysala temples are noted. The *adhishthana* pattern is more akin to the northern style in having tiers of superposed friezes of elephants, warriors, horses, *hamsas, makaras*, etc., the broad *pattrika*-like top tier depicting *Puranic* scenes in a series of narrative vignettes. The walls are embellished by niches crowned by pyramidal tiered superstructures and enshrining figure sculpture of varied iconography. The intervening parts are adorned further by pilasters carrying pyramidal, tiered, superstructural motifs on top. The *prastara* has a prominent eaves-like cornice. The superstructure is a scheme of close-set *hara* elements, essentially of *kutas*, rising one behind the other, each marking a storey, the topmost one carrying a short *griva* and octagonal *sikhara* terminating in a *stupi*. The middle of the front face of the upper *talas* is drawn forward into a *sukanasika* over the *antarala* below. The pillars inside the *mandapa* have square bases. The shaft and capital region up to the broad square abacus is smoothly rounded, turned on a lathe and polished, forming a series of bulges and curved necks, beadings, etc., usually later embellished by finely picked ornamentation. Often the axial series of the temple unit is surrounded by an open court and pillared cloister inside the *prakara* wall, having its *mahadvara* entrance only on one side, the front.

Among the hundreds of Hoysala temples of greater or lesser merit, the most well known and typical are the Hoysalesvara among the many temples at Halebid, the Chennakesvara temple at Belur (both in Hassan district; the two towns were the earlier and later capitals of the Hoysalas), and the Kesava temple at Somnathpur (Mysore district).

The Chennakesvara temple unit at Belur was built by Hoysala Vishnuvardhana in 1117 and consecrated to Vishnu with the name Vijaya Narayana. It now forms the principal unit in a complex of later temples, surrounded by a cloister and *prakara*, with a *gopura* entrance in the east on the axial line of the main unit, and a plain side entrance to its south on the same side. The present brickwork superstructure of the *gopura* is a much later renovation. As designed and completed by Vishnuvardhana it had the *vimana* of a beautiful stellate plan and an ornate sanctum doorway with a superbly carved over-door, and an *antarala* fronted by a similar ornamental doorway. The ornamental doorway was preceded by a large *navaranga*, the three sides of which had extended passages or closed porches, east, south and north, terminating externally into elaborately carved entrances with over-doors. The whole is raised on an *upa-pitha*, 1.5 m high, the plan of its open circumambulatory following the stellate plan of the *vimana* and its axial *mandapa*. In front of the three external openings of the *mandapas* are two short flights of steps down the *adhishthana* and *upa-pitha* heights, respectively, with two miniature *vimana* models posed at either end on the ground level and on top of the flight of steps over the *upa-pitha* platform. The bases of the peripheral pillars of the *navaranga* and its three porches were interconnected by *kakshasana* platforms over which a few generations later (in the time of Ballala II who built the tank at the north-east corner and the *prakara)*, perforated screen walls were fitted between the pillars, making the *mandapa* a closed one. The *adhishthana* tiers of the *vimana antarala* and *mandapa* are profusely carved with long lines of friezes of animals, men and narrative scenes. The walls carry sculptures of iconographic interest. The relieved bays on the three sides of the *vimana aditala*, which are almost buttressing miniature *vimanas*, have deep cells inside for sculptures of deities. The overhanging *kapota* of the *mandapa* is supported by numerous finely-carved female figures in graceful poses called *madanikas*. The superstructure of the main *vimana* is now lost. The pillars inside the *mandapa* are exquisitely lathe-turned or intricately carved, and a few of them carry fine, bold, figure sculptures. The raised coffer-like central ceiling of the *mandapa*, rising in eight tiers by stepped-up triangular slabs cutting the corners successively, forms a sort of octagonal hollow dome with all the tiers intricately carved. The apical covering stone extends down the centre as a large, intricately-carved lantern-like pendentive or *karnika*. The lowest tier of the ceiling is also supported, as it were, by *madanikas*, more beautiful than those outside, sprung from the square abacus of the lathe-turned pillars. The temple thus is a veritable museum of sculptures, large and small, and intricate vegetal, floral and animal carvings.

The Hoysalesvara, built about 1150, among the many other temples of the period in Halebid, is a composite of two similar *vimana* units, both dedicated to Siva, standing side by side on a common raised platform, a combination of two stellate *upa-pithas*. Each unit consists of a *vimana* of a star-shaped plan with *antarala* and *navaranga* in front, facing east. Each *navaranga* has three projected entrances in a cruciform manner with the northern arm of the southern *navaranga* joined to the southern arm of the northern *navaranga*, resulting in a common passage between the two. The *adhishthanas* of both the units are made up of elaborate animal or narrative friezes forming their respective tiers. Externally the inter-columnal spaces of the projected porches are screened by perforated windows above the level of the *kakshasana* platforms that join together the bases of the pillars. The walls of the *vimana*, the inter-connecting transept, and the walls of the *mandapas* are covered externally with large sculptural reliefs of remarkable fineness. The entrances of the porches, the *antarala* and the shrine chamber are framed by elaborately carved over-doors, with elegant *makara torana* lintels on top. The superstructures of both the *vimanas* are lost. The *upa-pitha* platform provides a broad open circumambulatory round both the units. Standing in front of the temple units, and at some distance from them are two open-pillared Nandi-*mandapas*, both asymmetrical and later additions, though of the same period, the southern one having a small shrine at its rear. Though incomplete as it stands now, the Hoysalesvara marks the climax of Hoysala art and architecture.

The Kesava temple, Somnathpur, is a fine example of one of the latest in the series of Hoysala creations. It was built in 1268 by Somanatha, a general of the Hoysala king. It is one of the most exquisitely carved temples of small size, resembling a jewel casket. It is a *trikuta* temple with three principal *vimanas* of equal magnitude, facing north, east and south, respectively, opening into a larger and closed common *mandapa* on its north, west and south sides. To its east is added a larger *navaranga-mandapa* closed by perforated screen walls over the *kakshasana* level. All the three shrines are dedicated to Vishnu in different forms. The whole is mounted over an *upa-pitha* platform of steller plan, as also are the three *vimanas* and the *mandapas* from base to apex. The platform provides a broad circumambulatory. This axial series is surrounded by an open court with a peripheral cloister of sixty-four shrines inside the *prakara* wall. The shrines are ranged on the rear half of the cloister close to the *prakara*, while the anterior half forms a continuous corridor with a pillared facade. In front there is a pillared entrance, *mandapa*, which perhaps had a superstructure of the pattern of a *gopura*. The *adhishthana* mouldings are exquisitely carved with friezes of men, warriors, elephants, horses, *hamsas* and *makaras*, the topmost tier having a series of narrative panels depicting incidents from the *Ramayana* and the *Bhagavata*. The wall niches have boldly moulded figure sculptures of gods and goddesses. The pillars inside the *mandapa* are all finely lathe-turned with gracefully carved mouldings. More interesting, however, are the coffered ceilings of the *navaranga*, as also those of the inner *mandapa*, and the outer porch, looking like inverted basketry, with elaborate carvings, floral, vegetal, serpentine, etc. of different patterns and including small sculptures of *dikpalas*, no two ceiling bays looking alike. **The** larger central bay is the most significantly wrought bay.

Of the temples of the Kakatiyas of Orangallu, or Warangal, the temples at Hanamkonda and Palampet are the most well known, and typical of their architecture and art. The so-called 'thousand-pillared temple' at Hanamkonda (Warangal district), built by King Prataparudra in 1162, shows well the transition from the late Western Chalukyan to the Kakatiya style. The main part consists of a *trikuta* or triple shrine of considerable dimensions and dedicated to Siva, Vishnu and Surya, all the three opening into a common *mandapa* on its west, north and east, respectively, and the whole standing over a common platform. The *mandapa* has open corners between the three shrines and on its two sides, and its pillars inside are lathe-turned. The *adhishthana*, the walls with pilasters and the *prastara* are repeatedly offset with projected bays, the central one on each side projecting the most and constituting by itself a small side *vimana* with a cella. The superstructures of all the three *vimanas* are lost. The most interesting part extant is the multi-pillared *mandapa* with about three hundred pillars, all richly carved. This is attached in front of the unit to an intervening Nandi-*mandapa*. Another interesting feature of this ruined temple within the fort is the elaborate free-standing *toranas* marking the entrances.

The temples at Palampet (Warangal district) form another interesting group. The main temple of the group constructed in 1215 stands on a high platform, with a Nandi-*mandapa* in front. It is enclosed by a massive wall. The main *vimana*, essentially square on plan, has its three sides offset prominently into five bays each, the central one of each side further offset forward and constituting a three-tiered replica of the main *vimana* on a lesser scale. The other bays have tall close-set pairs of pilasters carrying on their tops shrine-motifs which are replicas of the superstructures of the southern-type *vimanas* and northern-type *prasadas* alternately. The *haras* of the *talas* are indistinct, with more of the *kuta* element conspicuous. The *griva* too is abbreviated and less distinct and almost of the same width as the domical *sikhara*. The entire superstructure is of brickwork. Axially, a closed square *antarala* or *ardha-mandapa* connects the *vimana* with a large *navaranga* in front, which is surrounded by a peripheral platform with an outer series of thirty-two pillars and a circumambulatory. The most noteworthy feature is the array of brackets in the form of female figures, rising from the capitals of the pillars and strutting up the beams and the cornice. Twelve of these are almost life-size figures of slender build and in graceful poses. The rest are rearing *vyalas*, their hind legs resting on elephant heads. The bases of the peripheral pillars of the *mandapa* are also connected by a *vedi* and a balustrade forming the lean-back of the *kakshasana*. The interior of the *mandapa* is also full of sculptures, and the ceiling of the bays are ornate. The *hara* of the *aditala* of the *vimana* is also extended over the *mandapa* terrace. On the platform inside are a set of eight subshrines in four pairs, adjacent to each of the four corners of the *navaranga*. While the main structure is of reddish sandstone, the decorations are of polished basalt or hornblende, which are stones of the hard variety.

Among the three temples in Pillalamarri (Nalgonda district), the Erakesvara, now called Somesvara, consecrated in 1208, is like the great temple of Palampet, a complete unit of the Kakatiya pattern. It consists of a *vimana* with a *mukha-mandapa* in front that is provided with three projected porch entrances, preceded by flights of steps on the north, east and south, while the *garbha-griha* is attached to the west with a connecting *antarala*. The whole stands on a prominent and well-moulded *upa-pitha*. The wall of the *garbha-griha* over the *adhishthana* on each face has five prominently relieved pilasters, the central one wider than the lateral pairs, and the *prastara* on top has a slopy, flat, plain cornice. The recesses between the pilasters contain the usual short and slender pilaster motif surmounted by a shrine superstructure over its abacus. The superstructure of the main *vimana*, now ruined, appears to have been of four *talas* or storeys with a prominently projected *sukanasika* on the front side over the *antarala*, a Nandi placed on top of it. The *sikhara* on top also appears to have been square. The *mandapa* with offset sides has four carved pillars at its centre round a raised floor with a ceiling, which is a grid of nine squares, each containing a lotus.

The Namesvara temple in another part of the village, consecrated in about 1202 by Nami Reddi, is a more elegant structure with carving and sculpture richer than in the larger Erakesvara. It consists of the *vimana* facing east and open *mukha-mandapa* connected by an *antarala*. The *upa-pitha* is absent. The *mukha-mandapa* has a frontal porch. The *mandapa* is of the *navaranga* pattern with four central pillars round the centre of the floor and twelve more pillars on the periphery. Adjacent to the Namesvara is a triple-shrined unit with three shrines opening on the south, west and north of a common *mukha-mandapa*. The three shrines, all alike, are comparatively plain structures built of large slabs of stone with no decorations on their exterior. The shrines named Namesvara, Kamesvara and Kachesvara (now called Mukkanti Siva temple) were built by Nami Reddi at the beginning of the thirteenth century. The ruined brickwork superstructure has lost many of its distinctive features.

The temple complex at Ghanapur (Warangal district) inside the mud-fort at the centre of the village is another example of a Kakatiya temple complex. The nuclear structure dedicated to Siva is large with a *mandapa* in front and a number of lesser independent shrines of varied shapes on the four sides, some of them with *mandapas* and others without such an axial appendage. The main structure is like the great temple of Palampet in size, plan and elevation. It faces east. The *vimana* of 16.3m width at base is connected to the western side of a large *mukha-mandapa* through an *antarala*, the *mukha-mandapa* having openings with entrance porches on the other three sides, east, south, and north. The whole stands on a double plinth, as usual, the wider *upa-pitha* platform below and the *adhishthana*, or the real base of the structures above, leaving an open ambulatory all round. The superstructure of the *vimana* is unfortunately lost. Over the *adhishthana* of the *mandapa* there is the usual dwarf wall, or *vedi* parapet forming *kakshasanas* and supporting the shorter periph-eral pillars at the corners and on either side of each porch entrance. These pillars, as at Palampet, carry fine caryatid brack-ets springing from the top cubical part of the shaft and reaching up to the corbel and cornice. The bracket-figures represent *madanikas* in graceful poses, and *vyalas* surmounting elephants, each with a human torso emerging out of its gape. The walls of the *antarala* and sanctum are alternately relieved by flat pilasters and recessed, as in other temples of the type, the recesses containing a pilaster motif crowned by a shrine superstructure below a *patra-tala* arch or *torana*, the common motif of the Kakatiya temples. The bases of the main pilasters have relief sculptures of gods and dancers. Inside the *mandapa* there are minor shrines arranged on the periphery, five of them extant, as in the Palampet temple again. The roof of the *mandapa* is lost.

Axially there is a ruined *mandapa* in front of the eastern porch. The surrounding *parivara* shrines are of varied character, with or without a front *mandapa*. Some of them have tiered superstructures still extant with *sukanasika* projections, in some of which the *kuta sala* elements of the southern *vimana* are evident. Many of them have square *sikharas*. In one case at least the crowning part is of the *amalaka* type.

There are about a dozen temples, not very outstanding, inside the Warangal fort, many of them only small structures like the Virabhadra, Mandalamma, Rama, Vishnu, Venkatesa, Svayambhu, Nelasambhu, Jangamesvara, and Devi temples. The two small temples at Katachpur (Katakshapura) in the same district are *trikuta* with their superstructures lost.

The Kakatiya temples, though they derive mostly from the Western Chalukyan group, form a distinct category. They include single *vimana* units and *trikuta* units. The superstructure over the stone-built body in many cases, especially the larger temples, is of brick and mortar. The *trikuta* units are to be found among those at Panagal. The Rudresvara-Vasudeva-Surya complex at Hanamkonda is the best example of this type. One of the units is at Pillalamarri. This and the shrine to the west of the main temple at Palampet are also *trikuta*. The single *vimana* units, of which a typical example is the great temple at Palampet, show variations in plan, rise, and decorative details. Typically the *vimana* is connected by an *antarala* to a frontal *mandapa* with three porch entrances on the other three sides. The *mandapa*, after the *navaranga* pattern, has four central pillars, which are highly finished and are decorative, lathe-turned, with basal and top cubical sections on the shaft, with their faces sculptured, and an intervening polygonal belt. The jar-like *kalasas* or *lasunas*, with more straight sides than curved, are polygonal in section often and the *kumbha* is flattened in the form of a circular and lenticular disc with almost a sharp or narrow edge. The *phalaka* is large, square and thin in section. All this indicates an elaboration of the trends already noticed in the Western Chalukyan temples. The pillars in the *mandapa* of the great temple at Palampet and in the triple shrine of Hanamkonda are of black granite, lathe-turned and highly polished, while in the other cases they are of sandstone. Similar shorter peripheral pillars, over the *vedi* of the *mandapas*, as at Ghanapur and Palampet, often carry remarkable bracket-figures, of *madanikas* or of mythical animals. The sanctum and axial *mandapa* or *mandapas* are often raised on their own *adhishthana* over a common and larger *upa-pitha,* affording a circumambulatory platform round the entire structure and providing the first landing over the flights of steps from the ground level to the porch entrances over the *adhishthana* above. The scheme of *vimana, antarala* and *mandapa* with three porch entrances is found in the great temple at Palampet as also in the one at Ghanapur, the Reddigudi and some other shrines in the same place, the ruined temple on the tank-bund at Palampet, and the Erakesvara of Pillalamarri. The scheme where the *mandapa* preceding the sanctum and *antarala* has a single porch is to be found in the Namesvara of Pillalamarri, in a lesser shrine at Ghanapur and in Shrine IV at Palampet. There are others with a sanctum and an *antarala* alone, as found among the lesser shrines at Ghanapur and Palampet. In a few cases, the *antarala* is absent. The shrine comes directly behind the *mandapa* and hence the sanctum alone is present. The walls of the *garbha-griha* are sometimes plain in the simpler cases as in the one on the tank-bund at Palampet. The offsetting of the sides is not generally much pronounced. When alternately projected and recessed, the bays are broad, flat pilaster patterns, often with shrine-motifs at their bases. The recesses contain a slender pilaster carrying a shrine top at its apex over its abacus with a superposed creeper or *patra-lata torana* over it. The *kapota* of the *prastara* is not curved in section as it is in the earlier examples of the Pallavas and the Chalukyas. It is rather a slopy, straight, projected ledge, often large. The *prastara* over the *antarala* and the front *mandapas* carry, like the lower *tala* of the *vimana* superstructure, a *hara* of miniature shrines of the *kuta* variety, often in brick and mortar. These form the fore-runners of the typical arched niche-like miniature shrine series, the *chunchus* of the subsequent Vijayanagar *mandapa prastaras.* The *sukanasika,* projected in front of the *vimana* superstructure is an invariable characteristic, marking the Chalukyan derivation of the temples. The *antarala* and sanctum entrances are framed by over-door patterns, which incorporate in the composition of the *sakhas,* a vertical perforated *jalaka* window-pattern. The lintel has a *lalata bimba* of Gajalakshmi or other gods, often in the central loop of a wavy *torana* issuing from *makara* heads perched atop the door-jambs. The *prastara* over the door-frame, as in the earlier Chalukyan models, carries a series of miniature shrine tops. The relieved pilasters on the projected bays of the shrine walls have often shallow *devakoshthas* inside paired pilasters with *prastara* and shrine superstructures on top, single or in a row. In the extreme cases of the larger *vimanas*, the central bay is the most projected one with its *devakoshtha* niche and superstructure simulating a side *vimana* attached to the main structure. These miniature shrine tops here and elsewhere are of the *vimana* type with a square or circular *sikhara* or of the *prasada* type with an *amalaka* on top. Another characteristic decorative motif seen is a cruciform rosette, or a lotus with four petals spread crosswise, a pattern that one finds carried over to the Ikkeri area of the late Vijayanagar empire and the temples of the Keladi Nayakas there.

There are nearly fifty temples of the Kakatiyas known, but they are mostly in various stages of ruination. A few of these temples, however, are of the Kadamba-Chalukya *vimana* pattern which have been dealt with separately.

8

STRUCTURAL STONE TEMPLES: THE LAST PHASE

THE VIJAYANAGAR TEMPLES

After the early Muslim inroads into the south which had abated the hitherto continuous temple-building activity, there was apparently a temporary lull for less than half a century. The rise of the militant Vijayanagar empire to halt the Muslim conquest in the middle of the fourteenth century (which, in the process, soon encompassed the whole of the peninsula) almost gave a new and vigorous spurt to temple architecture by way of repairs or additions to existing structures, and erection of new ones. In their northern domain, the imperial rulers, with their capital at Vijayanagar or Hampi, inherited the architectural traditions as carried down till their times by the later Chalukyas, Kakatiyas and Hoysalas, and in their southern provinces the tradition as developed up to the times of the later Pandyas. Thus their temples in their northern domains in the Deccan, Andhra and Karnataka regions retain much that was of Chalukyan-Hoysala-Kakatiya inspiration, while their more southern constructions in Tamil Nadu and southern Kerala continued the traits of the Pallava-Chola-Pandya architecture. But as already stated, they made one significant change in so far as the northern regions were concerned: in all the places throughout their vast empire they adopted and spread the hardstone tradition and technique and building to the exclusion of the hitherto prevalent softstone constructions. In their vast capital of Hampi, now ruined, there are scores of temples, all of hard stone, exhibiting the traits from one of the two sources, the Chalukya-Rashtrakuta-Hoysala-Kakatiya series, and the Pallava-Chola-Pandya series. Their subsequent capitals at Penukonda (Anantapur district), Chandragiri

(Chittoor district), and Vellore (North Arcot), and their environs, and their provincial capitals or seats of viceregal Nayakas as at Vellore (North Arcot), Gingee (South Arcot), Thanjavur, Madurai, and Ikkeri (Shimoga district) also have temples of their period. In fact, the reign of the Vijayanagar rulers witnessed a greater activity in temple-building than had been the case in the times of the Cholas. Some of their temples are remarkable for the great size of their component structures, i.e. the *mandapas* and *gopuras*.

The choice of hardstone, as against the then extant softstone tradition, for the fabric of construction in the building activities, including temple architecture and sculpture, in the northern part or the home provinces of the Vijayanagar empire was a significant enough step. It marked a definite break and made the designers and the architect-sculptors think in terms of the new material and urged them to put forth their best, both in terms of number and quality that would reflect the aim and genius of the Vijayanagar epoch. It is to be noticed that the extensive and many-walled fortifications of cyclopean masonry, the massive gates and other defence works of the new capital city, which now form the celebrated 'Hampi ruins' centring round the earlier existing temple of Sri Virupaksha or Pampapati on the banks of the Tungabhadra amidst the chain of massive granite hills, as also the numerous temples that sprang up since, inside and outside the city were all built of the hardstones quarried from the local hills. This new capital was located on the right bank across the river with the old capital Anegundi on the left bank and came to be called Vijayanagar,[1] or the 'City of Victory' that lent the name

---

[1] Alternatively it was also called Vidyanagara in honour of the great saint-preceptor Vidyaranya. He was a *sanyasin* of the Sringeri Sankaracharya lineage ordained by the great pontiff Vidyasankara, also called Vidyatirtha and himself became the pontiff as second in succession to him. During Vidyaranya's sojourn in the Hampi area, as a *sanyasin* (in the times of Vidyasankara as pontiff of the Sringeri *matha*) he took both the royal brothers, the founders of the dynasty, Harihara I and Bukka, under his fostering spiritual care and as their constant preceptor friend, philosopher and guide played a momentous role in the events of the time, culminating in the foundation of the new Hindu empire of Vijayanagar. Under the aegis of the saint, Virupaksha I celebrated his coronation in the new capital on 18 April 1336 in the presence of God Virupaksha, undertaking to rule the kingdom as the agent of the deity, in token of which he adopted the royal sign manual *Sri Virupaksha* that continued as such ever since. Placing the royal insignia at the feet of his guru Vidyaranya, in all gratitude and reverence, he hailed him as the '*Karnataka simhasana pratishthapanacharya*' (the establisher of the throne of Karnataka), a title

also to the dynasty.

The urgent need for stone constructions in and around the new capital and the requirements of the know-how of the technique of working on the hard, adamantine stones, in which material the rocky terrain of Hampi and the neighbourhood abounded, was perhaps met from the further south where the craftsmen were for long centuries steeped in the hardstone tradition and possibly also from the Kakatiya region in the north, where sculpture in hardstone had come into vogue for some time since.[2] These should have helped the Vijayanagar craftsmen guilds even in their initial achievement which was considerable enough after the stagnation that ensued due to the invasions and upheavals.

The problem of a break or disruption of the continuity of the development of the *vimana* temple in hardstone that had all along been the choice and character of the farther south, to which area Vijayanagar hegemony soon extended in the reign of Harihara's contemporary and successor Bukka, was not so keen in that area. In Tamil Nadu and parts of Kerala that went into the Vijayanagar empire it was merely a task of continuing the then unbroken chain of the *vimana* temple forms by forging the new Vijayanagar

---

which the successive heads of the Sringeri *matha* have borne till today as also the royal honours conferred on the saint at that time by the emperor. This historical background will help in the proper appreciation of the zeal and fervour with which the founders of Vijayanagar and their successors entered into the tasks of reconstructing the shattered polity and religion of the country, repairing the damages wrought to the temples and institutions that were in existence in addition to constructing and founding many new ones and providing for their proper maintenance.

[2] Such migrations or importations of craftsmen guilds from one region to another are not unknown. A Mahabalipuram inscription in script of the seventh century, coeval with the date of the monolithic *rathas*, gives a list of a team of such artisans— a master architect-builder (*permutachchan*) from a place (Kevada(?)), a blacksmith (needed to temper the chisels for cutting hardstone) or Kollan Semakan by name hailing from Kalyani, etc. (*see* K.R. Srinivasan, *The Dharmaraja Ratha and Its Sculptures*, New Delhi, 1975, p. 45). Again "the vastly improved design and execution of the Virupaksha temple (Pattadkal) built by one of Vikramaditya II's queens was most likely due to workmen brought from Kanchipuram and to their direct imitation of the Kailasanatha temple which had come into existence in the Pallava capital some decades earlier." (K.A.N. Sastry, *A History of South India*, Third Edition, Madras, 1966, p. 452). There is inscriptional evidence to show that a guild of Dravida (Tamil) artisans had come for work in the Chalukyan country for the inscription refers to the settlement of affairs relating to the comparative status of the immigrants vis-a-vis the local artisan guilds.

links with the modulations and innovations introduced by the genius of the period as the Vijayanagar idiom. As such the evolutionary chain of the southern *vimana* order could be handed over at the end of the empire to the succeeding Nayak rulers for them to add in turn before leaving the heritage to be continued in post-Nayak times till today.

But nearer home, in the northern regions of the empire, the break is observed to be more pronounced, conditioned not only by the political invasion by iconoclastic rulers of alien faith but also other local and intrinsic causes. The change-over from a hitherto softstone vogue to one of rather quite novel and less tractable hardstone apart, the models left in the hundreds, though of great merit as great expositions and landmarks in the history of architecture, by the immediate predecessors, the Hoysalas and before them the Western Chalukyas, could not supply the want adequately. The very peculiarities of their plan and elevation could not afford the starting point for the Vijayanagar series. Either of them have become *cul-de-sacs*, so to say, that had taken far away from the main highroad of evolution[1] laid by their precursors, the Rashtrakutas and before them the early Chalukyas and codified in the architectural canons. The early Vijayanagar temple-builders and sculptors had perforce to hark back to the earlier developed forms and types obtaining in that cradle of temple architecture, viz. the early Chalukyan region that linked the north of India with the south and choose two rather basic and

---

[1] The very bold emphasis of the vertical off-settings or corrugations from plinth upwards to the apex below the crowning elements reminiscent of the *bhadras* or *ratha* projections of the northern *rekha-prasadas* against the suffused persistence of the horizontal divisions of the superstructure, especially expounded by the Western Chalukyan genre could not very well offer the desired model. For, the emphasis on the horizontal division resulting in the tiered nature of the superstructure was the *sine qua non* of the recognized southern *vimana* order. In such a perspective of the subdual, almost to the extent of obliteration in effect of the horizontal division and stratification, neither could the Hoysala genre satisfy. The similar but stellate vertical corrugations again extending from the very base to the near apex, more boldly emphasized in the Hoysala genre, could not satisfy the need. The tempting softness of the stone, coupled with the increased surface area to be carved, resulting from the vertical folds or offsets, had encouraged such profusions of sculpture and embellishment which could not very well be done with equal facility in the hardstone material that the Vijayanagar artisans took up for their work. The Hoysala mode, both in terms of prodigious output and cloying exuberance had almost spent itself out in the effort.

characteristically southern strains from among the early forms and the welter of their mutations that had since filled the landscape developed under the aegis of the succeeding dynasties.

Of the two types opted, one was the southern *vimana* form with a *sukanasa* as a type derived from early Chalukya-Rashtrakuta times. The other choice of equal antiquity and ubiquity in the area was the *Kadamba Nagara*, a Kadamba-Chalukya form (described in chronological series in the next chapter) with a superstructure formed by successively receding tiers, superposed one over the other, each tier made up of horizontal or slopy (in regions of high rainfall) or curved eaves-like *kapota* members—the smallest topmost tier carrying the *griva sikhara-stupi* combination. This latter form is akin to what obtains in the *pidadeul* shrines of Orissan vintage on the north-east and the *phansanakara sikhara* found in Gujarat and western India on the north-west of the Deccan.[2] The temples in Hampi and places round about, that constitute the maximum agglomeration of Vijayanagar fame, very patently exhibit this dichotomy, by their conformity with the one or the other of these two parent stocks and the most important ones of either class are noticed below and in the succeeding chapter.

The Vijayanagar temple-builders could soon catch up with the above two opted strains and fall into even strides in the development of the characteristically Vijayanagar temples, many of them eventually turning out to be massive and dignified structural models of great virtuosity and elevational clarity. But in the initial years of the nascent empire wherever faced with the challenge of raising up imposing edifices that would accord with the ambition and pride of the rising empire, the Vijayanagar architects have responded by making some bold and daring experiments and produced structures that would seem to be aberrant in the geographical and cultural context but yet exhibiting merit and fine composition. One such example, that is unique in more ways than one, will be the Vidyasankara temple in Sringeri (district Kadur-Chikmagalur, Karnataka)) located high

---

[2] The *Kadamba Nagara* mannerism in the superstructural tiers culminating in the *griva sikhara-stupi* apex, the southern *vimana* mannerism, was the most common combination. The *sukanasa* may or may not be present and the latter form is found adopted in secular constructions, too, as in the 'Lotus Mahal' in the *zanana* enclosure in Hampi and in the 'Kalyana Mahal' in the lower fort of Rajagiri in Gingee (district South Arcot).

up in the heaviest monsoon area of Malnad on the Western Ghats. It was in the Ikkeri (Keladi) viceroyalty of the Vijayanagar empire—and has been one of the principal seats of *amnaya mathas* founded by Sankara. The temple was built under the royal patronage of Harihara and Bukka under the behest of their guru, sage Vidyaranya, in commemoration of the earlier and illustrious pontiff, Sri Vidyasankara, also called Vidyatirtha, over the site of his disappearance.[1] The temple was founded in AD 1338 according to traditional accounts but a Sringeri inscription indicates the date as 1356. While the former date may refer to an earlier nuclear shrine raised on the spot, the latter date would indicate that the large all-stone temple now standing over the spot was in a completed stage by that year. Thus it would be seen that the temple was founded within a few years after the foundation of Vijayangar, the city and the empire.

The temple built in the local reddish granite is easily the largest among early Vijayanagar temples, consisting of the sanctum and axial *mandapa* combined into one unit. On plan, from foundation to the *aditala* and *mandapa prastara,* it is a double apse or *chapa,* the two large apses meeting each other by their open ends resulting in an elliptical shape that is rather elongated. The outer, curved apse ends face east and west respectively. The western half of this combination (ellipse) contains the sanctum and as such forms the *vimana* half while the eastern half contains a large pillared *mandapa*, there being a narrow north-south transept inside, separating the two. The whole stands over an

---

[1] It is said that Vidyasankara went into yoga in an underground tryst—an excavated pit which was covered up after his entry. Before the twelve years stipulated by the sage were over, the pit was opened out of curiosity at the end of three years, by some indiscreet disciples in the absence of the successor on tour only to find that all mortal traces of the sage had disappeared. The site of this *videhamukti* (AD 1333)) was sanctified by installing a Siva *linga* over it which soon got enshrined into a temple. The importance of this great *acharya* and saint (who in his spiritual effulgence, it is believed, continues to manifest himself, shedding subtle spiritual influence about the place, and even today inspires and guides the affairs of Sringeri) and the veneration in which he was held both by the royal house of Vijayanagar and the successive pontiffs on the *pitha* can be realized from the fact that the sign manual and seal of the *pitha,* whatever may be the individual name of the occupant pontiff, continues to be 'Sri Vidyasankara' even as the royal sign manual of all the Vijayanagar kings was 'Sri Virupaksha', the tutelary deity of Hampi. This is echoed also in the contemporary inscriptions and copper plate grants.

adhishthana raised up in turn by an *upa-pitha*, both of the same plan, elliptical, the lower *upa-pitha* of slightly greater overall length and width, resulting in the formation of a narrow open ambulatory on its top round the base of the *adhishthana*. The provision of an *upa-pitha*, or sub-base, an optional member solely intended to enhance the height and stature of the structure according to the texts, has been an invariable feature of the Chalukyan and its lineal cohorts. It follows in its tiers and mouldings the southern norms including a *kapota* with indistinct *kudu* ornamentation. The tiers of the *adhishthana* follow the later Chalukyan and Hoysala models in the form and ornate nature of its six projected tiers or mouldings and five recessed sculptured intervals alternating. They, as in Hoysala forms, are friezes of horses, elephants, lotuses and on top, cameos or panels in series illustrating episodes from the *Puranas* and a historical narration in sculpture of some local event.

The wall above forms the *bahya bhitti* or outer wall of the rear or western part of the structure surrounding the inner *antara bhitti* that contains the *garbha* or sanctum, thus rendering the *vimana* a *sandhara* one, while over the eastern part of the structure it forms the external wall enclosing the twelve-pillard *ranga-mandapa* inside it. In imitation of the Western Chalukyan models, the convex parts of the front and rear apses are each thrown at intervals into seven major vertical off-sets or *bhadras*, which are in turn offset further, resembling the *sapta ratha* mode of the Orissan temples or the northern *prasadas*. These are six doorways set into the six major offsets or bays, one each at the forward or eastern end, and at the hind or western end, with two more on each flank, south and north, the six so arranged that each apsidal half comes to have three—one terminal and two lateral.

Each portal or *dvara*, set inside one of the large *bhadra* projections, is provided with an ornate door-frame having a number of *sakha* components as is the wont with the Chalukyan and its derivatives and in the northern temples. The lintel has a Gajalakshmi relief and the introduction of a wide-set projecting door cornice over each one of the doorways is reminiscent of the Kakatiya mode. There is the usual river goddess panel at base of each jamb. The sill of each door-opening is reached by a flight of seven steps over the height of the *adhishthana* while below there is a corresponding *sopana* of six steps over the *upa-pitha* height, each flanked by a pair of elephant balustrades as in Hoysala examples. The eastern doorway forms the principal entrance.

The *bahya bhitti* right round exhibits a series of pilasters with capitals complete and the interspaces between the pairs of pilasters accommodate niches, of the *devakoshtha* or *torana* type. These enshrine a galaxy of more than sixty sculptures or sculpture groups of varied iconography, making the temple wall a veritable museum of sculpture and iconography. This is an imitation in the hardstone of what the Hoysala predecessors could do in their softstone fabric. The sculptures besides being Saiva, Vaishnava and Sakta, include the Buddha and Jina too, rendering the scheme quite eclectic. The six doorways are each guarded by a pair of doorkeepers, two of the six pairs being Saiva and two more pairs, Vaishnava *dvarapalas*, while the remaining two pairs are Sakta *dvarapalikas* as could be identified by the attire and the attributes they carry. On top of the wall runs the entablature with the usual *prastara* components but with the difference that the *kapota* or flexed cornice or eaves has a double flexure (a doucene or ogee section) instead of the simpler single-flexed *kapota* encountered in all the earlier eras. This is a typical Vijayanagar innovation. What is more, its underside is sculptured with a series of curved ribs and connecting cross-bars in imitation of the original timber frame of pristine *kapotas*, that was of curved metal sheeting nailed over the ribbed frame projected from the tops of the beams to serve as the eaves. This delicate imitation is to be seen in the *kapotas* of numerous Vijayanagar structures as for example in the famous *kalyana-mandapa* of the Varadaraja temple in Kanchipuram. Another characteristic Vijayanagar innovation, made as if to display the great skills their craftsmen had achieved in working hardstones, is the pendent links of stone chains cut out of the same corner stone of the *kapota* or cornice which is found round the eastern corners of this temple. This feat had become ubiquitous later.

The inner wall of the rear apse encloses the sanctum or the *garbha-griha* enshrining the principal Vidyasankara *linga* with a narrow *antarala* in front. On either side of the *antarala* and with door-openings facing east in line with that of the *antarala* are two cells, one on each side. The one on the south enshrines Ganapati, while the other on the north enshrines Durga, as had become the norm from the Chalukyan times.[1] Attached to the south, west and north of the sanctum part and as affluent sub-shrines, as in the case of some Western Chalukyan temples, are three affluent sub-shrines facing the respective directions. The one on the south enshrines Brahma with his consort Sarasvati, the one at the rear on the west, Vishnu with his consort Lakshmi and the one on the north has Mahesvara or Siva with his consort Uma. Thus the grouping round the main sanctum forms a *panchayatana* complex of five subsidiary shrines hugging close on to the sanctum sanctorum. The three door-openings in the outer wall of the rear apse, each come opposite the three affluent shrines of Brahma, Vishnu and Siva on the south, west and north. In front of the complex the front wall of the north-south transept has three openings, the central one opposite the *antrala* and the lateral ones, each opposite the Siva, Ganapati and Durga shrines while inside, the transept with provision of the openings one at either extreme of its rear west becomes continuous with the circumambulation or *pradakshinapatha* round the whole complex through the *sandhara* passage between the main outer and inner walls. The *antrala* front has two *dvarapalas*, one of which, curiously enough, is Hanuman while the other is sage Bhiringi.

Inside the eastern apse, or the eastern half of the structure is accommodated a large pillared *mandapa* with twelve peripheral pillars each of which is a huge monolith of the composite character that becomes the feature of Vijayanagar temples to come. Each pillar has a thick massive central shaft, the front of which is carved out as a huge rearing *vyala* mounted over a crouching elephant, the proboscis of both intertwined, the *vyala* bearing on its head the upper components or corbelled brackets, the topmost and most projected being a typical *pushpa potika* as had been evolved out from the late Pandyan types and developed in Vijayanagar times. On the outer face of each such caryatid column is cut out the *pillai-k-kal* or slender columnette attached to the main part only by its base and top, and having all the features of a typical pillar, the *potika* on top again, being a *pushpa potika*. The twelve columns

---

[1] In the Chalukyan temples and their derivatives, Durga and Ganapati often have separate small shrines facing each other in the *maha-mandapa* set a little distance in front of the *antarala*. In the temples of the Pallava-Pandyas and their derivatives they come to be accommodated in the northern and southern *devakoshtha* niches on the exterior walls of the *ardha-mandapa*.

form the outer series of a typical *navaranga* with the four usual central pillars eliminated. Yet the *navarnaga* design is betrayed by the raised ceiling with nine coffered bays on top, eight of them surrounding a central larger one. Inside the open gaps of each one of the *vyalas* the stone mass has been very dexterously cut out into a round ball which can be rolled inside but not taken out, another feat of sculpture by the craftsman as is common in the Vijayanagar *vyala* pillars. The twelve columns are each marked by one of the twelve signs of the zodiac or *rasi* in the regular order and are, therefore, called the *rasi* pillars, the arrangement of the pillars being such that the rays of the sun fall on each one of them successively in the order of the twelve solar months. On the floor of the *mandapa* enclosed by the twelve pillars is inscribed a large circle with many converging lines to indicate the direction of the shadows cast by the pillars when the rays of the sun fall on them through one of the three door-openings, north, east and south. This is a rare combination of astronomy and architecture. The passage outside the ring of the *ranga-mandapa* pillars and between them and the outer wall has a roof made up of two rising stages, each with an outward slope while that over the central *ranga-mandapa* the ceiling is raised up still further as a clerestory. The roofing in this highly rain-soaked region is adequately designed by the laying above of the long channel stones sloping out and placed together, the adjacent parallel edges of every two channels being covered by an inverted channel stone, hood-like. This pattern is found followed in many other temples of this area and the western coastal strip on the other side of the Ghats. The large central bay on the ceiling of the *ranga-mandapa*, inside, thus coming to have a greater depth—forming as it were a *nabhichchanda vitana*, bears a well-defined inverted lotus blossom with many seriate petals and a large pendentive central torus which is pecked by four parrots perched, topsy-turvy, on the petals immediately surrounding the central torus. This is a novel but significant pattern, occupying the central *vitana* in place of the sculptured panel with the icon of the main deity consecrated in the sanctum often surrounded by eight *dikpalas* or guardians of the quarters placed all round, as has been usual in the earlier series of temples in this Chalukyan area. In conjunction with the *rasi* pillars arrangement, the *rasis* being the 'houses' which the sun is supposed to aspect in order of the twelve months; the central lotus is symbolic of the sun.

The four parrots perched topsy-turvy around the torus of the lotus blossom in the ceiling of the *rasi-mandapa* of the Vidyasankara temple, Sringeri, are incidentally the first examples of the kind. Their pose is also true to nature, attesting to the acquaintance of the sculptor with things of nature. The ornithologist will be reminded of the species of the Indian parrot (*Psittacula*), commonly called the *lorikeet*, which is unique among Indian birds for its habit of roosting upside down like a bat. To the ascetic yogi, it will be a form of *sadhana* or penance (*tapas*).

The superstructure of the *vimana* or *garbha* part is an upward continuation of the inner wall or *antara bhitti*. It is a tall cylindrical tower of three upper *talas* of gradually diminishing circumference raised over the sanctum terminating in the *griva* that carries the *sikhara* with the *stupi* on top, while the roof over the *antarala* carries a large *sukanasa* projected from the front of the *vimana* superstructure. It is thus a *chatushtala vimana* with a *sandhara aditala*. The top of the *sandhara* passage between the outer and inner walls of the *aditala* is made up of a system of channel-and-hood stones, as over the *mandapa* half in front, the long stones radiating from the base of the second *tala* with a proper slope giving rise to a slopy *alinda*. The usual *hara* scheme characteristic of southern *vimanas* made up of miniature shrine aedicules is totally eliminated over this part, the second and third *talas* and over the anterior *mandapa* top, nor does the pattern of the superstructure follow the local Hoysala style. The *aditalachadya* or roof is marked externally by the abbreviated *adhishthana* mouldings of the second *tala* base, the *harmya* of which is raised tall with the vertcally offset *bhadra* projections, the corners of the offsets cantoned by pilasters of the order as in the case of the *tala harmyas* of the southern *vimanas*. There are three niches provided in the main *bhadras* of the three cardinals, south, west, and north while on the east comes the prominent *sukanasa*. The *prastara* of this second *tala harmya* or the *uparichchadya* is composed of seven tiers of curved cornices or *kapotas*. The third *tala* of slightly lesser elevation repeats the same pattern ending with its *uparichchadya* of five *kapotas*, superposed one over the other. The fourth *tala* of still lesser height, again of the same pattern, carries an *uparichchadya* of the three *kapotas*. This scheme is an adaptation of the system of *uparichchadya* coming successively over the main *talachchadya*, with a clear but short or indistinct recessed neck intervening between any two, as obtains in the temples of the Eastern Ganga and Kalinga vintage but is a modification of the same with the respective sets of cornices here, forming the *tala harmyas*. The top of the third *tala* carrying the *grihapindi* or base of the *griva* has four Nandis at the four corners or *vidiks*. The circular *griva* shows a ribbed pattern because of the offsetting as in the *talas* below and the domical globular *sikhara*, too, exhibits the same pattern of ribbing. The *griva sikhara* combination has four *maha nasikas* projected on the four cardinals, including the eastern face, where the third *tala* of the *vimana* rises clear over the top of the frontal *sukanasa*. The *maha nasikas* are framed in front each by an ornate *mukhapatti* that carries at its apex, a *kalasa* or *stupi* that rises up round the base of the larger main *stupi* placed over the crest or *mastaka* of the *sikhara* proper. All the five *stupis* are of metal and they together form a *pancha kalasa* scheme, that according to ancient Buddhist texts should be the character of a *divya vimana*. The *sukanasa* in front rises in two stages on top of the *antarala*, the lower forming the rectangular *harmya* part with a vestibule internally leading to the inside of the hollow superstructural *talas*. This rises to the height of the second *tala* or the *harmya* over the sanctum. The *sala* type roof or *chadya* over this vestibule, rising to the height of the next *vimana tala*, is again a system of superposed cornices. The *sukanasa* with its longer side, east-west, has a *torana mukhapatti* framing its front that has a framed door-opening leading into the vestibule in the lower rectangular face and the sculptured relief of dancing Siva inside the arch fronting the upper or roof part of the *sukanasa*, a feature that is common to temples of the Chalukyan and northern areas. The *vimana* super-structure which has a hollow interior has its shell of externally carved stone work supported by a stone scaffolding built inside, made up of upright and cross-pieces of roughly hewn stone props and beams, a feature not noticed anywhere else in the south.

Thus this unique temple, which is a bold experiment, as it were, in the blending of architectural features, borrowed from far and near, and cleverly harmonized with a unique plan and elevational lay-out, is an interesting early Vijayanagar production of great merit. The intention was to make it a sort of universal amalgam of different regional architectural styles with its eclecticism in the sculpture too, in view of the importance of the spiritual master, whom both the royal house and the heads of the spiritual seat venerated equally.

Among the temples in Hampi following by and large the traits of the southern group may be mentioned the Vitthala temple, which is one of the largest there. It is, in fact, a great complex planned and built at one time, with *vimana*, axial *mandapas*, *garuda-mandapa*, other *mandapas*, including *kalyana-mandapas*, cloister *prakara* and *gopuras*. It was commenced by Krishnadeva Raya in 1513 and was perhaps still not completed when the empire fell in 1565 after which the capital was shifted to Penukonda.

The *mandapas* and *gopuras* are, as in all Vijayanagar temples, remarkable for their great size. The *mandapas* are often of the thousand-pillared variety. The pillars and pilasters have elegant shafts. The lower part of the abacus, the *pali*, which was a plain doucene in the Pallava and early Chola temples and got scalloped into petals in the later Chola period, evolves still more into a floral form with the petals, *idal*. The corbel evolves into what is called the *pushpa potika*, characteristic of the Vijayanagar style, with a double-flexed arm extending, projected from the main block and scalloped at the free end as upturned petals with an incipient conical bud at the centre. The downwardly flexed arm has a horizontal connective bar below it, connecting the free tip with the main block. The *kumbha panjara* motif on the wall recesses of *vimanas*, *gopuras* and *mandapas* is made more ornate and elaborate. The cornice, which was till now thick and curved down, becomes large, much thin and with a double flexure, and extends far forward, often showing the imitation in stone of the wooden ribs of the frame-work supporting it. In the case of *mandapas*, like the *kalyana-mandapa* of the Varadaraja temple at Kanchipuram, one of the finest examples of such kind, the corners of the *kapota* have large stone chains dangling down, all the links, including the cornice stone-piece from which it hangs down being cut out of one stone. These *mandapas*, the *kalyana-* or *utsava-mandapas*, are noted for their fine and intricately-worked colonnades in hardstone. Some of the pillars with a series of small columns are cut out round the main central shaft, or with large animal sculptures or statutes all in a monolithic mode. The *aniyottikkals*, as they are called, are characteristic of the Vijayanagar style. The superstructure of the stone *vimanas* or *gopuras* are of brick and mortar, often with timber inside if they are not built in the corbelled or *kadalika karana* fashion. Such immense *gopuras* were added to the outer-most *prakara* of pre-existing temple complexes of importance and are called *rayagopurams*, sometimes as many as eleven storeys high, as in the Ekamranatha at Kanchi, the Arunachala at Tiruvannamalai (North Arcot district) and the large Siva temple at Kalahasti (Chittoor district), all built by the great emperor, Krishnadeva Raya (1502-1529).

The Vitthala complex stands inside a high-walled, paved enclosure, with three *gopura* entrances, south and north. There are also axial and accessory *mandapas* and ancillary shrines. The axial series consisting of *vimanas* with front *mandapas* stands on an ornate platform, carved with friezes of men, horses, *hamsa*, and small shrine motifs. The steps leading up to the frontal *agra-mandapa* are flanked by the large stone elephants. The *agra-mandapa* itself contains huge monolithic pillars with carved-out columnettes, or with large *vyalas* having riders on their backs. The hall has cruciform extensions in front and on the sides. The beams show carvings from the *Ramayana*. The superstructure of the *vimana* is of brickwork. The *hara* of the *aditala* is extended over the tops of the front *mandapas*. In front of the *agra-mandapa* stands the *garuda-mandapa* which is a lesser *vimana* fashioned in the form of a temple-car on chariot on stone wheels. On the northern side of the fore-court is the Amman shrine, while on the south is the beautiful though small *kalyana-mandapa*. There are also shrines for other attendant deities in the courtyard. The Krishna temple built by Krishnadeva Raya in 1513 is another handsome temple complex with the usual components of attendant shrines, the *mandapas* and pillared *malikas* and *gopura*.

The Pattabhirama temple at Hampi is yet another large temple complex of this kind. Built by Achyuta Raya (1530-1542), it is noted for its great size and huge proportions. The Achyuta Raya temple built in 1539 is another large structure inside a double *prakara* with *gopuras* and an Amman shrine, *mandapas* and cloister, designed on lines similar to the famous Vitthala temple, though it will not bear comparison with that superb creation. Its pillars are, however, handsome and it contains some fine sculptures.

The Anantasayin temple at Anantasayanagudi near Hospet on the way to Hampi is an example of a large oblong *vimana* with the brickwork superstructure having an immense *sala sikhara*. It is elaborated axially by a large pillared *mandapa,* and surrounded by other peripheral *mandapas* and an Amman shrine. The whole is enclosed within a *prakara* with a large *gopura.* It is the largest *sala*-type *vimana* known. The temple was dedicated to Anantasayin Vishnu, but the deity is now missing. The shrine front has three doors to render the head, body and feet of the reclining god visible from the *antarala.*

Besides the extension of the *hara* over the *mandapas*—a prevailing trait of Chalukyan extraction—there are other Chalukyan characters retained by some of the other temples in Hampi, and in the Deccan, Andhra and north Mysore area. Among them are the presence of the *sukanasika* in front of the *vimana* superstructure, the occurrence of the sculptures of the river goddess on the door-jambs, and ornate over-doors, often delicately carved in softstone and fitted over the plain granite door-frames, as in the temples at Tadpatri (Anantapur district). Then there is the *navaranga* pattern of the *mandapas,* as opposed to the linear multi-pillared type of the farther south, and free-standing *toranas* as in the temples on top of the hill at Chitaldrug (Mysore state).

The Hazara Rama temple was probably begun earlier and was completed by Krishnadeva Raya. This temple is devoid of the characteristic *gopura* but its *prakara* walls are decorated by friezes, externally depicting dance, music and folk festivals. The *maha-mandapa* in front of the main *vimana* is of the Chalukyan *navaranga* pattern and its four central pillars, in contrast to the greyish granite of the rest of the entire structure, are polished shining black, though of square section, and embellished with panels of sculpture and carvings. The *vimana* superstructure of brick has a prominent *sukanasika.* There is an Amman shrine *vimana* to its north, also of the same type. The walls of the open *agra-mandapa* and of the *vimanas* as also of the *prakara* on the inner faces around its north-east corner have panel sculptures which are narrative, depicting episodes from the *Ramayana* and the Krishna-*lilas.*

The Pampapati or Virupaksha temple, the most prominent temple in Hampi, and in worship, is a large complex, elaborated round a later Chalukyan temple nucleus. Its *agra-mandapa* of the Vijayanagar period is noted for its sculptured columns and contemporary ceiling paintings. The most interesting painting is a panel depicting the sage Vidyaranya, a lineal successor of

Sankaracharya and pontiff of the Sringeri *matha*, being taken in a procession in a palanquin with royal honours and paraphernalia to the Virupaksha temple. The hollow, tall, main, east *gopura*, built of brick in the corbelled fashion is one of the largest Vijayanagar *gopuras*. The Vijayanagar *vimanas* farther south in Tamil Nadu do not have the *sukanasika*. They conform more to the Pallava-Chola traditions and form a continuing link with temples of the earlier epochs.

THE POST-VIJAYANAGAR TEMPLES

After the fall of the central power following the disastrous battle of Talikotta in 1564 and the ruination of Vijayanagar city, the capital of the empire was shifted in succession to Penukonda, Chandragiri and finally to Vellore. The central power was much weakened. The Vijayanagar viceroys in the southern regions, the Nayakas, gradually assumed independent powers. Some of them fostered temple architecture and created some notable temples. They were the Nayakas of Vellore (North Arcot district), Gingee (South Arcot district), Thanjavur and Madurai in Tamil Nadu, and Ikkeri in north-west Mysore. The Nayaka period in Tamil Nadu witnessed the addition of elaborate *mandapas* of the hundred-pillared type , and larger *gopuras* with a greater number of plastic stucco figures on them, as at Vellore and Madurai, their tallest *gopura* superstructure being at Srivilliputtur (Ramanathapuram district) in front of the Vatapatrasayin temple. The closed ambulatory, flanked on either side by continuous platforms, with massive pillars set on their edges on either side of the sunken *pradakshina* path, and elaborately corbelled brackets on top spanning the gap above and nearly meeting each other, built during Nayaka and later times, form the celebrated 'corridors', as at Ramesvaram. The *kalyana-mandapa* of the Jalakanthesvara temple at Vellore, and a similar one in the eastern *prakara* of the famous Ranganatha temple at Srirangam, like the earlier Vijayanagar structure in the Varadaraja temple at Kanchi, are two of the great masterpieces of the time. They are of the multipillared type, having a facade row of remarkably sculptured columns carrying almost full-size monolithic figure sculptures of rearing horses with warrior-riders and retinue and other animal figures of the hunt.

Most constituents of the large temple complex at Madurai on all sides of the nuclear shrine are of Nayaka origin, mostly of the time of Tirumalai Nayaka (1623-1659), including the great *mandapas* and towering *gopuras* on all the four sides. The huge pillars have life-size portraits of royalty with consorts and retinue, or donor-chiefs; the sculpture are so cut out as to form along with the main shaft a common support to the capital. Other sculptures of gods, women in graceful poses, tribal folk like the *kurava* and *kuratti*—hunter and huntress—are also to be found in the composition on the pillars. The Pudu *mandapam* in the Minakshi-Sundaresvara temple at Madurai, and the front *mandapa* in the temple at Krishnapuram are notable examples in this respect among hundreds of others.

The Subrahmanya temple unit, with *vimana ardha-* and *mukha-mandapas* standing in the north-west court of the Brihadisvara temple complex, is a typical example of the Nayaka temple of the ornate variety and a real gem of its kind. Built of fine-grained granite, it exhibits in the mouldings of its *adhishthana* and pilasters of its wall some fine and intricate engraving. The characteristic *kumbha panjara* in the wall-recesses between pilasters is rendered highly ornate, as also the *pushpa potika* corbel of the capitals over the pillars and polygonal pilasters, with the pendent bud at the tip of the curved arm taking the shape of a full lotus bud. The double-flexed *kapota* is thin and elegant showing the ribbed supporting frame-work on its under side. The *griva* and *sikhara* of the square *vimana* are hexagonal, in conformity with the six-faced Shanmukha form of Subrahmanya installed in the sanctum. The *karnakutas* too of the *tala haras* of this multi-storeyed *vimana* are six-sided. This and other temples thus formed easily the pattern for the living art of the modern *sthapati* or temple-builder of south India.

Another feature initiated by the Nayakas of Madurai and continued thereafter is the employment of polished granite—the external faces of the plain carved or moulded stones, polished shining black, and used in the construction of small *vimanas* and their *ardha-mandapas*. Such work can be seen in the rock fort temple at Tiruchirapalli, Madurai, and other places.

The entire temple complex inside the Vellore fort including the *kalayana-mandapa* and *gopura*, as also much of the Virinchipuram temple near Vellore, is the work of the Bommi

Nayakas of Vellore. What we see, however, of temples or their ruins inside the extensive fort at Gingee and its neighbourhood is the creation of Gingee Nayakas. Similarly, there are many small Nayaka temples inside the Chandragiri fort.

What may be reasonably considered to be the quintessence of later Vijayanagar architecture and sculptural art, as evolved in the southern half of the Vijayanagar empire, is the unique example of a moderate-sized temple unit in the large Ranganatha temple complex in Srirangam. It may as well be considered to be the precursor of, or the model for, the exquisitely designed and ornately carved Subrahmanya temple unit of Nayaka times, inside the enclosure of the Thanjavur Brihadisvara temple complex. On the basis of an inscription from elsewhere it is believed by some scholars, following the epigraphist's report (A.R.E., 1937), that the Vaishnavite teacher of Kuruhurpura who was in charge of the Tiru-k-kulal-udina Pillai (Venugopala Krishna) temple at Halebid that was consecrated by the Hoysala queen, Umadevi, was during his visit to Srirangam, also, instrumental in consecrating a shrine for Venugopala in that temple complex.

There is a superbly built temple unit of Venugopala extant, with exquisite sculptures on its walls and very fine architectural features, also with a painted ceiling on its *agra-mandapa* (done in Lepakshi style). It is located inside the fifth south *prakara*, west of the *utsava-mandapam*, called locally *ranga-mandapam*. It is a temple unit by itself, facing east with a *dvitala vimana* that has an *aditala* built of fine grained white granite surmounted by a brickwork superstructure, *ardha-*, *maha-* and *agra-mandapas* preceding the *vimana*, in the order. The *upa-pitha* and *adhishthana* are of finely carved mouldings adorned by miniature shrine motifs or aedicules, at intervals, as in the Darasuram *mandapam*. The central *bhadra* reliefs on the walls of the *vimana* and the *mandapas* have *devakoshthas* crowned by *sala sikharas*, the niches containing lithesome sculptures of divine-looking damsels in various poses of suffused grace and beauty. The recessed wall spaces carry fully formed *kumbha panjara* motifs, in the *vimana* part, while in similar situations on the *mandapas* they are elaborately carved *vritta sphathitas*, the so called 'decorative pilasters', that is pilasters carrying on top a *panjara* crest, but devoid of the basal *kumbha* or *purna ghata*. The *pushpa potikas* are of the characteristic Vijayanagar type. These and the advanced architectural features as also the style of the extant paintings on the ceiling of the *agra-mandapa* or porch would only indicate a later Vijayanagar date (bordering on the Nayaka times that succeeded). It may perhaps be a Vijayanagar renovation of an earlier foundation during the Hoysala interregnum and not a standing Hoysala example as some scholars aver in the wake of the suggestion of the epigraphist. There are a few granite stone-built temples of the Hoysala times, built when a collateral branch of the dynasty ruled over parts of Tamil Nadu with the capital at Kannanur near Srirangam and Jambukesvaram. They are all built in the local regional style in logical continuation of the late Pandya temples of Tamil Nadu and consequently heralding features of the Vijayanagar temples of Tamil Nadu that followed.

Such temples of the Hoysala times are to be found in Kannanur, some 6 kms from Srirangam (Posalesvara, called locally Bhojesvara) and in Jambukesvaram, in the eastern part of the Srirangam island. There are a few more constructed by the Hoysala generals and administrators, in the Tiruchirapalli and Pudukkottai districts, for example the temple unit at Sembattur (Pudukkottai). These temples built during the Hoysala interregnum reveal in their architecture and sculpture only the local regional norms, and not of the Hoysala patterns as known in their home country (Karnataka) built of soft soapstone. The Srirangam Venugopala temple shows noticeably far advanced architectural and sculptural features of the local regional style. The sculpture of the tall, slender-built graceful maidens, perhaps many of them depicting *gopis*, besides *salabhanjikas* in different attitudes and poses, contrast with the short-built and buxom *madanikas*, of Belur, Halebid and similar feminine sculpture in other centres of Hoysala art. The Venugopala temple sculptures may bear comparison, if one is at all required, with the similar hardstone caryatid (*madanika*) sculptures of the Kakatiyas and, nearer home, with those at Krishnapuram and Tenkasi (Tirunelveli district) and in the Pudu *mandapam* and other parts of the Madurai-Minakshi-Sundaresvara temple.

The Ikkeri Nayakas have left temples of a Chalukyan affiliation in their capital towns of Ikkeri, Keladi, and in other places in their area. The Aghoresvara temple at Ikkeri (Shimoga district) is the largest and finest of the Ikkeri style of temples. Built of granite, it stands on a lofty and well-moulded *upa-pitha* platform.

Its five-storeyed square *vimana* is a double-walled *sandhara* structure, and the *tala* superstructure has the characteristic *sukanasika* projection. The *griva* and *sikhara* are octagonal. The square, closed-front *mandapa* has three projected openings—one frontal and two lateral with elaborate over-doors, as is also the case with the *antarala* and shrine doors inside. They are reached by flights of steps with ornamental balustrades. A horizontal band divides the exterior wall face into upper and lower halves. The upper half shows a series of pointed arches enclosing lattice windows with floral spandril decorations and rhomboid rosettes, introducing an element of Indo-Islamic motifs. The lower half shows a series of shrine fronts between paired pilasters. Inside, the *mandapa* is of the *navaranga* pattern with ornate pillars, some of which have the animal statutory characteristic of the Vijayanagar and post-Vijayanagar pillars.

The twin temples of Ramesvara and Virabhadra in nearby Keladi, the earlier seat of the dynasty, are built of greyish-green granite. The two separate *vimanas* have their front *mandapas* interconnected. The Ramesvara was built between 1499 and 1513, and the Virabhadra between 1530 and 1540. Both are *sandhara vimanas* with their walls made up of large slabs laid in longitudinal tiers and sparsely carved, as is commonly found in many of the smaller temples in Hampi, and in the northern area. The pillars inside the *mandapa* are in the typical Vijayanagar pattern and the ceiling slabs are carved with designs and motifs, some of them reminiscent of Indo-Islamic designs.

9

OTHER TEMPLE TYPES

THE KADAMBA-CHALUKYA STYLE TEMPLES

While the early Chalukyas took in the early norms of *vimana* architecture, developed them according to their own regional idiom and evolved the early forms of such types, they also devoted equal attention to the forms more prevalent in the region which was earlier dominated by the Kadambas of Banavasi. They took note of what was developing further north. Their geographical position astride the area of the Deccan, dividing the peninsula from the northern half of the subcontinent, made them susceptible to more influences than one. The result was that the cradles of early Chalukyan architecture and art, namely, Mahakutesvar, Aihole, Pattadkal and Badami, and lower down in Andhra-Karnataka region round about Kurnool in Satyavolu and Mahanandi—bordering the Eastern Chalukyan branch of Vengi—produced a mixed variety of temples: the northern, the southern, and those locally known as Kadamba.

The Kadamba-Chalukya or Kadamba-*Nagara* type in its simplest form has a square *vimana* body with a low superstructure that is a stepped pyramid of successively receding tiers, essentially eaves-like or of *kapota*-like form, often separated from one another by short recessed necks standing for the *talas*. The *kapota* tiers are decorated by relieved *kuda* motifs, particularly at the centre on each side. These in their vertical alignment simulate the *rekha* of a northern-style *prasada sikhara*. The separating necks, or *galas,* may be altogether absent or much abbreviated so as not to be visible. The topmost tier carries a short *griva* with a distinct *amalasila,* or *amalaka,* which has a ribbed globular or lenticular shape which is the characteristic top member of the northern *prasada* superstructure or alternately the *griva* may carry a *sikhara* with a *stupi* as in the southern *vimana* forms. The former resembles the so-called *pidadeuls* of Orissan architecture or the *phansanakara* edifices of the Gujarat region. In more developed forms with the *amalaka* crest, the corners of the tiers are further provided at intervals with similar smaller *amalaka* forms, the *karnamalakas*, as in the northern-style temples. It will be evident that this system of tiered arrangement of slopy roof slabs or cornices curved one over the other was best suited to a region of high rainfall, as was the original Kadamba region on the west coast. It witnessed further developments in the area of coastal Konkan and in the succeeding centuries spread even beyond to the east as far as the lower reaches of the Krishna and the Tungabhadra. The earliest structures in stone, as in some examples in Aihole, though possessing the *amalaka* head and the *karnamalakas*, lack the *sukanasika*, the invariable characteristic of north Indian temple forms. It may be said that this form with either type of top member and devoid of or with the *sukanasika* is more or less a cross between the typical northern *prasada* superstructure and the southern *vimana* form. This type is exemplified by the Mallikarjuna group (*c.* eighth century) near the Galaganatha temple at Aihole,[1] the Lakulisa temple on the way to the *bhutanatha* group in the Badami valley and in the Mahakutesvar group, all of the Badami-Chalukya-Rashtrakuta origin. The group of smaller shrines behind the Mahanandisvara temple complex at Mahanandi (Kurnool district), and the Papanasanam group of temples in Alampur, are of this type in the Eastern Chalukyan territory. Eight of the nine structures of the Lakshmi Devi temple complex in Doddagaddavalli (Hassan district, Mysore)[2] built in 1113 are of this type belonging to the Hoysala period. The Ganigitti Jain temple built in 1385, the similar Jain temple on the hill at Chippagiri (Bellary district), the group of *trikuta* shrines on the Hemakutam hill adjoining the Pampapati temple in Hampi, and two more just near its *gopura* as also another a mile north-east of Hampi are examples of such types built in the Vijayanagar

---

[1] Cousens, *Chalukyan Architecture of the Kanarese Districts*, Archaeological Survey of India, Vol. XLII, New Imperial Series, 1926, pl. XXV labelled "the back of the temple of Galaganatha and temple Nos. 37 & 38". These are also called Gandaragudi and Galaganatha.

[2] Narasimhachar, R., *The Lakshmi Devi Temple on Doddagaddavalli*, Mysore Archaeological Series, Architecture and Sculpture in Mysore, No. III, 1919.

period. It is perhaps because the Ganigitti and Chippagiri temples were of Jain dedication that Longhurst chose to call the temples on the Hemakutam hill as Jain too, though they are, from evidence found on them, Brahminical.[1]

A variant of this form, looking like a cross between the tiered *talas* of the southern *vimana* and the schematic and undifferentiated *bhumis* of the northern *prasada*, often with *amalakas* compressed at the corners, is also to be found distributed over the same region in different periods. In this type, each of the *bhumis* is differentiated by simple, short, pilastered and recessed walls that divide the entire pyramidal superstructure into square sectioned strata. The top is crowned by a *griva, amalasila,* and *stupi*, as is usual in northern *prasadas*. This is exemplified by the Galaganatha at Aihole, with a plain stepped-up superstructure with *karna malakas* (temple No. 10 of Cousens).[2] The Mallikarjuna temple at Aihole is an example of this kind without the *karnamalakas*. The other structures standing inside the enclosure of the Mahakutesvara temple complex, except the Makutesvara and the Mallikarjuna which are southern *vimana* type and the Sangamesvara which is of the northern *prasada* type, are variants of the Chalukya-Kadamba style. Similar temples are to be found at Terala near Nagarjunakonda (Guntur district). In the Kadamba territory itself, as at Hangal, Belagami, and other places, the type assumes a form which has a tiered superstructure of receding horizontal slab-like components, a series of upright lotus, bud-shaped projections or 'dentils' along their upper edges in addition to *kudu*-like ornament at the centre, a square *vimana*-type *sikhara* on top, and a *sukanasika* in front. This type became more common in the northern territories of the Vijayanagar empire, as at Hampi.

THE NORTHERN STYLE *PRASADA* TEMPLES OF THE CHALUKYAS AND THE RASHTRAKUTAS

The *prasada*-type structures with square bodies and proportionately immense curvilinear superstructures quite different in form

---

[1] Longhurst, A.H., *Hampi Ruins*, Government of India publications, Delhi, Third Edition, 1933.

[2] *Ibid*, pl. XIX, Aihole temple No. 10 from south-west.

and composition from the superstructure having tiered *talas* with *haras* of the *vimanas* were also built by the early Chalukyas in Aihole and Pattadkal along with the other types, as mentioned earlier. These also came to be built in other parts of Karnataka and Andhra. The *sikhara* in these temples connotes the entire super- structure over the part enclosing the sanctum, forming a single unit called the *anda*, differentiated into nodes defined by small gooseberry-shaped *karnamalakas* at the corners, all compressed in such a manner that a clear-cut storeyed division, as in the *talas* of a southern *vimana*, is not revealed. There are only undifferentiat- ed *bhumis*. This *sikhara* of the *rekha-prasada* carries on top a *gala* or *griva* that holds up the large *amalaka*-shaped *amalasara* or *amalasila* with a *stupi* or *kalasa* finial on its top. Thus it would be clear that what is termed as the *sikhara* in a northern *rekha-prasada* is not to be equated with what is known by the same name in the southern tiered *vimana*. The smaller *amalakas* found squeezed in at the corners of the superstructure of the *prasada*, hence called *karnamalakas*, are the only basis for differentiating the *bhumis*. These northern-type *prasadas* in the Karnataka and Andhra region of the peninsula, with their characteristic Chalukyan idiom, despite their individual variations, form a group that stands quite apart from such *prasada* temples of western, northern or eastern India. Their *adhishthanas* generally follow the patterns found in the southern *vimana*, and the body is provided with a clear *prastara* entablature separating the superstructural part over it. The square plan or quadrature is relieved by three or five bays on each face from base to top, the relieved parts being called *rathas*, making the temple *tri ratha* or *pancha ratha*, as the case may be. The most characteristic and conspicuous *sukanasika* is projected from the front side of the superstructure over the *antarala* roof and is almost as wide as the front face of the *sikhara* at its lowest part and projecting forwards, to an extent equal at least to half, if not two-thirds, the basal width of the *sikhara* in the earlier examples. The axial *mandapas* are, however, of the same pattern as those of the *vimana* temples of the region, and their flat roofs help to make the projected *sukanasika* more evident than in the northern-style temples elsewhere, in which the *sukanasikas* hardly exceed in width the central bay or *bhadra* projection. Besides the *mandapas*, these northern-style temples of the Chalukyan area share much in common with the local *vimana* types in respect of their pillar forms, door-frames, sculptures, particularly *dvarapalas* on either side of the entrances, iconography and other features of embellishment.

The Huchchimalligudi, the Huchchappayyagudi, and the Tarappagudi in Aihole, the Siddhanakolla near it, the Mallikarjuna in Mahakutesvara, and the Kadasiddhesvara, the Jambulinga, the Papanatha, the Kasivisvesvara and the Galaganatha in Pattadkal are the most important of such examples to be found in the Badami Chalukyan territory. The Huchchimalligudi, the Huchchappayyagudi, and the Mallikarjuna are the earliest of this group. These are generally *tri rathas* with front *mandapas*. The outer wall is plain or decorated and often provided with a pillared porch. The former ones are of *sandhara* type, while the latter one is of the *nirandhara* type, though they are similar in general outward form to the first.

The Kadasiddhesvara and the Jambulinga at Pattadkal are the simplest ones. They have a sanctum with a *tri ratha sikhara* and a *mandapa* in front. The Kasivisvesvara is *pancha ratha*, while the Galaganatha is *sandhara* with three sides of the sanctum outer wall conspicuously projected as flat-roofed porches, and with a *tri ratha sikhara*. The Papanatha has a low and linear plan with a stunted *sikhara* over the main edifice which appears to be too small in proportion to the whole length made up of the disproportionately large *antarala* in front of the sanctum, with a *mandapa* and a portico as its front. The most interesting feature is the *hara* of *salas* with *karnakutas* at the front corners and a few *panjaras* in between that extend continuously over the roof of the axial *mandapas*, a southern feature appropriate only to the *vimana* type of temples. The Sangamesvara in the Mahakutesvara group is of the *tri ratha* lay-out with a pillared *mandapa* in front. The presence of a chute in the form of groove ending as an oblong opening on top of the *adhishthana* on its northern side as a water outlet from the floor of the sanctum is an interesting feature.

In the Eastern Chalukyan area comprising the district of Kurnool, Mahboobnagar and Guntur, we have such *rekha-prasada*-type temples built from the seventh-eighth centuries. In the *navabrahma* complex of nine temples in Alampur, all except the *tarakabrahma*, which is of the southern *vimana* type, are of this variety. They mostly date earlier than AD 713 when, as stated in an inscription, the *prakara* enclosing the whole group was built by

Isánacharya. They are mostly *nirandhara* while a few are *sandhara*. Each unit consists of a sanctum with a well-proportioned *tri ratha sikhara,* an *antarala* and pillared *mandapa* with a two-tiered flat roof. The whole axial series has a single entrance in front and a continuous wall surrounding it, forming also the outer wall of the cell in the *sandhara* type. The exterior wall faces are richly carved with niches, surmounted by *udgama* motifs containing fine sculptures and lattice windows. The carvings are fine, and reminiscent of the central Indian and Rajasthani styles. The Balabrahma is the most advanced and elaborate specimen of the group.

The Mahanandi group of temple units, also enclosed by a common *prakara*, consists, among other structures, of six miniature shrines of varying types in one group and four smaller shrines in another behind the principal Mahanandisvara, which is a *sandhara rekha-prasada* with a *tri ratha* type *sikhara*, datable to AD 750. The Bhimalingesvara and Ramalingesvara of the complex at Satyavolu (Kurnool district) that form the principal units of the group are both *nirandhara* with a *tri ratha sikhara*, over a square body. They, in addition to having the *adhishthana* akin to that of the southern *vimana* type, show also a *vyala vari* or *vyala mala*, a frieze of *vyalas* in the entablature, an invariable component of the *prastara* of the southern *vimana* temples, and absent in all the other *rekha-prasadas*. The larger Ramalingesvara has a sanctum, *antarala* and axial *mandapas* in front. The shrine wall is plain but for a *devakoshtha* niche on each side. Among the diminutive shrines are to be found specimens with square, rectangular and apsidal plans. The square one is similar in form to the Huchchimalligudi with a stepped-up series of six horizontal *kapota*-like tiers crowned by an *amalasara*, an example of the Kadamba-Chalukya model.

The Panchalingesvara, also near Kurnool, though much renovated, also belongs to this class. It is *sandhara* in plan and its present superstructure is a modern renovation in the Kadamba-Chalukya style. It has a pillared *mandapa* in front with a central raised clerestory roof and lateral wings with slopy roofs. It contains an inscription of Vijayaditya's time, about AD 750. Another well-preserved temple of this type is to be found in Bandi Tandrapadu nearby with a *nirandhara* body, having carvings of Ganesa, Durga and Kartikeya on the relieved *bhadra* niches on its sides. The *sukanasika* in front of the *sikhara* is prominent.

The Somesvara at Chebrolu, and the Panchalingesvara at

Panchalingula also belong to this category. The miniature shrines found in the Yelesvaram excavations are akin to the diminutive experiments found in the Satyavolu and Mahanandi complexes.

This type of *rekha-prasadas* soon fell out of vogue in these areas; it could not extend any further south into the Tamil territory.

THE KERALA TEMPLE TYPES

The Kerala temples form a class by themselves because of the material used in their construction that includes timber to a large extent, as was the case everywhere in south India before the advent of the stone *vimanas*. Though in a few places the *vimana* temples of the medieval and late medieval periods and styles (as in Tamil Nadu) are to be found, the vast majority have their bases and walls built of granite and laterite, respectively, with the roof of wooden planks, or tiles, or sheet metal over timber frames, and their forms are adapted to suit the high rainfall of the region. While the *adhishthana* of the *vimana* or *srikoyil* is of moulded stone with all parts resembling those of the *adhishthana* of the southern temples, the walls are usually of laterite blocks which are abundant in the area, and can be cut and shaped easily when freshly quarried. Because of their rough and pitted surface, the walls are heavily plastered and the few decorations are picked out in stucco. The walls form a good ground for mural paintings which take the place of relief sculptures. The Kerala temples are thus noted for their rich colour paintings executed on the lime-plastered walls in fresco technique. The roof timbers rest directly on the wall plate on top of the walls, and converge in gable form to meet at the top. The roofing material covering the timber framework is clinker-built. It is made up of laminated wooden planks overlapping one another and covered over by clinkertiles or tiles highly heated in kilns with a vitreous or glassy smooth surface that makes them waterproof. It is this fish-scale-like overlapping pattern of tiles that is found reproduced in the covering plaster of the brick-and-mortar *sikharas* of the southern *vimanas*. The roof may alternatively be of metal sheet—copper or brass, which is again found imitated even in the earliest monolith-ic models at Mahabalipuram, the Draupadi *ratha*, for instance. Like the Draupadi *ratha*, the Kerala temples in their simplest form

have only the four essential parts instead of six of the simple
vimana, namely, the *adhishthana* or base, the *bhitti* or wall, the
skikhara or roof, and the *stupi* or finial. The *prastara* and *griva*
below the ultimate roof are eliminated. The entablature and *hara*
may be seen in storeyed forms only. The usual plan for the *srikoyil*
or *vimana* is the square or the circle and the apsidal. The rectangle
is more common for the *mandapas* and *gopuras* which are called
padi-p-pura. The rafters of the roof project beyond the wall,
forming well-formed eaves-like *kapotas*. These are often additionally supported by a carved wooden frame-work with carved
wooden brackets sprung from the walls, caryatid-like. In larger
vimanas the body is *sandhara* or double-walled with a
circumambulatory, or *idai nali*, round the shrine chamber, the
inner wall rising up to form a second *tala* as it were, and carrying
the conical or pyramidal gable roof. The circumambulatory has a
roof at a lesser level which slopes down from the middle height
of the inner wall and projects eaves-like over the top of the outer
wall. The conical or slopy main roof has dormer, or *nasika*,
projections, which are called *kilivasal* locally, with finely-carved
wooden *torana* frames fronting them. Their entire forms, or at
least their fronts—*mukhapatti*, retain the arched or horse-shoe
shape in most cases, while in some they are simply triangular.
The local name *kilivasal* (parrot entrance) is suggestive of the
name *sukanasika*. It is not also unusual for the outer wall to be
circular, with the inner one round the sanctum square, or vice-
versa. Normally, there is only one entrance on the east or west of
the *srikoyil*. On the remaining three sides there are niches or false
doors. In some cases, the entrances are found on both east and
west, the space inside the shrine chamber being divided into an
eastern and a western half by a transverse wall, each half
containing a different deity. In front of the entrance is a flight of
stone steps flanked by stone side-slabs or balustrades, which
contain rich relief sculptures, the banister or coping being shaped
in the form of an elephant trunk issuing from a *vyala* mouth, or
similar interesting patterns. The *pranala*, or water-outlet, projected from the northern side, is of a characteristic shape—thick,
long, cylindrical and tube-like, with a narrow bore made through
it, simulating a straight elephant's trunk emerging out of a *vyala*
mouth. Externally, it is often ribbed and divided into ringed
nodes at intervals and supported below by a *bhuta* or *gana*. The

srikoyil has a detached small front *mandapa*, often square with a slopy roof, called the *namaskara-mandapa*. Externally, the quadrangular open court is surrounded by a *prakara* with a cloister, or *malika*, locally called *nalambalam* or *chuttambalam*. There may be more quadrangular enclosures, the outermost with the main *gopura* entrance or *padi-p-pura*, in front, occasionally with additional ones on the rear and on the sides. Besides the inner *prakara* which is simpler, larger temple complexes like the Vadakkunnathan temple in Trichur have an outer *prakara* with storeyed *gopura* entrances on all the four sides, and detached halls or *mandapas* in the court, like the *rangasala* or *kuttambalam*, for operas, dances and similar performances, for which Kerala is noted, especially dance-dramas and pantomime shows, like *Kathakah Ottantullal*, etc. In the Vadakkunnathan temple, the subsidiary shrine for Sasta, at the north-east corner of the outer court is apsidal with a timber-and-metal sheet roof.

Most of the Kerala temples now existing are not very old, the oldest dating from medieval or post-medieval times. The cldest ones, because of the perishable fabric of construction, have been lost, but for their stone *adhishthanas* and sculptures of gods, *dvarapalas*, etc. These give us an idea of the continuity from at least the tenth century AD if not earlier.

Such temples with prominent slopy or pent roofs, or ridged-roofs on gables, are to be found extensively distributed over the entire monsoon-swept littoral, from Kanyakumari in the south to south Kanara and Goa on the north. Their *srikoyil* or *vimana* plans include the circular, which is more frequent, the elliptical, the square, the oblong and the apsidal, and they rise often in more than one storey. When storeyed, the lower storeys have their slopy or pent roofs resting on rafters with their overhanging eaves on the outer walls further supported by brackets sprung from the outer wall and sloping down from beams on hooks fixed at a higher lever on the inner wall. The top storey over the innermost wall is covered over by a conical or four-sided *kuta* roof with a single finial in the case of circular, octagonal, and square structures, or by a ridged *sala* or *sabha* type on gable walls, with a row of *stupis* in the case of the oblong and apsidal structures. The *adhishthana* is invariably of granitic stone, while the walls and superstructure may be of granite, laterite or brick and timber. The roof is made of planks, metal sheet or tiles, or even thatch in extremely humble cases. Most of these temples, some with original foundations dating from the tenth-eleventh centuries, have been considerably renovated and reconstructed in their upper parts in recent centuries and as a result do not reveal much that can be attributed to or interpreted as evolutionary trends.

Usually what goes unnoticed is the internal make-up and structural contents of the *srikoyil*, since, by ritual, tradition and convention, the interior of the Kerala temple is totally inaccessible to any except the ordinated priesthood. What one perceives of the *srikoyil* is in fact an external shell, as it were, of a core *vimana* or *garbhakudya* inside. The internal core containing the *garbha* or sanctum is in essentials a *vimana* form as found elsewhere in the south, often with a full complement of its *angas* in the tiered superstructure over the cella, including the crest or *sikhara*, or more commonly ending up with its *griva*; in either case the superstructure is raised up over the cella by the system of internal corbelling or *kadalika karana*. The pedestal of the principal deity on the sanctum floor is called the *pithika*, and the space all round it inside the cella, the *vithika*, the wall of the cella itself being called the *antara mandala*. The circuit outside the *antara mandala*, in which are erected the rings of pillars to support the external roofing, is the *antara hara*, which is circumscribed by the *antara bhitti* or inner wall of the *srikoyil* between which and the *bahya bhitti* or outermost wall, in a *sandhara* structure, runs the ambulatory passage called the *idai nali*. The plan of this nuclear unit often does not correspond with the ground plan of the *srikoyil* and its plinth and it is usual to find that the cella is square, inside what is externally a circular or apsidal structure or vice versa. The ultimate external conical (domical) or ridged roof either covers the inner *sikhara* over the nuclear inner structure like an umbrella with its *stupi* or it is made to rest on the top of the *griva* itself, forming *sikhara* with *stupi* as common to both.

The eaves (*avalambana*) of this *sikhara* is extended and rendered slopy on all sides (with dormer projections or *nasikas* projected out of the faces) in order to overhang and shelter the *tala* face below the external superstructure even as the *chadyas* or projected, slopy eaves from the various levels below do in respect of the parts below them, the lowest among them, in the case of a multi-storeyed structure or the *avalambana* of the single main roof or *sikhara* in the case of the *ekatala* or single-storeyed structure coming to overshadow the main outer wall that rises over the *adhishthana* of the structure.

While, essentially, the nuclear fane or the sanctum sanctorum is of the usual *vimana* type as found developed in the mainland part east of the Western Ghats, the outer *srikoyil* structure is an adaptation to form a protective armour, so to say, shielding the inner core from the excessive and continuous monsoon precipitation of the western littoral, much like an umbrella—single- or multiple-tiered—or a shell. The plan of the *srikoyil*, as mentioned earlier, is generally square, or may be oblong or elliptical when intended to house reclining deities, or circular, or apsidal, the apse arms having often a proportionately greater width to approximate in shape a semi-circle, as suggested by the descriptive name *chapa* (bow). The roofing or *sikhara* is *kutagara* or domical, the sides converging to an apex with a single *stupi* or *salakara* with gable ends, extended, with a longitudinal ridge on top carrying a row of *stupis*, in either case, as appropriate to the plan and shape of the structure below. In addition to the simple, single-storeyed *srikoyil*, two- and three-storeyed types are also common. But judging from the local texts and from the extant models of *srikoyils* a *talachchanda* of more than three storeys does not seem to be contemplated or attempted. The *nirandhara* (single-walled) *ekatala* structure is devoid of a *sukanasa*, while the *sandhara* (double-walled with an annular passage in between) *ekatala* structure of any plan has of necessity a *sukanasa*, as dictated by its very *sandhara* nature, as also the double or triple-storeyed ones. The multi-storeyed types exhibit a *hara* scheme of aedicules at top of each tier or *tala* (equated with the term *griva* in Kerala texts), of successively diminishing height in their arrangement one over the other. The true *sandhara* nature may be inferred, even from outside, by the fact that superposed eaves of the multi-storeyed structure (that are, of course, separated from one another, in the vertical plane, by the intervening *tala* or *griva*) comes over the *hara* elements of the *tala prastara* below, as an overhanging *chadya*. This, because the respective *chadyas* emerge from what would otherwise be the *kapota* tier of the *tala prastara* in a southern *vimana* prototype. In the *nirandhara* pattern with a thick wall, the *hara* aedicules would appear to be placed over the line of emergence of the *chadyas* or eaves, since it is a case of the *chadyas* being sprung at convenient levels and strutted up in position by the carved brackets sprung from the wall itself. Internally the support for the *sikhara* roof and the successive *chadya* eaves below is afforded by the top of the *garbhakudya* in combination with the system of walls and concentric rings of pillars of graded heights on which the skeletal framework of beams, sloping rafters, cross-pieces that are further secured by the planking over is constructed. The actual water-proof covering is laid over the planking in the form of clinker tiles, or metal sheeting (copper or brass). This accords with the regional climatic requirements, and the steep slant of the *sikhara* sides and the *chadya* eaves not only drain quickly the heavy rain-water and throw it away, but also protect painted stucco or wooden sculpture work wrought over the faces of the *tala* walls and the main wall below. Thus a diligent comparative study would indicate more a taxonomic homology with the parts of the southern *vimana* type with such modifications as called for by the local climatic environment, especially in respect of the *sikhara* and *chadya* forms, than a seeming analogy with the Orissan *pidadeuls* or the *phansanakara* styles of western India, or even the canopied temples of the sub-Himalayan tract.

The intervening parts of the *idai nali*, immediately in front of the door-opening of the *garbhakudya* and lying between it and the outer principal door-opening of the *srikoyil* fronton constitutes, functionally, the *ardha-mandapa* part in the scheme and thus comes to have a *sukanasa* superstructure over it as a frontal projection of the main *srikoyil* superstructure. This, as in the Chalukyan temples and its cohorts, will be in addition to the *maha nasikas* on top of the *srikoyil*.

In front of the outer door-opening is the flight of steps. It may be a single flight of steps or *sopana marga*, laid in front of the door providing direct ascent. Or, often, there is a landing laid in front of the doorway with lateral flights of steps, one on either side. While the frontal *sopana marga* is flanked on either side with *surulyali* balustrades, with sculptured outer faces, the lateral flights have each of them, a similar balustrade flanking the front edges of the steps with carvings. The front of the central block with the landing on top of it likewise contains sculptures. These balustrade sculptures along with the *dvarapala* figures form the only significant stone sculptures in the *srikoyil* make-up.

Perhaps one of the largest complexes in this series of temples is the Vadakkunnathan, or Tenkailasam, or Sri Mulanatha temple, perched picturesquely on a low hilly promontory in the centre of Trichur town, which itself is almost at the centre of Kerala territory. From its inscriptions the temple is known to have been in existence from the twelfth century, though its foundations could have been much older. The nuclear structures inside the *nalambalam* or inner *malika prakara* are the three independent shrines standing almost in a line north-south, all of them facing west. The circular *srikoyil* of Vadakkunnathan, the most northerly of the row, has its sanctum cells divided by a transverse diagonal wall. The western half enshrining Siva has its own door-opening and flight of steps in front with a detatched *namaskara-mandapa* in front. The eastern half is dedicated to *devi* Parvati with a door opening on the east. The northern and southern faces have · false doors, or *ghanadvaras*. Over the moulded stone *adhishthana*, the outer wall of the *sandhara* structure and its *prastara* show the characteristic reliefs of pilasters and miniature shrines of the *kuta*, *sala*, and *panjara* models, as in the Tamil Nadu temples. The slopy conical roof of metal sheet covers these by its overhanging eaves supported by brackets sprung from the wall at intervals. The inner wall rising up further actually carries this immense conical roof, or *sikhara*, with a single metal *stupi* on top. The most southernly of the group is the two-storeyed shrine of Rama, square on plan, with its *adhishthana*, walls, and *prastara* relieved five times on each of its four faces. The central reliefs on the side and rear faces, corresponding to the door-opening on the west, have false doors inset between the pilasters carrying the *sala* motif on top. The corner bays have the *karnakutas* at the corners and the intervening ones, the *panjaras*. The narrow recesses have lesser shrine motifs on paired pilasters. These *kuta*, *sala*, *panjara* reliefs are overshadowed by the overhanging eaves of the pent roof sloping down from hooks and beams, set higher up on the face of the inner wall, and resting on the wall-plate of the outer wall, the overhanging eaves further supported by intricately carved caryatid-like wooden brackets sprung from the top region of the outer wall again. The inner wall rises up to a further level, carrying the four-sided domical ultimate roof, or *sikhara*, also of metal sheet, with a *stupi* on top. The *sikhara* roof has four *nasikas*, or dormers at the middle of its four sides. In between the Rama and Siva shrines, there is a third shrine dedicated to Sankaranarayana, or Harihara, circular in plan and two-storeyed in its rise. Its *adhishthana* and wall are likewise relieved, the larger bays in the middle of the north, east and south sides being *sala* patterns, with a false door inside a *stambha torana* front with a *makara* arch on top. The other bays correspond to the *kuta* or *panjara* patterns—all two-storeyed models—while the recesses have again such two-storeyed models of lesser size with *sala sikhara* motifs on tops of shorter and more closely set pairs of pilasters. On the southern side of the Vadakkunnathan shrine, on the floor of the open court, is the Saptamatrika group, the component deities being represented by a row of *padma pithas* alone, a characteristic of Kerala temples. All the three central shrines have *mukha-mandapas* on the west. There is also a smaller shrine for Ganapati, interposed between the Siva and Harihara temples. The walls of the shrines are richly painted and the timberwork and brackets ornately carved. The *nalambalam* or pillared corridor, surrounding the nuclear group, has on its outside a large, wider open court, with a paved circumambulatory passage immediately to its outside. The lesser shrines for subsidiary deities like Krishna, Nandi, Parasurama, and Sasta are also located in the outer court. The shrine of Sasta on the south-west is an elegant, small, east-facing *ekatala*, apsidal structure, *gaja-prishtha-kara*, appropriate to Sasta, whose vehicle is the elephant. It is perhaps the smallest apsidal structure in the Kerala mode of construction. In the north-west corner of the outer court is the large *kuttambalam* or opera-hall, rectangular in shape, and built in typical Kerala style. Inside is a central pavilion with exquisitely lathe-turned pillars which, in addition to the carved pillars of the hall and the woodwork of the ceiling, add to the splendour of the structure. The whole complex is surrounded by a massive stone *prakara*, with four-storeyed gateways on the four cardinal sides with slopy gable roofs, standing as good examples of *gopura* construction in the Kerala style.

Another large and important temple complex in the south of Kerala is the Padmanabhasvami or Anantasayin temple in Trivandrum, which was wholly reconstructed in the last two centuries. The stone-built central shrine is appropriately oblong on plan to enshrine the reclining form of Anantasayin Vishnu. It is two-storeyed with pent and gable roof patterns for its storeys.

The walls are painted and there are subsidiary shrines for deities like Krishna, Kshetrapala, Narasimha, Sasta, Garuda, etc. The open-pillared *mandapa* round the complex, with stone pillars, and the eastern *gopura* of stone body and brickwork superstructure are in the style of Tamil Nadu temples, while a subsidiary entrance to the north of the *gopura* is in the traditional Kerala pattern with a gable roof and *kilivasal nasikas*.

The *srikoyil* of the celebrated Guruvayur temple, dedicated to Krishna, is square and two-storeyed with metal-sheet gable roofs, as in the above two cases. It has the *chuttambalam* and *prakara* encircling it. The other noteworthy temples, single-or more-storeyed and built of laterite, brick and wood, and roofed by metal sheet or tiles, are the Siva temples at Tiruvanchikalam, Tali (near Kozhikode), Taliparambha, Tiruprangode, Perumanam, Trikkandiyur, Trittala and Sukapuram, the Rama temples of Trichchambaram and Tirunavay, and the Bhagavati temple at Kodungallur. The Tiruvanchikalam shrine is square on plan and ashlar-built, double-walled and two-storeyed, the lower slopy roof resting over the outer wall, and the upper one over the raised inner wall, both of metal sheeting. The upper roof in its overhanging eaves, further supported by wooden brackets profusely carved, has four *kilivasal nasikas* projected from the sloping sides. The walls contain some good sculpture and carving. The top *stupi* is of gold-plated copper.

The Taliparambha temple is almost similar, quadrangular on plan and double-walled, with the roof in two storeys. The lower pent roof slopes down on the top of the shorter outer wall and the upper pyramidal or *kuta* roof cap the top of the inner walls. In front there is the *namaskara-mandapa* with a sloped roof and two projecting gables at either end. The remnants of a large *gopuram* demolished during Tipu Sultan's invasions are still extant.

The Tali temple near Kozhikode is again another structure of the same kind, square, double-walled, and two-storeyed, the roofs made of modern tiles. The *adhishthana* and the walls show the usual five reliefs on both the side and rear faces, the central widest with a *sala* over the *prastara,* and a false door inset into a *torana,* placed between the wall pilasters below; the extreme bays relate to the *karnakutas*, while the intermediate ones, the smallest, to the *panjaras* of the *prastara*. The recesses show narrow windows between close-set pairs of pilasters carrying *panjara* tops reaching to the level of the *kapota* of the *prastara*. Its stone sculptures are of a fine quality as also the wood-carving on the ceiling of the *namaskara-mandapa*.

The Rama temple of Tiruvangad in north Kerala is unique in having a rectangular *srikoyil* with a linear orientation, that is, with the entrance on one of the shorter sides of the oblong structure. It is two-storeyed. The front elevation on the face with the main doorway is almost vertical, while the two longer sides and the shorter rear side have the slopy pent roof at the lower level, and the ridged gable roof at the higher level with three *stupis* in a linear row on the ridge along the longitudinal axis. The roofs are of copper sheeting. In front there is a *mukha-mandapa*, also oblong, but with its long axis transverse to that of the *srikoyil* and provided with *stupis* over its transversely-oriented ridge. All round there is a *nalambalam* of lesser height.

The Krishna temple at Trichchambaram, noted for its excellent wood-carvings illustrating scenes from the *Bhagavata*, has a *srikoyil* square on plan and *sandhara* in its make-up, with the roof of both the storeys covered with copper plate. The lower pent roof is extended forward, as the *sukanasa*, with a front triangular gable face over the *idai nali* or linear *antarala-mandapa*, in front of which is an independent *namaskara-mandapa*. The upper four-sided pyramidal roof has projected *kilivasal nasikas* on its four sides, with arched or horseshoe-shaped front; there is a single *stupi* on top. The Tirunavay Vishnu temple also belongs to the same category. The Perumanam Siva temple dedicated to Erattayappan is a three-storeyed version of the kind with a frontal *antarala* projection of two storeys in front, and the top pyramidal roof unique in being octagonal. It is raised over an eight-sided neck with *kilivasal nasikas* projected from each of the eight octant faces. The lower roofs are made of tiles and the octangonal *sikhara* of metal sheet.

The twin temples of Rama and Lakshmana standing side by side, in Tiruvilvamalai, the former facing east and the latter west, are interesting. Both are of the same plan and rise, square, *sandhara*, and with a projected gable roof from the lower tier over a linear front *antarala-mandapa*. The roofs are made of metal sheeting and the four-sided pyramidal *sikharas* have four *kilivasal nasikas* and single metal gold-gilt *stupis* on top. The walls are decorated with sculptures, the *dasavatara* sculptures on the

Lakshmana temple being particularly noteworthy. The Rama temple has undergone renovation recently.

The Rama temple at Tiruprayar has a circular *ekatala srikoyil* and is noted for its ancient wood-carvings. The *namaskara-mandapa* has profuse wood-carvings, while the wall of the shrine has interesting mural paintings. The *srikoyil* at Vaikom is similar, circular and *ekatala*, with an immense conical copper-sheet roofing, and a single *stupi*. The *srikoyil* of Thrikotithanam, another ancient structure, is likewise of circular plan but two-storeyed, as also is the *srikoyil* of Payyanur, which has a boldly moulded stone *adhishthana* and finely carved caryatid brackets supporting the eaves of the lower pent roof. The Siva temple at Ettumanur, noted for its paintings, especially of Nataraja, has a simple *ekatala srikoyil*, which is also circular on plan.

While the small Sasta shrine in the outer precincts of the Vadakkunnathan temple at Trichur stands for a simple *ekatala* apsidal, or *gajaprishtha vimana*, the Siva temple at Tiruvannur exemplifies a two-storeyed and larger version of the type. The pent roof covering the storey below and the apsidal ridged roof above, with a gable front, has a row of three *stupis* on top. The Subrahmanya temple at Payyanur is another example of a two-storeyed structure of the *gajaprishtha* class with a square *namaskara-mandapa* and a transversely oblong *mukha-mandapa* in front, all metal sheet-roofed, and having a tiled *nalambalam* of a lesser height running all round. The decayed temple at Tiruprangode, and the one at Tiruvannur near Kozhikode, are yet other examples of the same class. The comparatively modern Ananthavinayakar temple at Madhur in north Malabar, also *gajaprishtha*, has its roof in three tiers, the two lowest ones with pent roof and tiled; the upper lean-to-roof and the ultimate apsidal roof are of copper sheeting.

The Bhagavati or Durga temple at Kodungallur of ancient fame is now a total modern renovation, of course in the indigenous style. The main *srikoyil* is two-storeyed with a subsidiary Siva shrine to its left.

Among the temples with southern style *vimanas*, akin to those of the adjoining districts of Tamil Nadu, and more or less concentrated in the south Travancore and Kanyakumari regions, may be mentioned the Guhanathasvami temple of stone of Kanyakumari of the middle Chola period, with the superstructure lost; the Parthivasekharapuram temple, four-storeyed with the superstructure in brick and mortar over the stone body of the late Chola or Pandya period, and the Banatirtha temple with *tritala vimana* of the late Vijayanagar period, with the *vimanas* all square on plan. The Parasurama shrine in the Tiruvallam temple complex and the Valiya Udaiyadichapuram shrine with a stone body and brickwork superstructure are examples of *dvitala* and *tritala vimanas* of *vritta* or circular plan of the sixteenth century and later. The largest temple complex of this kind is the one at Suchindram, with structures inside dating from the ninth-tenth centuries AD, a *chitrasabha* built in 1410, a *mandapa*, called the Chempakaraman *mandapam*, built in 1471, and the *gopura* built in about 1545.

The Kanara temples, as Cousens calls them, form an interesting group, though small in number, characterized by their plain sloping roofs of stone slabs with a peculiar arrangement for closing in the sides. This is adapted to the excessive rainfall of the place that makes for the deep gradient of the roof, and its extension much downwards to cut off the beating rain. The sides of the halls inside are closed by screens and often they are storeyed. Inside they often contain lathe-turned pillars, but in general the columns are short, squat and clumsy, rather degenerate Chalukyan forms. Their affiliations have been mentioned earlier and besides the Ketapi Narayana temple, we have examples of such temples in Bhatkal itself, also in Mudabidri and its neighbourhood.

Glossary of
Indian Architectural Terms

adhishthana: Basement of a *vimana*, a *mandapa*, or similar structure, forming a distinct architectural feature supporting walls and pilasters or pillars, and consisting of distinct moulded tiers.

alpa nasika: Projected front end of an apsidal shrine resembling a *kudu* arch over pilasters, originally functioning as a small opening or fenestrated window, usually in *kutas*, *koshthas* and *panjaras*.

alpa vimana: Small, one-storeyed *vimana*. The parts are *adhishthana*, *bhitti* or *pada prastara*, *griva*, *sikhara* and *stupi*. It is usually without a *hara*.

amalaka, amalasara, amalasila: Ribbed, lenticular or globoid part resembling the *amalaka* (Indian gooseberry fruit) crowning the top of the northern-style *sikhara* as its characteristic; also adopted as the top of the Kadamba-Chalukya forms, sometimes as an alternative to the *griva sikhara* component of the southern *vimana* form.

anarpita hara: String of miniature shrines (*hara*) on the edge of each *vimana tala*, distinct from the body of the upper *tala* or storey, with intervening space (opposite of *arpita*).

antara bhitti: Inner wall of multiple-walled *garbha-griha*, or sanctum, or storey.

arpita hara: *Hara* or string of miniature shrines on the edge of each *vimana tala* that is applique to the body (*harmya*) of the upper *tala* or storey without any intervening space (opposite of *anarpita*).

ardha-mandapa: Pillared hall immediately in front of the principal shrine or distal half of a *mandapa* with two seriate pillars, as in rock-cut cave-temples.

ashta parivara: Lay-out of central shrine with eight surrounding sub-shrines (including the Nandi shrine) in the cardinal and corner directions.

aytana: Shrine; *vimana*.

ayatasra vimana: *Vimana*, oblong on plan and covered by a wagon-top roof.

bahya bhitti: Outermost wall of a multiple-walled sanctum or storey (opposite of *antara bhitti*).

bhadra: Central relieved or projected part from each side of the body of the *vimana* or *prasada* as distinct from the corner projection (*karna*).

bhadra sala: Oblong, wagon-topped miniature shrine of *ayatasra* type in the centre of each side of the *hara* over the storeys of the *vimana*.

bhitti: Wall.

bhitti torana: Ornamental festoon on the wall, usually a *makara torana* supported by two pilasters (*see torana, makara torana*).

bhumi: Stage in the curvilinear superstructure (*sikhara*) or *anda* of a northern-style temple, often marked off at the corners by compressed *amalakas*—the *karnamalakas* or *bhumiamalakas*.

bhuta: Goblin.

chaturmukha: Shrine or *vimana* opening on all four sides.

chitra potika: Corbels with embossed carving or painting of creepers, flowers, etc.

devakoshtha: Niche on walls of shrines and *mandapas* containing sculpture of deity; often crowned by *torana* or shrine motif, *kuta sala, panjara,* or *kudu,* or *udgama*.

gala, griva: Neck; usually the clerestory raising up the roof (*sikhara*) with light and air-openings (*nasikas*) on its sides in the *vimana* types. The neck is below the *amalaka* in *prasada* types, but without *nasikas*.

garbha-griha: Shrine-cell, or sanctum sanctorum, or cella.

gopura: Main gateway; the storeyed structure over the entrance or entrances through the enclosing walls to the premises of a temple, palace, or city.

hara: String of miniature shrines over each terrace (*tala*) of the storeyed *vimana* consisting of *kutas, koshthas,* or *salas* and *panjaras*, interconnected by cloister-lengths or balustrades simulating cloisters (*harantara.*)

harantara: See hara.

kadalika karana: Successive inward offsetting or corbelling-in of the roofing slabs or brick courses over walls to reduce the space to be roofed over to an ultimate small opening on top that can be covered by a slab overlapping like a banana bunch.

Kadamba-Chalukya: Variant primarily of the *rekha-Nagara*-style *prasada*, or temple, in which the superstructural tiers comprise *kapata* (cornice) and *kantha* (neck) and are capped by a circular *griva* or *gala* (neck), and an *amalasara*, often without the *sukanasika*.

kalasa (*lasuna*): Wide-mouthed vase; lowermost member of the pillar capital, so-called after its shape. Also the vase-shaped finial over the *amalaka* of northern temples.

kalyana-mandapa: *Mandapa* or hall in which the ceremonial wedding of god and goddess in the form of *utsava murtis* or processional bronze icons is celebrated annually in south Indian temples.

kapota: Dove, pigeon; overhanging cornice, usually flexed, projecting beyond the principal beam to throw off water from the terrace beyond the beam and joist-end or the recesses of the *adhishthana* like the *kumuda* and *padma*.

karnakuta: Miniature *sama-chaturasra* (square) shrine at the corner of each storey of the *vimana* over the *prastara*, with a single *stupi*. It is rarely *vritta* (circular) or *ashtasra* (octagonal) on plan.

karna sala: Miniature *ayatasra* (oblong) shrine with barrel-vault roof placed at the corner of each *tala* of a structure, usual in *gopuras*.

kattu: Intervening octagonal or polygonal portion between the bottom and top squares of a pillar.

kilivasal: Kerala term used for the *nasika* (*see nasika*, and *sukanasika*).

koshtha: Same as a *sala*.

kshudra nasika: Short *nasika*; projected front end of a miniature apsidal (one or two-storeyed) shrine with arch over pilasters functioning as a small opening, usually found in the *harantara*.

kudu: 'Nest'; an arched or horse-shaped opening projected out of a flexed cornice (*kapota*), originally perhaps intended for entry of roosting birds (*kapota*) but in later examples filled with human figures *mithuna*, etc.), surmounted by a finial. The arch is usually a *makara torana*.

kudya-stambha: Pilaster shown as relief on wall surface.

kumbha: Member of the pillar capital coming above the *kalasa*, and *tadi*, and bulbous in form. Originally a flattened carinate vase with a short, narrow mouth.

kuta: Shrine of square plan (*sama-chaturasra*) with four-sided converging roof and single finial, or circular or octagonal with domical roof and single finial, or *stupi*.

lalata bimba: 'Crest figure'; chief decorative motif or figure on the frontal of any entrance or door-lintel, sometimes extending to the over-door.

maha-mandapa: Pillared hall immediately in front of the *ardha-mandapa*, or *antarala*, or the proximal half of a *mandapa* with two seriate pillars, closed or open, in cave-temples.

maha nasika: Projected nose-like part from the sides of the *griva* and *sikhara* showing the frontal aspects of apsidal *vimanas* and having pillars with surmounting arched *toranas*.

makara torana: Entrance decoration with a festoon—straight or arched, spanning the tops of two columns, the festoon or *torana* being a decorative garland or scroll issuing from mouths of *makaras* (crocodiles), placed over the capitals of the supporting *stambhas*. Such *makara toranas* are found over the *devakoshtas* or *mandapa* entrances, or walls (*bhitti torana*).

malasthana: Apex of pillar or pilaster shaft below capital with looped garland (*mala*) hanging from the *padma bandha*.

mandapa, mandapam: Open or closed pillared or astylar hall.

mukha-mandapa: First or frontal *mandapa* of a series at the entrance of a temple, often synonymous with *maha-mandapa* in earlier temples.

nasika: 'Nose'; projected arched opening (window). See *alpanasika*, *kshudranasika*, *mahanasika* and *sukanasika*. In Kerala temples it is called *kilivasal*, or parrot-beak entrances.

natya-mandapa: Dance-hall. See *nritta-mandapa*.

navaranga: *Mandapa* with four pillars surrounding a central bay, twelve more on the periphery in alignment with the central pillars, enclosing eight more bays, surrounding the central one and making nine bays in all; characteristic of Chalukyan temples and their derivatives.

nida: Miniature apsidal shrine; same as *panjara*.

nirandhara: Devoid of a closed circuit or ambulatory round the cella, the wall of the cella being single and thick (as opposed to *sandhara*).

nritta-mandapa: See *natya-mandapa*.

oma: Basal *pitha* of pillar or pilaster.

pada: Pillar (*stambha*).

padma: Lotus; capital-member (doucene) below the *phalaka* (abacus), shaped like a lotus with petals.

padma bandha: Broad fillet, ringing the top of the shaft of a pillar, marked by decorative bands between rows of lotus petals, separating the shaft from the capital.

pali: Capital member, same as *padma*, but without scalloped petals.

panjara: Miniature apsidal shrine; same as *nida*.

parivara devatas: Also called *avarana devatas*, or subsidiary deities in shrines called *parivaralayas* or *parivara*.

patta: Plain or decorated band occupying the median face of the corbel, as if binding the rolls of *taranga* mouldings of the corbel.

pattika: Projected top slab of the platform or *adhishthana* in line with the vertical norm or *manasutra*—a major moulding of considerable thickness.

phalaka: Abacus; wide plank on top of the terminal *saduram* or moulded capital of pillar supporting the corbel, or *potika*.

pidadeul: Structure with stepped or tiered superstructure over the sanctum as in Kadamba-Chalukya temples. The term is used in Orissa (Kalinga) architecture for the *mandapa* in front of the main *prasada*, called *jagmohan*, or smaller individual shrines with such superstructure (as distinct from *rekhadeul*).

pitha: Pedestal, base.

potika: Corbel-bracket over pillar. See *taranga potika, makara potika, chitra potika*.

pranala: Spout projected like a gargoyle to discharge water.

prasada: Northern-style temple, as distinct from the *vimana* form of the south.

prastara: Entablature, consisting of mouldings over walls and pillars, viz. the *uttira* (beam) *vajana, valabhi, kapota, alinga,* and *antari*.

ranga-mandapa: Equivalent of *navaranga*, corresponding to the *maha-mandapa* of southern *vimana* temples.

ratha: Chariot; monolithic *vimana*.

rekha-prasada: Typical northern-style sanctuary form with curvilinear superstructure, or *anda*, emphasized by the *bhadra* projections on the sides, and by *rekhas* (curvilinear lines) crowned by a neck and *amalaka* with *kalasa* on top.

sabha-mandapa: Mandapa with shrine of Nataraja in the southern temples, generally facing south.

saduram: Square basal, intermediate or terminal section of a pillar separated by octagonal, polygonal or circular intermediary parts.

sala shrine: Vimana of *ayatasra* type (oblong on plan) with barrel-vault roof and a series of *stupis* on its ridge.

sala sikhara: Sikhara peculiar to *sala* shrine, barrel-vault, wagon-top or inverted, keel-shaped.

sandhara: Structure with a closed or covered circuit passage or ambulatory round the cella or the sanctum as in a double-walled structure (opposite of *nirandhara*).

snapana-mandapa: Mandapa in which the *abhisheka* (or *mandapa*) or ceremonial bathing of processional idols of bronze is performed during festivals.

sikhara: Roof of the *vimana* over the *griva*, domical or four-sided with a single finial, vaulted with many finials on the ridge, or apsidal with many finials over the horizontal part. The entire superstructure (*anda*) is of northern *prasadas*.

stambha: Pillar (*pada*).

stambha torana: Entrance decoration or free-standing decorated entrance without doors and with a festoon spanning the tops of two columns, the festoon primarily being a garland of leaves and flowers, later on taking the form of one or more curved and decorated cross-bars, or a floral and foliar festoon arch issuing out of *makara*-heads, placed on top of the supporting columns.

stupi, stupika: Finial, morphologically the *ushnisha*, taking in later times the form of a *purna ghata* or *purna kumbha*, forming the topmost or ultimate member of the *vimana, gopura*, or any other structure.

sukanasika (also *sukanasa*): Integral forward projection of the tiers of the superstructure below the *griva* and *amalaka* level in northern *prasadas* coming over the *antarala* and forming its roof; has a *nasika* front, enclosing bas-relief sculptures inside the arch. In adaptations in the southern *vimana* types, as in the Chalukyan and its derivatives, the forward projection, primarily of the front *nasika* or *maha nasika* or the dormer of the *griva sikhara* region alone, in smaller simple *vimana* types and along with the forward projection of the *talas* in storeyed types, the whole coming over the terrace of the lower *antarala* or *ardha-mandapa*.

tadi: Saucer-shaped capital-member above the *kalasa* and below the *kumbha*.

tala: Storey of the *vimana* or *gopura*.

taranga: Wave; wavy roll-ornament of the corbel resembling the 'reed' moulding or 'reeding' of European classical architecture.

taranga potika: Corbel-bracket with roll- or *taranga*-moulding.

torana: Free-standing ornamental foliar and floral festoon forming entrance supported by two upright columns and often interlaced vertically; (*jala torana*): copies in wood and stone with greater elaboration and carving, or taking the form of *makara torana*, mounted on two pillars. It precedes the main gateways (*gopuras*) of cities, palaces and temples. It is often erected temporarily (as is common in south India) on festive occasions on roads leading to cities, palaces and temples. When adorning the doorway as a *dvarasobha*, it is called a *griha dvara-torana*, or the face-of-a-wall (*bhitti*) *torana*, where it often frames a niche or *devakoshtha* or suggests an opening *ghanadvara*. When free-standing, it is designated *stambha torana*.

trikuta, trikutachala torana stambha: Pillar or pilaster supporting *torana*; three *vimanas* connected by a common *adhishthana* in a line or placed round a common *mandapa*, as in Chalukyan types.

udgama: Fenestrated pattern of coalescent *kudu*-like arches and half-arches, typical of northern-style temples and found in the facade arches of Buddhists cave-temples; used in northern temples as crest over *devakoshthas* also in place of the miniature shrine tops of such figure niches on walls of shrines and *mandapas*.

upana: Lowermost part or footing of the basement or *adhishthana*, projecting beyond the vertical norm and surmounted by the *jagati*. It forms the lowermost visible part of the *vimana*, the uppermost limit of the same being the *stupi*.

upa-pitha: Additional moulded platform or sub-base below the basement or *adhishthana* with mouldings repeating those of the *adhishthana*, or often reduced in number, or simpler.

utsava-mandapa: *Mandapa* in which the processional deities of bronze are kept during celebrations.

vedika: Railing.

vimana: Shrine from *upana* to *stupi* (base to finial), the whole shrine consisting of *adhishthana* (basement), *pada* (pillars) or *bhitti* (walls), *prastara* (entablature), *griva* (neck or clerestory), *sikhara* (head or roof), and *stupi* (finial) in the case of simple *vimanas* *(ekatala)*; with *talas* (storeys) intervening between the lowermost *prastara* below and the *griva*, *sikhara*, and *stupi* above in storeyed *vimanas*.

vyala: Leonine figure.

vyala mala, vyala vari: Decorative friezes with *vyalas* usually as part of the *adhishthana* and on top of the entablature of each *tala*, marking the ends of the cross-joists in original timberwork.

Index

Karnataka/Kannada region, 3, 4,
13, 16, 18, 33, 55, 148, 149n,
171
*Kanataka simhasana Pratishtha-
panacharya*, 149n
Karnika, 140
Karrali, 108
Kartikeyasvami temple, Nagarj-
unakonda, 20
Kartikeya (god), 7, 17, 21, 68, 70,
109, 173
Kasi-Varanasi, 132
Kasi-Visvesvara temple at
Lakkundi, 137
Pattadkal, 172
Katuchpur/Katakshapura, 145
Kathakali (dance), 176
Kattu, 39
Kaumara, 33, 50
Kaval maram (royal totem tree), 10
Kaveri (river), 15, 34, 45, 108
Kaveri-p-pattinam (port city), Bud-
dha-*pitikai* at, 15
Kaviyur (cave-temple at), 51, 53,
54
Keladi (city-temple at), 166
Keladi Nayak (*see* Ikkeri Nayak)
147, 166
Kerala, 4, 6, 16, 18, 33, 40, 45, 48,
52-53, 124, 150, 176, 177, 180,
181, 183
Kerala-style temples, 81, 174, 176,
177
Keri (Goa-Vaital temple at), 116
Kesava temple, Somnathpur, 139,
141
Ketapi Narayana temple at
Bhatkal, 115
Khandagiri (Jain cave at), 24
Kilivasal (Nasika), 175, 182, 183
Kilmavilangai (cave-temple at), 40
Kinnari, 37
Kiratarjuniya; Kirata (Siva), 45, 53
Kirtivarman (king), 31

Kodumbalur (temple at), 110
Kodungallur temple, 183, 184
Kollan Semakan (blacksmith), 150n
Konark, Sun temple at, 135
Kondane (Buddhist cave), 25
Koneri *mandapam* (cave-temple),
42
Kongu, 46
Konkan, 59
Kontgudi temple, 113, 114
Ko-Perunjinga (chieftain), 134
Koranganatha temple, 111
Korravai (goddess), 16, 17
Koshta, 78, 91, 121
Kottam (temple), 16, 17
Kottapalle, 72
Kotikal-*mandapam* (cave-temple),
38, 40, 83
Kottukkal (cave-temple), 52, 53,
54
Koyil (temple), 15, 17
Kozhikode (Calicut), 182, 184
Kubja Vishnuvardhana (king), 54
Khumbarvada cave (25), Ellora,
63
Krishna district; god, 4, 45, 70,
165, 182, 183; river, 29, 72
valley, 10
Krishna I (king), 94
Krishna Devaraya (king), 160-61
Krishna-*lilas*, 162
Krishna-Nappinnai, theme of, 45
Krishnapuram temple at, 164
Krishna-sila (hard blackstone), 107,
130
Krishna temple at Grurvayur, 183;
at Hampi, 161; at Srirangam,
165; at Trichchambaram, 184
Kshatriyasimhesvara, larger *vimana*
of Shore temple,
Mahabalipuram, 99
Kshetrapala, 183
Kshudranasika, 78, 82
Kudavelli brick temple remains

Nagara (style of *vimana*), 77, 86, 88, 89, 106, 112, 118, 123, 131, 168

Nagaram (temple), 16, 17

Nagarjuni hills (Bihar), 23

Nagarjunakonda, 12-13, 18-19, 22, 27, 170

Nagesvara temple (at Kumbhakonam), 111, 134

Nakkalagudi temple (Biccavolu), 123

Nakula-Sahadeva *ratha* (monolithic *vimana*), 22, 79, 86, 88, 92

Nalambalam, 176, 180, 181, 183

Nalanda, 26n

Naltunai Isvara temple (at Punjai), 111

Namakkal (cave-temples at), 46, 50, 52, 53

Namaskara-mandapa, 176, 180, 182, 184

Namesvara temple (Pillalamarri), 143, 146

Nami Reddi (chieftain), 144

Nandi (Bana, capital city) temples at, 112

Nandi (of Siva temples), rock-cut, 66, 67, 71, 77, 88, 94, 95, 97, 99, 103, 109, 125, 128-29, 131, 132, 141, 143, 181

Nandivarman II Pallavamalla (king), 105, 107

Nangavaram (temple at), 109

Nappinnai (Krishna's consort), 45

Nara-Narayana, 107

Narapatisimha Pallava Vishnu-*griha* (in Shore temple complex), Mahabalipuram, 99

Narasimha, 42, 47, 50, 52, 53, 70, 107, 182

Narasimha (king, Eastern Ganga), 134

Narasimhavarman I Mamalla (Pallava king), 38, 40, 73, 85

Narasimhavaraman II, Rajasimha (Pallava king), 98, 100, 102

Narayana-bali (ceremony), 31

Narttamalai, cave-temples at, 51, 53, structural temple— Vijayalaya Cholisvaram at, 110

Nasik (Buddhist caves near), 24, 25

Nasika, 26, 62, 71, 82, 89-91, 96, 97, 117, 119, 120, 122, 133, 175, 177, 180, 182, 183; *kilivasal*, 176, 182, 183

Nataraja, 17, 127, 130, 135, 184

Natya-sala-mandapa, 34

Natya-sastra, 127, 133

Navabrahma complex of temples (Alampur), 172

Navalinga temple (Kukkanur), 135, 136

Navamurtis (Vishnu forms), 107

Navaranga-mandapa, 26, 59, 65, 84, 122, 136, 138, 141, 143, 145, 162, 167

Nave, 26, 84, 121

Nayaks (rulers), 14

Nayakas (Nayaks) of Gingee, 149, 163; of Ikkeri (Keladi), 59, 149, 163, 166; of Madurai, 149, 163; Thanjavur and of Vellore 149, 163-65

Nayak paintings, 127; temples, 163,166

Nayanmar (Saiva saints), 4, 17, 32, 109, 127, 131

Nelasambhu temple (Warangal), 145

Nida (panjara), 79, 80, 90, 92

Nidhis, 61, 70

Nilakanthesvara cave-temple (Kunnathur), 49

Nirundhara (vimana), 56, 80, 89, 92, 117, 123, 135, 172-73, 178

Niruti, 128

Nolamba (dynasty) architecture,

Printed at Bosco Society For Printing & Graphic Training, Okhla Road, New Delhi - 110025